DisplayWr
Made Easy

Gail Todd

Osborne **McGraw-Hill**
Berkeley, California

Osborne **McGraw-Hill**
2600 Tenth Street
Berkeley, California 94710
U.S.A.

For information on translations and book distributors outside of the
U.S.A., please write to Osborne **McGraw-Hill** at the above address.
A complete list of trademarks appears on page 457.

DisplayWrite 4 Made Easy

1234567890 DODO 8987

ISBN 0-07-881270-4

Acquisitions editor, Jeffrey Pepper
Technical reviewer, Stephen Cobb
Project editor, Fran Haselsteiner
Cover art, Bay Graphics Design Associates
Cover supplier, Phoenix Color Corp.

Contents

II Advanced Word-Processing Features

Introduction

If you have never used a word-processing program before, you are in for a wonderful experience. After only a few hours' practice with the DisplayWrite 4 word-processing program, you will be finished with your correction fluid and typewriter erasers forever.

With a word processor, your text appears on the monitor screen as you type it there. You can make any corrections or changes that you want. You can move around words, sentences, and even paragraphs with just a few quick keystrokes. You can experiment with different margins and line spacing. Then, when your text is exactly the way you want it, you can print it—and print as many copies as you want. If you aren't completely satisfied, you can easily make alterations and print it again.

What Makes DisplayWrite 4 Special

Advanced features are known in computer talk as "bells and whistles," and DisplayWrite 4 has all the bells and whistles a word-processing program can have. These extra features are designed to turn complex, tedious typing jobs into quick and easy ones. For example, DisplayWrite 4 can number all your footnotes and place each one at the bottom of the appropriate page. The program can produce outlines and tables, making all the necessary calculations.

DisplayWrite 4 can even perform calculations for you and insert the result of a computation in any location you designate. It can provide special symbols for foreign-language and technical writing. It can also let you "program" certain function keys so that you can execute up to 500 keystrokes simply by pressing two or three keys.

If you have previously been using DisplayWrite 3, you will find in DisplayWrite 4 all the features you have been used to plus handy new ones like Notepad and Paper Clip. DisplayWrite 4 even has a Voice feature that lets you incorporate verbal instructions into your files. You will also find that the new program is streamlined—faster and easier to use.

How to Use This Book

Chapter 1 of this book teaches you how to set up your system to use DisplayWrite 4. Chapter 2 shows you how to create simple documents and how to print them. That information is all you need to get started. However, to reap the benefits of the DisplayWrite 4 program, you should gradually become familiar with all the material in the 16 chapters of Part I. When you have, you will be a proficient DisplayWrite 4 user, able to write and edit a wide variety of documents quickly and have them formatted and printed to your exact specifications.

Part II—Chapters 17 through 22—teaches you how to use the advanced features of DisplayWrite 4. Read the chapters in this part one by one, when you want to learn to use a particular feature. For example, when you want to learn how to create tables with DisplayWrite 4, read Chapter 19, "Creating Tables."

Part III—Chapters 23 through 25—teaches you how to create repetitive documents. These are documents such as form letters in which most of the text remains the same from document to document but which also have some text elements (such as names, addresses, and even entire paragraphs) that change. DisplayWrite 4 has a number of features that enable you to produce many copies of repetitive documents with minimal typing.

As you use this book, you will be instructed to type certain text on your keyboard. Any text that you are to type will be shown in boldface, like this:

Type **this text.**

There are also many times when you will be asked to hold down the Control key (marked CTRL on most keyboards) and to press another key simultaneously. If you see "press CTRL-E," you are being asked to press the Control key and the E key simultaneously. If you see "press "ALT-E," you are being asked to press the ALT key and the E key simultaneously.

What This Book Won't Do

Before you use this book you should have some familiarity with your computer. This book will not teach you where the switches on your computer are nor how to put a disk into a disk drive. Nor will this book try to teach you how to use the DOS operating system. When using DisplayWrite 4, you will find it helpful to know a few simple DOS commands, particularly FORMAT and COPY.

A Word to the Wise

No matter how careful you are, the text files that you produce with DisplayWrite 4 can become corrupted or erased, for any number of reasons. Hard disks can malfunction; floppy disks can get lost or even stolen. Therefore, it is important that you periodically make backup copies of all the important text files you produce with DisplayWrite 4. You can use the DOS COPY command or the DisplayWrite 4 Copy command for this purpose.

WRITING AND EDITING WITH DISPLAYWRITE 4

1

Setting Up
Your System

This chapter describes the equipment you need in order to use DisplayWrite 4. It shows you how to install DisplayWrite 4 on your system. It also lists the mouse types and printers you can use and discusses the difference between Character mode and APA mode.

What Equipment Do You Need?

Before attempting to use DisplayWrite 4, check that you have the correct equipment, as described in this chapter.

Computer Requirements

To use DisplayWrite 4, your computer must have either a hard disk and one floppy-disk drive or two floppy-disk drives.

Systems that can run DisplayWrite 4 include the IBM PC, the IBM PC XT, the IBM PC AT, the IBM Portable Personal Computer, the IBM 3270 Personal Computer, and compatible computers.

If you are using a non-IBM computer, check with your dealer to be sure your system can run DisplayWrite 4.

The Operating System

Computers that can run DisplayWrite 4 use the DOS operating system. To use DisplayWrite 4, you must have one of the following DOS versions: 2.10, 3.0, 3.10, or 3.20.

Memory Requirements

The *absolute minimum* memory required to operate DisplayWrite 4 is as follows:

- 310K on a hard-disk system
- 341K on a floppy-disk system

Additional memory is required for background printing, voice notes, printer drivers, Enhanced Graphics Adapter cards, and Color Graphics Adapter cards. See the *DisplayWrite 4 Technical Reference* manual for exact memory requirements. If you are using an IBM PC AT, you can use the 512K Memory Expansion option.

Monitors

Any compatible monitor with an 80-column display will work—it can be either monochrome or color. If you use a color monitor, you will be able to select the colors of the display.

Printers That Work with DisplayWrite 4

You can install up to three printers to work with Display-Write 4. The program is designed to work with the following printers:

- IBM 3812 Pageprinter
- IBM 3852 Model 2 Color Jetprinter
- IBM 4201 Proprinter and IBM 4202 Proprinter XL
- IBM 5152-2 Graphics printer (many Epson printers and printers sold as IBM-compatible can also work if installed as an IBM 5152-2 Graphics printer)
- IBM 5201 Quietwriter and IBM 5201-2 Quietwriter
- IBM 5216 Wheelprinter
- IBM 5223 Wheelprinter E
- IBM 5219 FFTDCA printer (this printer must be attached to an IBM System/36)
- IBM 5140 PC Convertible System Printer

Printer Tables for Supported Printers

For each printer that works with DisplayWrite 4, the system supplies a *printer table*. When you specify a printer during installation, DisplayWrite 4 automatically selects the correct printer table for your printer. (These tables are on the original DisplayWrite 4 Volume 1 disk if you have 720K disks or on the original Volume 3 disk if you have 320K disks.)

Printer Tables for Nonsupported Printers

If your printer is *not* one of the printers just listed (or an equivalent), you may still be able to use DisplayWrite 4 with your printer.

The DEFAULT.PFT Printer Table DisplayWrite 4 supplies a printer table, DEFAULT.PFT, that you can use with nonsupported printers. This table enables you to print simple text. You will *not* be able to change pitch or typestyle or use any of your printer's advanced features.

Creating Your Own Printer Table Using the default printer table DEFAULT.PFT as a base, you can also create your own printer table (see Appendix A) to enable you to use all of your printer's features. *DisplayWrite 4 Technical Reference* warns that "The Printer Function Table Tasks are intended for use by programmers, technicians, or experts on printer functions." However, you can do no harm by trying to create your own table. If it doesn't work, you don't have to use it.

Getting a Printer Function Table from Another Source Your printer dealer or printer manufacturer may be able to supply you with a printer function table for your printer. In addition, Koch Software Industries, 11 West College Drive, Building G, Arlington Heights, Illinois 60004 (312-398-5440) provides programs such as PC Em-U-Print and FONTastic that enable many printers (including laser printers) to work with DisplayWrite 4. Contact the company for more information.

Using a DisplayWrite 3 Printer Table If you created a special printer table for use with DisplayWrite 3, you can use the same table with DisplayWrite 4. Installation of your DisplayWrite 3 table is explained later in this chapter.

Optional Equipment

Optional equipment you may use with DisplayWrite 4 includes the following:

- A mouse
- The IBM Voice Communications Operating Subsystem and the IBM Voice Communications Adapter card (to use "voice" with DisplayWrite 4, you will also need a speaker and a microphone)

Mouse Types That Work with DisplayWrite 4

You can use the following mouse types with DisplayWrite 4:

- Microsoft mouse (serial version)
- Microsoft mouse (bus version)
- Visi On mouse (two-button optical)
- Mouse Systems PC mouse (three-button optical)

The Microsoft (serial version), Visi On, and Mouse Systems mouse types attach to serial interface communications boards. The address of the communications port can be either COM1 or COM2. The Microsoft (bus version) mouse attaches to a parallel interface circuit board that comes with the mouse.

DisplayWrite 4 is designed to work with a two-button mouse. The first button is used to select; the second button is used to escape. If your mouse has three buttons, the third button has no function in DisplayWrite 4.

Voice

DisplayWrite 4 lets you include *voice notes* in your files. These notes can explain your text, give instructions to readers, and so forth.

If you plan to use voice notes with DisplayWrite 4, you must install the Voice Communications Operating Subsystem program, using the special setup process that comes with it. This will create on your hard disk a subdirectory called VCAPI that contains the necessary files. If you do not have a hard-disk system, you cannot use voice notes.

Before You Install DisplayWrite 4

Make sure you have the items described next before you run the DisplayWrite 4 install program.

To install DisplayWrite 4 in a floppy-disk system, you will need six blank, formatted disks if you are copying onto 360K disks; two blank, formatted disks if you are copying onto 1.2Mb disks; and four blank, formatted disks if you are copying onto 720K disks.

For both hard- and floppy-disk systems, you need the name and model number of your printer, as well as the addresses of the printer ports to which your printers are attached (for example, LPT1). You also need the name of your mouse and the address of the port into which the mouse is plugged (for example, COM1).

Storing Your Document Files in a Subdirectory

If you have a hard disk, the program will create a special directory during the installation process for the Display-Write 4 program files. This directory is called \dw4. Additionally, you will be asked if you want to set up a special directory in which to store the documents you produce with DisplayWrite 4.

It is a good idea to set up this directory as a subdirectory of \dw4. You can give this subdirectory any name, such as \data or \text. To set up this subdirectory during installation, type the drive and path of the subdirectory when DisplayWrite 4 prompts you to "Type the drive and directory or just the drive, where you want your documents stored."

For example, to store your documents on your C drive in a subdirectory of your \dw4 directory,

type **c:\dw4\data**

See Appendix C for a fuller discussion on working with subdirectories.

Installing DisplayWrite 4

To install DisplayWrite 4 on a hard-disk system:

1. Turn on your computer and monitor and enter the date and time if necessary.

2. When you see the DOS prompt, insert the original DisplayWrite 4 Volume 1 disk into drive A.

3. Type **a:install** and press ENTER.

4. Follow the instructions on the screen to install the program.

5. When you are finished, press the CTRL, ALT, and DEL keys simultaneously to reboot the system.

6. If you need to stop the installation process before it is complete, press CTRL-BREAK.

To install DisplayWrite 4 on a floppy-disk system:

1. Turn on your computer and monitor and enter the date and time if necessary.

2. When you see the DOS prompt, insert a blank, formatted disk in drive A.

3. Insert the original DisplayWrite 4 Volume 1 disk in drive B.

4. Type **b:install** and press ENTER.

5. Follow the instructions on the screen to install the program.

6. If you need to stop the installation process before it is complete, press CTRL-BREAK.

Note: If, during installation, you specified your own printer function table (or one that was supplied to you by an outside source), use the DOS copy command to copy the table to your \dw4 directory (hard-disk users) or to your Volume 3 program working disk (floppy-disk users). You must do this before you can use the table to print.

Safeguarding Your Disks

Put your original DisplayWrite 4 disks away in a safe place. From now on, if you have a floppy-disk system, you will be using the working copies that you made with the setup program.

Creating the Subdirectory for Your Documents

If you have a hard disk and during installation you directed the system to set up a subdirectory for your DisplayWrite 4 documents, you now must create this directory. During the installation process, the system *automatically* creates the directory \dw4 for the DisplayWrite 4 program files. However, it does *not* automatically create the subdirectory for your documents.

To create the subdirectory for your documents, you must use the DOS MKDIR command. For example, if, during installation, you designated that a subdirectory \data of the \dw4 directory be used to store your documents, you would enter, at the DOS prompt:

mkdir c:\dw4\data

This would create the directory \data as a subdirectory of the \dw4 directory on your C drive.

Installing a DisplayWrite 3 Printer Table with DisplayWrite 4

If you created your own printer table for DisplayWrite 3, you can convert and use the same table with DisplayWrite 4. Follow these steps:

1. Copy the DisplayWrite 3 table to the \dw4 directory (hard-disk users) or to your Volume 3 working disk (floppy-disk users).

2. At the DOS prompt, type **dw4**. When you see the IBM logo screen, press ENTER. This loads the program.

Note: If you are a floppy-disk user, you need the Volume 0 working disk in drive A when you type **dw4**. After pressing ENTER, you must replace the Volume 0 working disk with the Volume 1 working disk. Exact procedures for loading DisplayWrite 4 are described in Chapter 2.

3. You will see the DisplayWrite 4 menu. In Chapter 2 you will learn more about making menu selections. For now, use the TAB key to move to a menu selection. The selection will be highlighted. Then press ENTER to choose the selection. Select Profiles as shown in Figure 1-1.

4. Select Revise Table. Read the screen of information (but don't get discouraged), and press ENTER.

5. You will see the Revise Printer Function Table Selection menu. For Table Name, type in the name of your DisplayWrite 3 table, as shown in Figure 1-2. Then, using the TAB key to move from item to item, type the Printer Number and the Paper Handling choices. (If the defaults are correct, do not make changes.) Press ENTER.

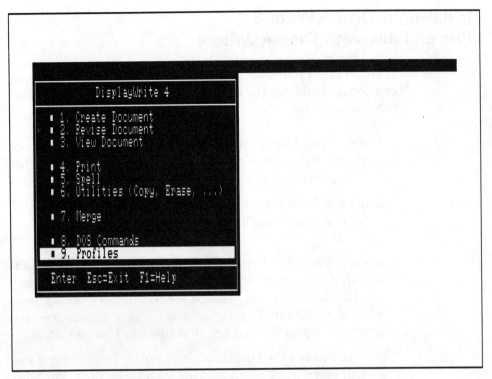

Figure 1-1. The DisplayWrite 4 menu with Profiles highlighted

6. In the Convert to Printer Function Table menu, type in the name of the new printer function table if necessary (it will probably be already typed in for you), and press ENTER.

7. Choose Function Selection Tests. Then select Run All Tests. Turn on your printer and follow the instructions on the screen to run the printer tests.

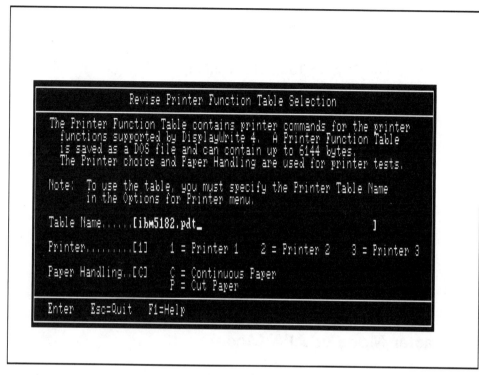

```
┌─────────────────────────────────────────────────────────────┐
│          Revise Printer Function Table Selection             │
│                                                               │
│ The Printer Function Table contains printer commands for the  │
│   printer functions supported by DisplayWrite 4.  A Printer   │
│   Function Table is saved as a DOS file and can contain up to │
│   6144 bytes.                                                 │
│   The Printer choice and Paper Handling are used for printer  │
│   tests.                                                      │
│                                                               │
│ Note:  To use the table, you must specify the Printer Table   │
│        Name in the Options for Printer menu.                  │
│                                                               │
│ Table Name......[ibm5182.pdt_                        ]        │
│                                                               │
│ Printer.........[1]    1 = Printer 1    2 = Printer 2    3 = Printer 3 │
│                                                               │
│ Paper Handling..[C]    C = Continuous Paper                   │
│                        P = Cut Paper                          │
│                                                               │
│ Enter   Esc=Quit   F1=Help                                    │
└─────────────────────────────────────────────────────────────┘
```

Figure 1-2. Typing in the name of your DisplayWrite 3 table

8. When you have completed the tests, you will be returned to the Function Selection Tests menu. Press ESC twice and choose End and Save from the End/Save menu.

9. You will be at the Profiles menu. You must now enter the name of the converted table into your profile. (Profiles are explained in detail in Chapter 15.) From the Profiles menu, choose Revise Profile. Then press ENTER to accept the name of the default profile.

10. Choose Work Station. Then choose Options for Printer # (depending on which printer you are dealing with).

11. When you see the Options for Printer menu, tab to Printer Table Name and type in the new name. Press ENTER.

12. Press ESC twice and choose End and Save from the End/Save menu.

13. You will be returned to the Profiles menu. Press ESC to return to the DisplayWrite 4 menu. Follow the prompts to return to DOS.

14. If you have a floppy-disk system, use the DOS copy command to copy the new table to your Volume 3 disk.

Character Mode or APA Mode?

When you installed DisplayWrite 4, the system chose *Character mode* as the display type for your monitor. In Character mode, the characters you see on your screen are ASCII characters. However, DisplayWrite 4 also supports *APA (All Points Addressable) mode*, which allows you to see a greater number of characters. In APA mode, the system displays EBCDIC characters on your screen. Table 1-1 shows some differences between Character mode and APA mode.

Note: There are 127 ASCII characters, but not all of them are displayable. For example, the first 32 ASCII characters are control characters such as line feed or carriage

Character Mode	APA Mode
Each menu item that can be selected has a box in front of it.	Each menu item that cannot be selected is lowlighted.
With a monochrome display, text to be underlined appears underlined on the screen. With a color display, text to be underlined appears in a different color.	Text to be underlined appears underlined on the screen.
Superscripts and subscripts are not displayed above or below the line on your screen.	Superscripts and subscripts are displayed above or below the line on your screen.
The mouse cursor displays as the reverse video of the cursor character.	The mouse cursor displays as an arrow.

Table 1-1. Comparing Character Mode and APA Mode

return. There are 191 EBCDIC characters, and they are all displayable.

To run DisplayWrite 4 in APA mode, you must have either a Color Graphics Adapter card or an Enhanced Graphics Adapter card installed in your computer. (With a Color Graphics Adapter card, your APA mode display will be black and white, even if you have a color monitor.) You can also use APA mode with an IBM PC Convertible Liquid Crystal Display.

If you want to change your system from Character mode to APA mode, you must change the batch file that loads DisplayWrite 4 into your system. This process is explained in Appendix D.

Using the Keyboard Template

Your DisplayWrite 4 program comes with a long gray strip called the *keyboard template*. One side of the template shows the DisplayWrite 4 keys that are common to all of the keyboards that use DisplayWrite 4.

Notice that each key is divided into a top and bottom half. The top half shows the character or feature that you get if you press the key with DisplayWrite 4 loaded in your machine. The bottom half, if it is totally shaded, shows the feature that you get if you press that key and the CTRL key simultaneously. If the bottom half is partially shaded, it shows the feature that you get if you press that key and the ALT key simultaneously. Figures 1-3*a* through 1-3*e* show individual keyboards with DisplayWrite 4 functions marked on each key.

The other side of the template lists the specific keys that DisplayWrite 4 uses. Set this template near your keyboard for quick reference. You are now ready for Chapter 2, which shows you how to write and edit text with DisplayWrite 4.

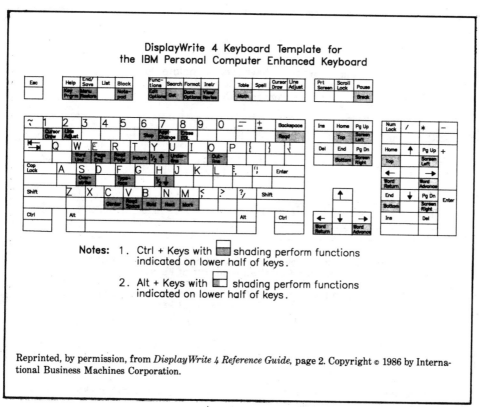

Figure 1-3a.   Keyboard template for the IBM Personal Computer Enhanced Keyboard

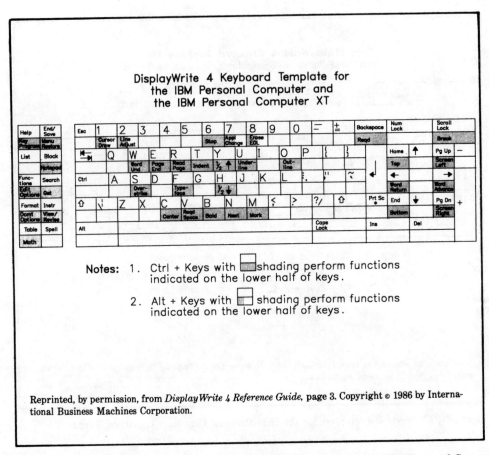

Figure 1-3b.   Keyboard template for the IBM Personal Computer and the IBM Personal Computer XT

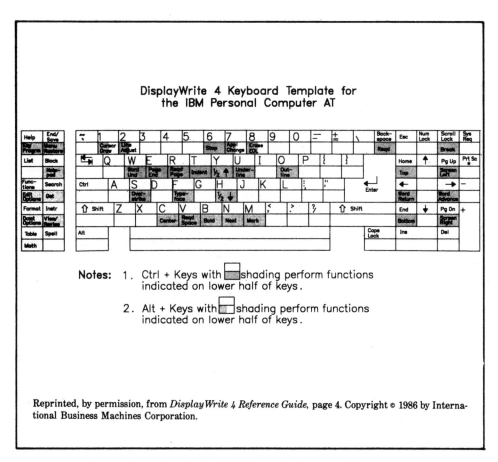

Figure 1-3c. Keyboard template for the IBM Personal Computer AT

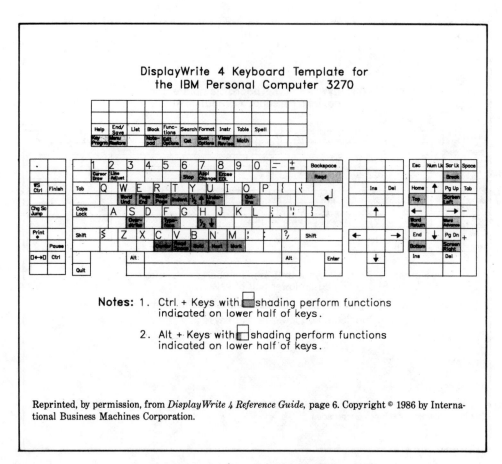

Figure 1-3*d*. Keyboard template for the IBM Personal Computer 3270

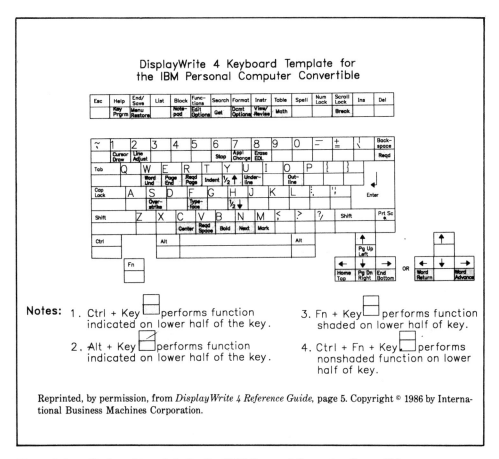

Figure 1-3e. Keyboard template for the IBM Personal Computer Convertible

2

Getting Started

This chapter shows you how to load DisplayWrite 4 into your personal computer, how to use the program to write a simple letter, how to save the letter on disk, and how to print a copy.

Loading DisplayWrite 4

Before you can proceed with this chapter, you must have completed the DisplayWrite 4 setup program described in Chapter 1. This program copies the DisplayWrite 4 files into a DW4 directory on your hard disk or onto floppy disks (the number depends on the size and type of the floppies you are using). If you are using a floppy-disk system, you will also need a blank, formatted disk to hold the letters, reports, and memos that you will produce with DisplayWrite 4.

Note: With a floppy-disk system, you might think it simpler to keep your programs and your writing all on the same disk so you don't have to keep track of so many disks. This is not a good idea, for two reasons. First, there is only so much storage space on a disk, and your program disks are already quite full because of the programs on them. If you start filling a program disk with documents, you will quickly run out of storage space. Second, as you add and delete your own writing on the disk, you might accidentally erase or damage some of your important programs.

Starting the Program

To load from a fixed-disk system,

1. Turn on your computer and monitor and enter the date and time if necessary.

2. When you see the DOS prompt,

   type **dw4** and press ENTER.

To load from a floppy-disk system, follow these steps:

1. Put the Volume 0 disk in drive A and the blank formatted floppy in drive B. Close the drive door.

2. Turn on your computer and monitor.

3. Enter the date and time if necessary.

4. When you see the DOS prompt,

   type **dw4** and press ENTER.

5. Insert the DW4 Volume 1 floppy in drive A

   and press ENTER.

Note: The IBM Voice Communications Operating Subsystem program works only on a fixed-disk system. If you are planning to use this program with Displaywrite 4, type the command **audiohf** at the DOS prompt *before* you load DisplayWrite 4. If the Voice Communications program is not on the default drive, you must specify the drive as well—for example, **audiohf [d]**.

You will see an attractive display introducing the program.

Now

press ENTER

to see the DisplayWrite 4 menu shown in Figure 2-1.

Using Menus

Notice that the top of the menu shows the menu's title—in this case simply "DisplayWrite 4." Below that is the list of menu items. A small box in front of an item means that you can choose it at the current time. Notice that the top item is

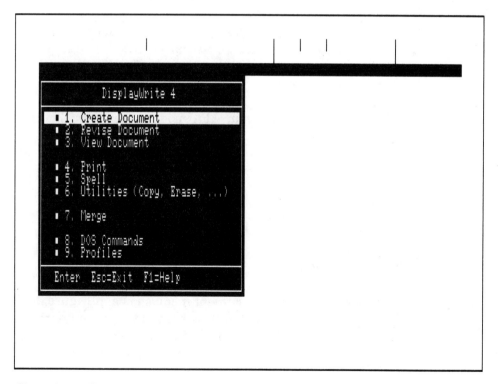

Figure 2-1. The DisplayWrite 4 menu

highlighted. Also notice that one letter in each menu choice is underlined or in a different color. At the bottom of the menu is the *select line* which lists keys used for such frequently used tasks as selecting a menu item, exiting the menu, or obtaining help.

You can make a menu selection by using any of the following methods:

- Simply press ENTER if the item you want is already highlighted. If not, press the UP or DOWN ARROW key or the TAB key to move the highlighting to your choice, and then press ENTER.

- Type the number or letter representing your choice. For example, to choose Print, you could type either **4** or **p**.

- If you are using a mouse, move the mouse cursor (which appears as an arrow or box on the screen) to the item you want and then click (press and release) button 1 on the mouse. Or you can press button 1 and hold it down, move the mouse cursor to the item you want, and then release button 1.

Note: If your display is in APA mode rather than Character mode (see Chapter 1), you will not see boxes in front of selectable items. Instead, selectable items will appear brighter than non-selectable items.

Since you are going to create a letter, you want to choose Create Document from the menu. To choose this selection,

press ENTER.

You will see the Create Document menu shown in Figure 2-2. Notice that this type of menu requires you to type in information, rather than to make selections.

You are now ready to pick a name for your document.

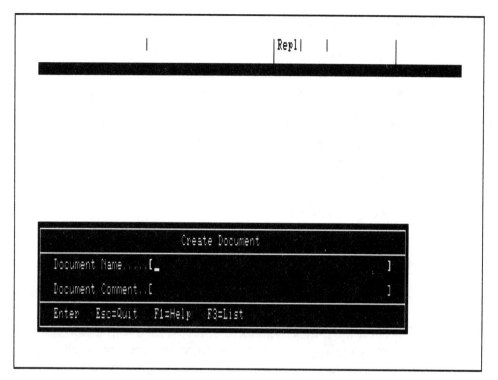

Figure 2-2. The Create Document menu

Naming Your File

Each piece of writing that you produce with DisplayWrite 4 will be saved on your disk as a separate *file*. A popular analogy compares a disk to a file drawer; the separate letters, tables, reports, and memos are equivalent to file folders that go into the drawer.

Each time you create a file, you must give it a unique name. Use this name whenever you want to interact with the file in any way, such as to look at it, revise it, or print it.

The file's name can consist of two parts: the *filename* and the file *extension*. In DisplayWrite 4, a filename can be from one to eight characters long. The extension consists of a period followed by one to three characters. If you don't include an extension in your file's name, DisplayWrite 4 will add the extension .DOC. (If you don't want any extension, type a period after the filename.) You can enter your file's name in uppercase or lowercase characters or a combination of both. DisplayWrite 4 always displays the name in uppercase.

Following are some examples of valid names:

ACCOUNTS.FEB
POSTCARD.SUE
CHAPTER.2
123
HOMEWORK.TXT
BASEBALL

On a hard-disk system, DisplayWrite 4 will automatically store your files in whatever directory you specified during the installation process. If you didn't specify any directory for your documents, they will be stored together with your program files in the DW4 directory.

On a floppy-disk system, DisplayWrite 4 will store your files on your data disk in drive B, because drive B is the *default drive*. This is the drive the system assumes if you don't specify any other. When you want to revise or print a file, DisplayWrite 4 will automatically look for it on the default drive.

If you want your file stored in a different directory or on a different drive, you must type a *path* or a *drive specifier* before the document name, to tell DisplayWrite 4 where to store the file. (See your *Disk Operating System* manual and Appendix C for information on using directories.)

Pick filenames that remind you of what is in the file. When DisplayWrite 4 prompts you for a file's name, you do not have to type in the default extension .DOC. Table 2-1 summarizes the rules for naming files.

Filename	Extension (Optional)
Consists of 1-8 characters	Consists of a period followed by 1-3 characters
Characters may include letters A-Z and numerals 0-9	Characters may include letters A-Z and numerals 0-9
Characters may include $ # & @ ! % ( ) - _ { } ' ' ~ ^	Characters may include $ # & @ ! % ( ) - _ { } ' ' ~ ^
May be entered in uppercase or lowercase letters, or in a combination of both	May be entered in uppercase or lowercase letters, or in a combination of both
	May be omitted by typing a single period after the file name. Otherwise, if you don't include an extension, the program will append the extension .DOC

Table 2-1.   Rules for Naming Files

Now you can start creating a file.

Type **example.1,**

but do not press ENTER. Instead, press TAB or use the DOWN ARROW key to move to the Document Comment item.

Type **practice file** and press ENTER.

You will see an almost blank screen. This is called the *typing area*. (The Document Comment entry is optional. To go directly to the typing area without entering a document comment, simply type the document name and press ENTER.)

Note: You can edit information that you type into a menu. See Table 2-2 to learn how to make menu corrections.

Key	Function
TAB or UP and DOWN ARROW keys	Move you from one menu item to the next. Use SHIFT-TAB to move back up the screen
BACKSPACE	Erases letters to the left of the cursor
LEFT and RIGHT ARROW keys	Move you left and right through your text
ALT-8 (the Erase End of Line key)	Erases any text from the cursor to the end of the line
INS	Toggles you back and forth between Replace mode and Insert mode
CTRL-F2 (the Menu Restore key)	Restores the menu's original default selections

Table 2-2. Editing Text in Menus

Entering Text

Now

press ENTER again

and you will be in the typing area. You are going to type a letter of recommendation for a friend. If, while you are typing, you see any mistakes in the sample letter or things that you would like to change, ignore them for now (you will revise this letter later). Type the letter exactly as shown in Figure 2-3, pressing the ENTER and TAB keys the number of times indicated.

Don't panic when you see lines of text disappear one by one from the top of the screen. They haven't vanished forever. Your letter will be all there when you print it out.

To use DisplayWrite 4, you must understand the function of the screen cursor and of several keys.

The Cursor

The cursor is the flashing line on your screen that shows where the next character will appear. As you type, the cursor moves to the right of each new character.

(TAB eight times) ──────────── December 8, 1986 *(ENTER*
                                                        twice)
Ms. Anne Summerson *(ENTER)*
Pharmotics, Inc. *(ENTER)*
144 East 18th Street *(ENTER)*
Flint, CA 59840 *(ENTER twice)*

Dear Ms. Summerson: *(ENTER twice)*

I would like to recommend Mr. Sam Flite for the position of
assistant office manager of Pharmotics, Inc. I have known
Mr. Flite for six years. He is a good worker and gets along
well with people. *(ENTER twice)*

In addition, Mr. Flite has excellent office skills. He can
organize tasks and meet deadlines. He is also a good
writer, and can produce clear reports without excess
verbiage. *(ENTER twice)*

Mr. Flite is also well-educated. He has a B.A. degree in
Business Administration. *(ENTER twice)*

Mr. Flite has an excellent personal appearance. He is a
very natty dresser. He always looks good when he comes to
the office and certainly will be able to represent your firm
at business meetings. *(ENTER twice)*

I am sure you will find Mr. Flipe an asset to your company.

(TAB eight times) ──────────── Sincerely,

(TAB eight times) ──────────── Henry Woodcourt

Figure 2-3. The EXAMPLE.1 file

If you have a mouse, the mouse cursor will look like an arrow or box and will move freely as you direct it with the mouse. To align the regular cursor with the mouse cursor, click button 1 on the mouse.

The Arrow Keys

On the numeric pad on the right side of your keyboard are four arrow keys, pointing up, down, right, and left. You can use these keys to move the cursor to any location in your text. When you press an arrow key, the cursor moves one space in the direction indicated by the arrow. The next letter you type will appear wherever the cursor is after you have moved it. Take a few moments now to practice using the arrow keys to move the cursor. You will notice that you cannot move past the end of your file. Try it and you will get the message

```
> Cannot move past end.
```

The BACKSPACE Key

Press the BACKSPACE key to correct any typing mistakes you make. BACKSPACE moves the cursor backward, erasing the character to the left of the cursor. When you have erased your mistake, type in the correct character. Note that BACKSPACE only works for the current line. If you are at the left margin, pressing BACKSPACE will not move you to the previous line.

The TAB Key

The TAB key indents your text a set number of spaces and works exactly the same way as the tab key on a typewriter. With the default setting, the cursor will jump five spaces each time you press TAB. Figure 2-3 shows you each time TAB is pressed to create the sample letter.

The ENTER Key

One big difference between typing with DisplayWrite 4 (and other word-processing programs) and typing with an ordinary typewriter is that DisplayWrite 4 automatically knows when to begin a new line when you type a paragraph. This feature is called *wordwrap*, because text that goes past the right margin is automatically "wrapped around" to begin a new line. However, you will often need to end one line at a particular place and begin another—for example, to end a paragraph, to end a short line, or to insert a blank line in your text. In such a case, you press ENTER. This is the same as using the carriage return on a typewriter. Figure 2-3 shows you each time ENTER is pressed to create the sample letter.

The Status Lines, the Menu Bar, and the Scale Line

At the top of the screen, above the typing area, are two lines of information. These are called the *status lines*. Below them is a *menu bar* that lists some of the keys you may need as you create and revise your file. Below the menu bar is a line that looks like a ruler. This is called the *scale line*. The status and scale lines give you important information about your text.

The Status Lines

The parts of the status lines are identified as follows:

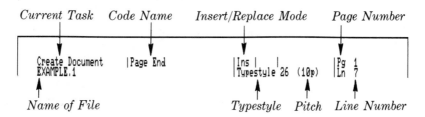

Many of these identifying labels will become more meaning-
ful as you read further in this book.

The Menu Bar

The menu bar lists the keys you can use at a particular time
to select DisplayWrite 4 functions. When you enter the typing area to create or revise a document, the menu bar looks
like this:

The menu bar keys have the following functions:

F2 (the End/Save key)	Lets you save your file or exit without saving.
F4 (the Block key)	Displays the Block menu so you can make text revisions.
F5 (the Functions key)	This is a "reminder" key. Use it to refresh your memory about which keys to press for which tasks.
F6 (the Search key)	Initiates Search and Search and Replace features.
F7 (the Format key)	Takes you to the Format menu so you can make format changes in your document.
F8 (the Instructions key)	Displays the Instructions menu. This key has a role in a variety of features such as Voice Notes, Merge, Keep, Footnotes, and so on. You will learn how to use it later on in this book.

To make selections from the menu bar, press the function key indicated or position the mouse cursor on your selection and click button 1.

The Scale Line

The scale line looks a lot like the scale line on a typewriter. The numbers on the line represent inches. Since standard printing paper, like standard typing paper, is 8 1/2 inches wide, the tiny rectangle between the 8- and 9-inch marks shows you the right edge of your paper. The scale line is shown here:

```
▌....2.....__....3.....__...4....▵...5....._....6...._....7...»....8....▪....9....
▲
```

The << and >> symbols show the current margin settings. In this example, the left margin is set at 15 and the right margin is set at 75 (multiply the scale-line number by 10 to figure the margin setting). Tabs are five spaces apart, as indicated by the underscores. You will learn how to change the margin and tab settings and design your own format for each file in Chapter 6.

Saving Your File

Each time you finish a writing session, you must save your text on your hard disk or on your floppy disk. Otherwise, your work will disappear forever the moment you turn off your computer.

To save your file,

press F2 (the End/Save key).

You will see

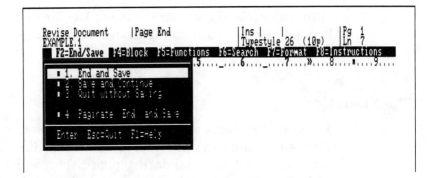

Next

choose End and Save.

This action saves your entire file on disk and must always be performed when you are finished working.

Note: The Save and Continue choice saves to disk the work you have done so far and then returns you to the typing area. Paginate, End, and Save paginates your file in addition to saving it. Pagination is recommended after revisions and when you use certain features like footnotes and outlines.

After saving the file, the program returns you to the DisplayWrite 4 menu so that you can print your letter or perform another word-processing task.

Printing Your File

Make sure that your printer is turned on and properly loaded with paper. Then, from the DisplayWrite 4 menu,

choose Print.

Then, from the Print menu,

choose Print Document.

You will see the Print Document menu. Notice that DisplayWrite 4 has already entered the document name for you.
(The system will assume that the file you want to print is the
one you have been working on. If it is not, just type in the
new name over the old.)
   This menu looks quite complex. In fact, it does not even fit
on one screen. You press PGDN to see the rest and then press
PGUP to return to the first screen. At this time, however, you
need not be concerned with the printing options.

   Press ENTER,

and your letter will be printed. If for any reason you need to
interrupt the printing process, press CTRL-BREAK.
   When printing is complete, you will be returned to the
DisplayWrite 4 menu. The following message will appear at
the bottom of the menu:

`Processing complete for EXAMPLE.i`

Read Chapter 7 if you have any difficulty printing your letter
or if you want to learn about printing options.

Using the Help Program

DisplayWrite 4 offers a *context-sensitive* Help facility that
provides you with information while you are using the program. *Context-sensitive* means that the program knows where
you are when you ask for help and will provide information
about the task at hand. To invoke Help,

   press F1 (the Help key).

If you are using a floppy-disk system, follow the prompt and insert the Volume 5 (Help) disk.

The left side of the screen displays the screen you were on when you invoked Help. On the right side of the screen, you will see a Help panel providing information about your task. For example, if you invoked Help after pressing F2, you would see a screen like Figure 2-4.

Notice the "2 of 6" message on the upper right of the screen. This means that you are looking at page two of six pages of information relating to your topic. You use the PGUP and PGDN keys to move through the Help panels. PGUP takes you to earlier panels; PGDN to later ones. Try moving through

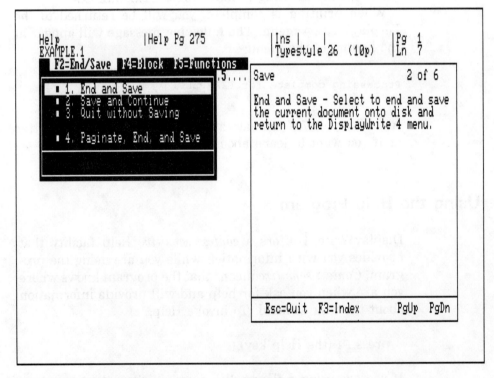

Figure 2-4. Invoking Help

Figure 2-5. Displaying the Help index

the Help panels now with PGUP and PGDN.

To display an index of all available Help topics, press F3. You will see the first page of a five-page index (see Figure 2-5). You select an item from the index in the same way that you select an item from any DisplayWrite 4 menu. For example, to see information about the Cursor Draw feature, use the TAB key to go down the list to Cursor Draw and then press ENTER.

When you are finished viewing Help panels,

press ESC to "quit."

Exiting DisplayWrite 4

When you are finished working with DisplayWrite 4, you must always exit DisplayWrite 4 and return to DOS. *Do not simply turn off your computer when you have completed a work session.* To exit DisplayWrite 4,

press ESC from the DisplayWrite 4 menu.

Then, to return to DOS,

press ENTER.

You will see the DOS prompt and can then use your computer for another task.

3

Moving Around
the Screen

*This chapter shows you how to use the List Services key to
select a file from a file directory and how to move to different
parts of your text in order to make revisions.*

Displaying a Directory

Now you are going to return your EXAMPLE.1 file to the
screen in order to revise it. First, load DisplayWrite 4 (see
instructions in Chapter 2). This time choose Revise Document from the menu. At the Revise Document screen, you
will be prompted for the document name.

You could just type in the name and press ENTER. Suppose,
however, you don't remember the name of your file. It isn't
difficult to remember now, when you have only one text file,
but how about when you have written 30 or 40 letters? Of
course, if you are familiar with DOS, you know that you can
use the DIR command to display a list of files in any directory before you even load DisplayWrite 4. But you would still

have to write down or remember the name so you would have it handy when DisplayWrite 4 prompts you for it.

Fortunately, DisplayWrite 4 lets you display a directory of your files whenever you need to, simply by pressing F3 (the List key). Instead of typing in the name of your file,

press F3.

You will see the List Services menu shown in Figure 3-1.

The Comments with Directory choice lets you see any comments that you entered when you created your file. For

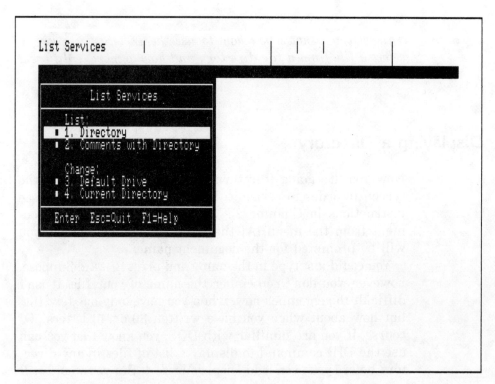

Figure 3-1. The List Services menu

now, you will view just the directory without comments.

Press ENTER.

You will be prompted for the directory name. Since you want to see a listing of files in the *default directory,* where your data files are, you do not need to type a directory name at this time.

Press ENTER.

You will see the screen display in Figure 3-2.

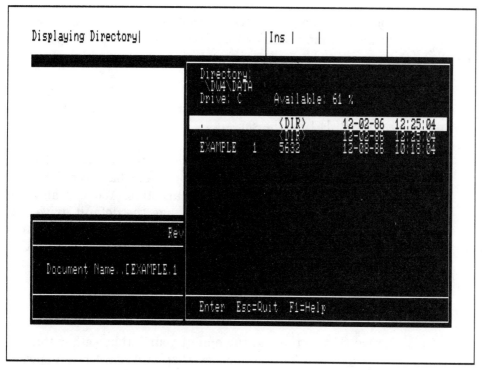

Figure 3-2. The Directory Display

Selecting a File from the Display

The Directory Display not only lists your files, it gives you other important information as well. It shows you the size of each file in bytes and the date and time the file was created. It also tells you how much space you have left on your disk. If you have a floppy-disk system, it is important to check that you have enough room on your disk to save the file you're working on.

You will probably find that the most helpful aspect of Directory Display is that it lets you select your file directly from the directory without your having to type the entire name. Just tab down to the file you want (at present there is only one) and press ENTER. Right now,

Tab down to EXAMPLE.1 and press ENTER.

You will return to the Revise Document screen, but now the document name EXAMPLE.1 will be typed in for you.

Press ENTER,

and you will find yourself in the typing area with EXAMPLE.1 on the screen.

Note: You can use the global characters * and ? to display a subset of your files in a directory. See Chapter 14 for more information on DOS global characters. You can also use the List Services feature to change the default drive and the current directory. You may want to use these features if you are working with subdirectories (see Appendix C).

Paper Clip

Notice that you are at the end of your letter, rather than at the beginning. This is because DisplayWrite 4 has a special Paper Clip feature that marks the cursor location at the time you save your file. Then, when you load the file for revision, DisplayWrite 4 returns you to the place where you were when you last worked on the file.

During any working session, you can disable Paper Clip so that the cursor will be at the beginning of any file that you load. To disable Paper Clip, press CTRL-F5 and set Return to Paper Clip to No. To disable Paper Clip permanently, you can change the system defaults (see Chapter 15).

Moving Through Your Text

In the previous chapter you saw that you can move the cursor in any direction by using the four arrow keys. Now you will learn some other ways to move around the screen.

Note: The keys you use to move around the screen are not the same in DisplayWrite 4 as they are in DisplayWrite 3. If you are a DisplayWrite 3 user who has just upgraded to DisplayWrite 4, consult Table 3-1 for a quick summary of cursor and screen movement keys.

What happens if you press the UP ARROW key until you get to the top of the screen, and then keep pressing it? Try it— you will see your text *scroll* up the screen a line at a time. In the same way, you can make your text scroll down the screen by continuing to press the DOWN ARROW key after you get to the bottom of the screen. The idea of scrolling can be confusing because when your text is scrolling up, you see it moving down. Just remember that scrolling up means moving toward the beginning of your file, and scrolling down means moving toward the end.

If you try to scroll past the beginning or end of your file, the program will send you the message "Cannot move above start" or "Cannot move past end" and nothing else will happen. To erase the message, move the cursor away from the edge.

Key	Function
(↑ UP ARROW)	Moves the cursor up one line
(↓ DOWN ARROW)	Moves the cursor down one line
(← LEFT ARROW)	Moves the cursor left one space
(→RIGHT ARROW)	Moves the cursor right one space
CTRL- ← (CTRL-LEFT ARROW)	Moves the cursor to the first character of a word or to the previous word if the cursor is already on the first character
CTRL- → (CTRL-RIGHT ARROW)	Moves the cursor to the first character of the next word
HOME	Moves the cursor to the beginning of the line
END	Moves the cursor to the end of the line
CTRL-HOME	Moves the cursor to the top of the page
CTRL-END	Moves the cursor to the bottom of the page
PGUP	Moves the screen window up
PGDN	Moves the screen window down
CTRL-PGUP	Moves the screen window left
CTRL-PGDN	Moves the screen window right
F6. Then select Go to Page	Moves the cursor to the specified page

Table 3-1. Cursor and Screen Movement Commands

Moving to the Beginning or End of a Line

Place the cursor in the middle of a full line of text in EXAMPLE.1.

Press HOME.

Notice that the cursor jumps instantly to the extreme left, as shown here:

I am sure you will find Mr. Flipe an asset to your company.

Press END

and the cursor jumps to the right edge of the typed line:

```
I am sure you will find Mr. Flipe an asset to your company.
```

Moving Word by Word

Now put the cursor on any word in your file (except the last). Next

press CTRL-RIGHT ARROW (the Word Advance key).

The cursor jumps to the first letter of the next word. If you are on the last word in a line, the cursor will jump to the first word in the next line.
Now put the cursor in the middle of any word (except the first).

Press CTRL-LEFT ARROW (the Word Return key).

The cursor will jump to the first letter of the word. If you are already on the first letter, the cursor will jump to the first letter of the previous word.

Moving to the Beginning or End of a Page

Press CTRL-HOME.

The cursor will jump to the first line of the page. When you are in the middle of a file consisting of several pages, pressing CTRL-HOME again will take you to the first line of the previous page. Now

press CTRL-END.

The cursor will jump to the last line of the page. When you

have a file of several pages, pressing CTRL-END again will take you to the last line of the next page. Practice using these keys a few times.

Moving to a Different Page

Right now your text file is only one page long, but when the file contains many pages, you will want to move quickly to any page you choose. You can do this easily. To move to a selected page,

press F6 (the Search key).

From the Search menu,

select Go to Page.

Type the desired page number, press ENTER, and you will find the cursor on the top line of the selected page.

If you want to go to the last page of your file, but you don't know exactly how many pages it has, type a number that you are sure is greater than the number of pages in the file. For example, type **20** for a ten-page file. After you press ENTER, you will be at the last page of your file.

Moving the Screen Window
with PGUP and PGDN

If your file is large, only a portion of text is visible on the screen at any time. The screen is like a window through which you can see your text moving. Two keys, PGUP and PGDN, let you move the screen window so you can view different portions of your text. These keys are particularly useful when you are working with large tables.

Putting a Line of Text at the Top or Bottom of the Screen   PGUP and
PGDN let you place the text line of your choice at the top or
bottom of the screen. To move the screen window so a line of
text appears at the top of the screen, put the cursor anywhere
on the line; then

    press PGDN.

The screen moves down until your line of text is at the top of
the screen.
    To move a line of text to the bottom of the screen, put the
cursor anywhere on the line; then

    press PGUP.

Your line of text is at the top of the screen.

Putting a Character at the Screen Edge   You can also use the PGUP
and PGDN keys to move the screen window to the left or right.
    To move the screen window so a selected character appears
on the left edge of the screen, put the cursor under the character, as shown here:

```
organize tasks and meet deadlines.  He is also a good
```

    Press CTRL-PGDN (the Screen Right key).

The window moves right until your character appears at the
left edge of the screen. Has most of your sample letter disap-
peared? You can get it back again with CTRL-PGUP (the
Screen Left key).
    When you are working with long lines of text (perhaps for
a large table or chart) you can use CTRL-PGUP to move the
window so that a character appears at the right instead of

somewhere in the center portion of the screen. Right now, if you try this you will get the message

> Cannot move past boundary.

You get this message because the system refuses to move the screen window left of the left margin.

Table 3-1 summarizes the cursor and screen movements discussed in this chapter. Go on to the next chapter to learn how to revise text. If you can't continue right now, be sure to save your file before you leave DisplayWrite 4.

4

Inserting, Deleting, Moving, and Copying Text

This chapter teaches you how to make simple text revisions and how to display codes during the revision process.

Viewing a Document

Before revising a file, you may wish simply to look at it to see whether you want to revise it or not. To view a file,

choose View Document from the DisplayWrite 4 menu.

Type in the document name, and then

press ENTER.

You can move through the text using any of the keys discussed in the preceding chapter. When you are finished viewing the file,

press F2.

You will return to the DisplayWrite 4 menu.

The advantage of using the View Document feature is that you are prevented from accidentally changing your file while looking at it. You can also use View Document to look at DisplayWrite 3 and revisable-form text documents.

Now you will revise EXAMPLE.1.

Displaying Codes

Choose Revise Document from the DisplayWrite 4 menu. Load EXAMPLE.1 and position the cursor at the beginning of your file. Run your cursor down the left edge of the screen; on the top status line you will occasionally see various terms, such as Tab and Required Carrier Return. These are called *code names*. Whenever a code name appears, you will also see a special symbol above the cursor, as shown here:

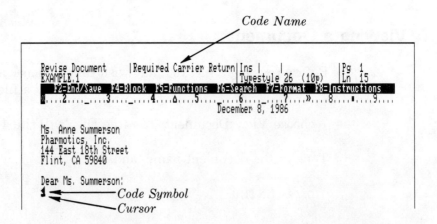

DisplayWrite 4 inserts into your text a number of codes that tell the system when to perform certain functions. Among the many codes are the Carrier Return code, Tab code, and Page-End code. Ordinarily, you cannot see a code unless the cursor is directly under it—in which case the code symbol appears above the cursor and the code name appears on the top status line.

When you are revising text, however, it is often helpful to be able to see all the codes all the time. To display codes,

press CTRL-F5 (the Edit Options key).

You will see the Edit Options menu shown in Figure 4-1.

Type **y** and press ENTER

to set Display All Codes to Yes.

You will be returned to the typing area. Your entire text

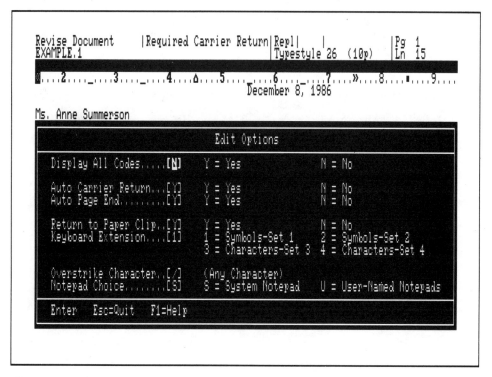

Figure 4-1. The Edit Options menu

will be peppered with codes. (When you are finished with all revisions, you can suppress the code display by pressing CTRL-F5 again and choosing No for Display All Codes.)

Inserting Text

There are two ways to add text to a file in DisplayWrite 4: the *insert* method and the *replace* method. Insert is the default. Look at the top status line and you will see Ins to the right of the code name area. This indicates that you are in Insert mode.

Insert Mode

You are going to insert a new sentence into the skimpy paragraph about Mr. Flite's education. Move the cursor to the beginning of the word "He" and type in the sentence as shown:

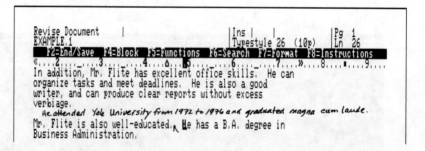

What happened? As you typed, the sentence beginning with "He" was pushed to the right and the new text *inserted* after it. Now move the cursor to a different line, and your new paragraph will instantly be rearranged into lines of appropriate length, as you see here:

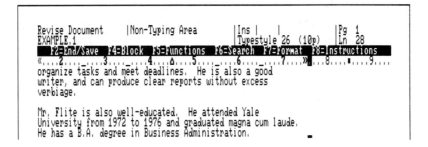

Replace Mode

Press the INS key on your keyboard. Now look at the second status line; the word "Ins" has changed to "Repl." You are now in Replace mode. (The INS key acts as a *toggle;* to change back to Insert mode, you just press INS again.)

Now you will make some text changes while in Replace mode. First, put the cursor under the "m" in the word "magna," as you see here:

```
University from 1972 to 1976 and graduated magna cum laude.
```

Type the letters

summ

The new letters replace the old, and the word "magna" has become "summa."

Now go down to the last sentence in your letter and correct Mr. Flite's name. Use Replace mode to change "Mr. Flipe" to "Mr. Flite." Then return to Insert mode.

Deleting Small Amounts of Text

You have already learned how to delete a character simply by backspacing over it: each time you press BACKSPACE, the character to the left of the cursor disappears. A second way is to use the DEL key to delete the character the cursor is on.

Deleting Single Characters

Go to the second paragraph of EXAMPLE.1. Place the cursor under the first "e" in the word "excess."

```
writer, and can produce clear reports without excess
```

Press DEL six times.

You will see the unnecessary word "excess" eaten up, one letter at a time. Move the cursor to a different line, and your lines will adjust automatically.

Deleting Codes

You can use the DEL key to erase codes as well as single characters. Right now you don't have much reason to erase the codes, but when you learn additional techniques—such as underlining, centering, and overstriking—you will need to know how to erase codes if you want to cancel instructions you have given to DisplayWrite 4.

Now, with Display All Codes set to Yes, move the cursor under the little triangle after the line

```
Ms. Anne Summerson.◄
```

You know that you're on the right spot if the status line

reads Required Carrier Return.

Press DEL.

You will be prompted as follows:

```
> Press Enter to delete this code, or move the cursor.
```

Since you want to delete the code,

press ENTER.

What happened? You can see that two lines of text joined together:

```
Ms. Anne SummersonPharmotics, Inc.
```

That's because you deleted the Required Carrier Return code that separated them. Press ENTER to restore the code, and you will see the two lines jump apart.

Notice that two different carriage return symbols are shown in your text. One is for a required carriage return (also called a *hard* carriage return). This symbol appears when you press ENTER to force a line to end at a particular spot. The other symbol is for a *soft* carriage return. This symbol appears at the end of a word-wrapped line.

As you insert and delete text, word-wrapped lines will adjust automatically, but lines ending with a required carriage return will always terminate exactly where you press ENTER.

Deleting a Blank Line

You can use the DEL key to delete a blank line between lines of text (such as between paragraphs). Simply put the cursor anywhere on the blank line and press DEL. The cursor will jump to the left of the line, under the Required Carrier Return symbol. Press ENTER in response to the prompt, and the line will be deleted.

Block Moves

The DisplayWrite 4 Block function lets you "cut and paste" your writing electronically. That is, you can arrange your text in various ways, moving sentences and paragraphs around until they are exactly where you want them. You can also use the Block function to delete large sections of text. You can even change your mind and restore a block of deleted text *without retyping it*. This chapter teaches you how to use the Move, Copy, Delete, Restore Delete Block, and Mark functions.

Deleting a Block

It would be tedious to delete a large quantity of text by pressing DEL over and over again, letter after letter. Instead, use the Block function to delete more than a word or two. For example, go to the fourth paragraph of EXAMPLE.1. You are going to delete the inappropriate sentence "He is a very natty dresser."

Put the cursor under the letter "H" in the word "He."

Press F4 (the Block key).

You will see the Block menu shown in Figure 4-2. Select Delete. You will be prompted as follows:

```
> Move the cursor to the end of the block; press Enter.
```

Using the cursor movement keys in the usual way, move the

cursor two spaces past the period at the end of the sentence. Your block of text will be highlighted. If you make a mistake, press ESC and start over.

When you have highlighted the block,

press ENTER,

and the block of text will disappear. (Include all punctuation and spaces in the block you are deleting, or you will have to delete them separately.) Move the cursor to a different line and the line endings will be readjusted.

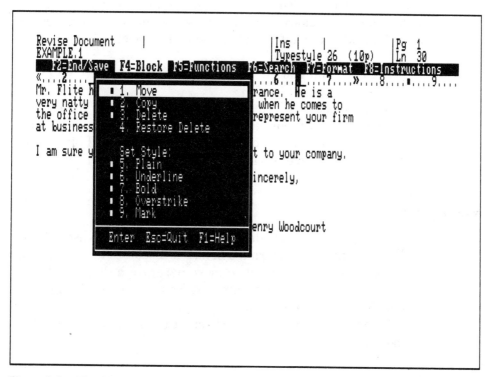

Figure 4-2. The Block menu

Note: There is another way to highlight blocks of text. After you have selected Delete, type the last character of the block you want deleted. The text will be highlighted from the cursor to the first occurrence of that character. The next time you type the character, the text will highlight to the second occurrence. Keep retyping the character until you get to the end of the block. This method is quite handy when you want to delete a sentence. Just type a period after you select Delete, and the cursor will usually jump to the end of the sentence.

Undoing a Deletion

If you change your mind and want to restore a deleted block of text, DisplayWrite 4 lets you undo the deletion. To restore a deleted text block, move the cursor to the first character (or code) that you want to appear *after* the block.

Press F4 and choose Restore Delete.

The last block that you deleted will be restored. You can restore this block in any text location and as often as you want, but you can only restore the most recently deleted block, and only while you are working on the current document.

Moving a Block

Now suppose you decide that your letter should discuss Mr. Flite's personal appearance before it discusses his education. In other words, you want to move paragraph three so that it comes after paragraph four. You can do this easily in DisplayWrite 4 with a block move.

Place the cursor under the first letter of the block you want moved:

```
Mr. Flite is also well-educated.  He attended Yale
```

Press F4 and choose Move.

Now, in response to the prompt, move the cursor to the end of the text you want moved (including all codes). In this case, go to the blank line after the paragraph about Mr. Flite's education, so you can include the Required Carrier Return code.

As you work, you will see the block becoming highlighted. (Remember, if you make a mistake, press ESC and start over.) The highlighted block will look like the one that you see in Figure 4-3.

Press ENTER,

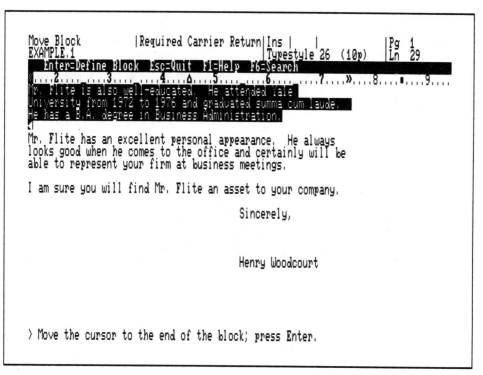

Figure 4-3. The text block to be moved is highlighted

and you will be prompted as follows:

```
To where? Move cursor; press Enter.
```

Move the cursor to the exact spot where you want the blocked text to begin. In this example, the cursor should be placed as shown here:

```
I am sure you will find Mr. Flite an asset to your company.
```

Don't worry about the text already there; it will be taken care of automatically.

Press ENTER,

and your paragraph is moved to the new location.

You can see that this feature saves you tedious deleting and retyping. Instead of deleting the text where you no longer want it and retyping it where you do, you can move the text from its old to its new location with one quick move.

Copying a Block

Sometimes you want a block of text in a new location, but you want the block to remain in the original location as well. The procedure is much the same as for a block move: press F4, but this time select Copy from the menu. Highlight the text to be copied just as you did for the block move, put the cursor where you want the copy to appear, and press ENTER. Your text block will appear in both the old and the new location.

Storing Text in Notepad

DisplayWrite 4 has a Notepad feature which lets you move or copy a block of text to a special "notepad." Then, whenever you want to, you can recall the block to any location you desire. Notepad has two advantages over the regular Move Block and Copy Block features.

- You can recall the text in Notepad either to the same file or to a different file. With regular block moves you can only recall the text to the same file.

- You can end a working session and shut off your computer. When you resume working, your text will still be stored in Notepad, ready for you to copy or move.

Notepad is a handy way to store text that you may be using in a variety of files—for example, an address that you frequently use, or your salutation in a letter. Only one item can be stored in the Notepad at a time. When you store a second item, it overwrites the first.

To use Notepad, position the cursor on the first character of the block you want to define. Next,

press CTRL-F4 (the Notepad key) to display the following:

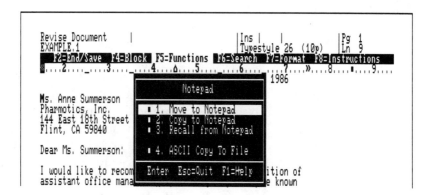

Choose Move to Notepad to remove the block from your file and store it in Notepad, or choose Copy to Notepad to leave the original block and also place a copy of it in Notepad. Then, following the prompt, move the cursor to the end of the block and press ENTER. The text will be stored in Notepad.

To recall the text block from Notepad, go to the location where you want the block to appear. (Remember that this can be the same file or a different file.)

Press CTRL-F4 and choose Recall from Notepad.

The text will appear at the cursor location.

Note: You can create and name your own Notepads instead of using the default $NOTEPAD.DOC. To change the Notepad name for a working session, you must first display the Edit Options menu by pressing CTRL-F5 when you are in the typing area. From the menu, select User Named Notepads. Then, when you later select Notepad with CTRL-F4, you will be prompted for the new Notepad name. You can also change the Notepad name permanently by changing the system defaults (see Chapter 15).

Blocking Text with a Mouse

When you block text with a mouse (either for Block with F4 or for Notepad with CTRL-F4), you block the text *before* you choose the action. First position the mouse cursor at the beginning of the block. Then align the mouse cursor with the text cursor by pressing and holding button 1 on the mouse.

Now *quickly* release and then hold button 1. This begins the block definition. While still pressing button 1, drag the mouse to the location where you want the block to end. Then release button 1.

Now you may select Block or Notepad and choose your action.

Revision Marking

The Revision Marking feature lets you mark text blocks that you have added or deleted during the revision process. Insertions are identified by both bold and underlining. Deletions are identified by overstriking.

Revision Marking makes it easy to see what you are doing to a document while you are working on it. Then, during pagination (see Chapter 5), the underlining and bold are stripped from text insertions, and the overstruck sections are deleted.

Marking Insertions

There are two ways to mark text insertions: with CTRL-M (the Mark key) and with the Block menu.

Marking Insertions with CTRL-M   Position the cursor at the location where you want to begin marking an insertion.

Press CTRL-M.

Type the insertion.

Press CTRL-M again

to end marking. The inserted text will be underlined and highlighted.

Note: How the text actually looks depends upon your monitor. It may be highlighted or underlined or may appear in a different color. However, it will definitely look different from regular text.

Marking Insertions with the Block Menu   To mark insertions with the Block menu, type the insertion first. Then position the cursor under the first character or code tobe marked.

Press F4 and choose Mark.

Move the cursor to the end of the block and

press ENTER.

The text block will be marked for insertion.

Marking Deletions

There are also two ways to mark text to be deleted: with CTRL-S (the Overstrike key) and with the Block menu.

Marking Deletions with CTRL-S   Move the cursor under the first character or code of the text you want deleted.

Press CTRL-S.

Then move the cursor past the last character or code of the deletion.

Press CTRL-S again

to end marking. The inserted text will be overstruck. (All you will see on the screen will be the overstrike character. However, if you move your cursor through the deletion, you will see your original characters.)

Marking Deletions with the Block Menu   Position the cursor under the first character to be marked.

Press F4 and choose Overstrike.

Move the cursor to the end of the block.

Press ENTER.

The text block will be marked for deletion.

Note: You can change the overstrike character from the default / (slash) by pressing F5 in the typing area and changing Overstrike Character to the desired character.

Adjusting Line Endings

You have already seen that paragraphs are automatically realigned after you add or delete text. However, you can get an even neater right margin after revisions by using either F12 (if your keyboard has this key) or ALT-2 (the Line Adjust key). This key will fit as many words as possible within your designated margins and prompt you to make hyphenation decisions when words cross the margins. However, the key will not suggest how you should hyphenate the words.

Use this key with short pieces of writing. When you begin writing text files of many pages, you will use the pagination feature (see Chapter 5) to adjust margins and hyphenate text. However, with one-page documents or short portions of text, you will probably find it quicker and more convenient to use Line Adjust.

Look at the paragraph beginning "Mr. Flite is also well-educated." The right margin of this paragraph is more ragged than you might find acceptable for a business letter. To straighten it, move the cursor to the beginning of the first line you want adjusted:

`Mr. Flite is also well-educated.  He attended Yale`

Press ALT-2.

The word "University" pops up to the same line as "Yale."

Move the cursor along the word "University" until you reach an appropriate hyphenation point, as shown here:

```
Univer_sity
```

Press ENTER,

and the word is hyphenated at the place you designated. Continue pressing ALT-2 until you get to the end of the paragraph. Figures 4-4*a* and 4-4*b* show the paragraph before and after Line Adjust.

```
Mr. Flite is also well-educated.  He attended Yale
University from 1972 to 1976 and graduated summa cum laude.
He has a degree in Business Administration.
```

Figure 4-4*a*. Paragraph before Line Adjust

```
Mr. Flite is also well-educated.  He attended Yale Univer-
sity from 1972 to 1976 and graduated summa cum laude.  He
has a degree in Business Administration.
```

Figure 4-4*b*. Paragraph after Line Adjust

If, during Line Adjust, you don't want to hyphenate the word "University" at all, you can move the entire word to the next line by putting the cursor under the first letter of the word and pressing ENTER. To keep the entire word on the current line, move the cursor one space past the end of "University" and press ENTER.

Note: The hyphens that the system inserts between syllables in a word are called *soft hyphens* because, if you later revise your text so that a hyphenated word falls in the middle of a line, the hyphen will automatically disappear. In the paragraph you have just adjusted, the word "University" contains a soft hyphen. The words "well-educated" contain a *hard hyphen*, or one that will remain in text.

Pagination After Revision

When you reach the bottom of a page, DisplayWrite 4 automatically saves that page on disk and begins a new page. If you are using default settings, this break will occur after line 60.

If you revise your file, however, by adding and deleting text, DisplayWrite 4 will not automatically readjust your pages. For example, if you type a full 60-line page and then add a 10-line insert in the middle of the page, your page will now be 70 lines long and will probably run off the paper when you print it out. Therefore, whenever you revise your text, you must use DisplayWrite 4's Pagination feature to readjust your page endings. See the next chapter to learn how to paginate your text.

Table 4-1 lists the keys used for inserting and deleting text and identifies their functions.

Key	Function
BACKSPACE	Deletes the character to the left of the cursor
DEL	Deletes the character the cursor is on
INS	Toggles back and forth from Insert mode to Replace mode
F4	Deletes, moves, and copies blocks of text
CTRL-F4	Invokes Notepad
ATL-2 or F12	Adjusts line endings for short portions of text
CTRL-F5	When "Display All Codes" is set to Yes, makes all codes visible on the screen
CTRL-M	Inserts a "Begin Mark" or "End Mark" code into your text, which begins or ends insertion marking
CTRL-S	Inserts a "Begin Overstrike" or "End Overstrike" code into your text, which begins or ends overstriking

Table 4-1. Keys Used for Inserting, Deleting, Moving, Copying, and Marking Text

5

Determining Page Breaks

This chapter describes DisplayWrite 4's automatic pagination feature and teaches you how to paginate your document after revision.

Automatic Pagination

As you entered text for the first time, you probably noticed the small triangle moving along to the right of the words you were typing, as you see here:

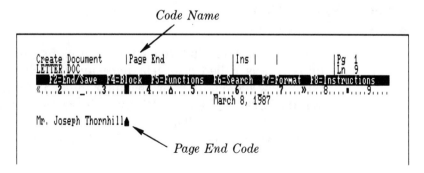

Code Name

```
Create Document    |Page End            |Ins |    |          |Pg  1
LETTER.DOC                                                    |Ln  9
    F2=End/Save  F4=Block  F5=Functions  F6=Search  F7=Format  F8=Instructions
  «....2...._....3....▪....4....▵....5....┬....6....┐....7....»....8....▪....9....
                                  March 8, 1987

Mr. Joseph Thornhill▴
```

Page End Code

This is a Page End code. When you complete the last typing line of each page (the default is 60 lines), DisplayWrite 4 *automatically* saves the page and positions the cursor at the start of a new blank page. It does this by inserting a Page End code at the end of the last typing line. The Page End code that you see moving along is the Page End code for the last page in the file.

You can also start a new page at any time by pressing CTRL-E (the Page End key). This inserts a Page End code at the cursor location.

Note: If you are upgrading from DisplayWrite 3, you will notice that the pagination features work differently in DisplayWrite 4 from the way they do in DisplayWrite 3. In DisplayWrite 3, you have to press CTRL-E whenever you want to begin a new page; the program does not automatically break your text into pages when you reach the last typing line. If you want to make DisplayWrite 4 work the way DisplayWrite 3 does (that is, you want to make all page-ending decisions yourself), in the typing area press CTRL-F5 (the Edit Options key) and change Auto Page End to No.

Notice also that DisplayWrite 4's terminology is different from DisplayWrite 3's. *Manual pagination* in Display-Write 3 is called *automatic pagination* in DisplayWrite 4; *automatic pagination* in DisplayWrite 3 is simply referred to as *pagination* in DisplayWrite 4.

Decimal System Numbers and What They Mean

The page number that you see on the right side of the top status line is called a *system page number*. Each time you start a new page (either by reaching the end of a page or by pressing CTRL-E), DisplayWrite 4 increments the system page number by one. These numbers indicate where you are in a file; they do not appear on the printed copy.

If you revise your text to insert a new page between two existing pages, DisplayWrite 4 will give the new page a *decimal system page number*. For example, if your file is two pages long and you add a new page between page 1 and page 2 (by pressing CTRL-E), the status line will read "Pg 1.1," as shown here:

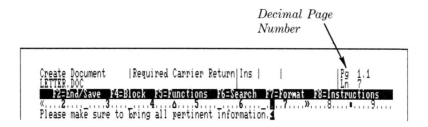

Decimal Page Number

DisplayWrite 4 does this in order to keep intact the page numbers that follow. If you later add more pages between page 1 and page 2, DisplayWrite 4 will assign system page numbers of up to two decimal places.

If you paginate your file (see the next section, "The Pagination Feature and When to Use It"), DisplayWrite 4 will divide your file into pages of even length and assign them new system page numbers, eliminating any decimals.

Limitations of Automatic Pagination

Automatic pagination seems like a simple, effective method. It is certainly suitable for short documents and documents with few revisions. But automatic pagination does have definite limitations.

One problem is that if you make revisions, you *must* keep track of where you are on a page. For example, if you have a full 60-line page and you add 30 new lines of text in the middle of the page, DisplayWrite 4 *will not* rebreak your text into even-sized pages—your new page will now be 90 lines long.

If you then simply press F2 to save your work, your 90-line page will run off the paper when you print it out.

Similarly, if you delete text from a page, your revised page will now be too short. When you print out this page, you will have extra space at the bottom of the paper.

To solve this problem, DisplayWrite 4 has a special *Pagination* feature. During pagination, old Page End codes are wiped out and your text is redivided into pages of even length. Pagination also activates any changes that you have made in your document format, as well as other features such as footnoting and outlining.

Inserting Required Page End Codes

Suppose you later plan to use the Pagination feature (which will readjust your page length), but you also want to end certain pages at specified points. For example, suppose you are typing a report with three main sections, and you want each section to begin on a new page. You can take advantage of the Pagination feature *and* specify page breaks by inserting Required Page End codes in your file.

To insert a Required Page End code in your file, position the cursor where you want the page to end. Then

press CTRL-R (the Required Page End key).

A Required Page End code is inserted into your file. During pagination, DisplayWrite 4 will begin a new page when it encounters this code.

Note: One peculiarity of DisplayWrite 4 is that if you are on the last page of your file when you insert the Required Page End code, the system also inserts a regular Page End code. If you are not on the last page, the system only inserts the Required Page End code.

The Pagination Feature
and When to Use It

When you use the Pagination feature, DisplayWrite 4 counts lines for you and divides your text into pages that fit within your chosen margins. This option lets you use the Dictionary Hyphenation feature of DisplayWrite 4. Use the Pagination feature for long text files, for files that have been revised extensively, for files with format changes, and for files containing footnotes and outlines. (For simplicity, this book will use the words "paginate" and "pagination" when referring to the Pagination feature.)

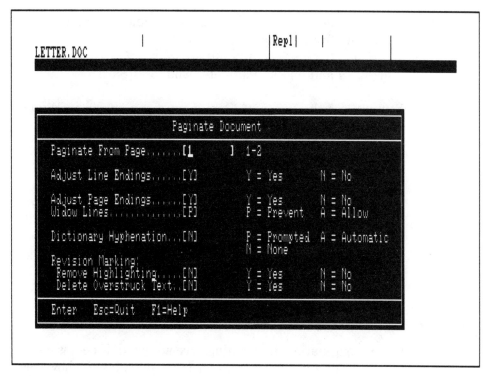

Figure 5-1. The Paginate Document menu

You can paginate at any one of three times, as follows:

- To paginate while working on a file, press CTRL-F7 and choose Paginate Document.

- To save a file and paginate, press F2 and choose Paginate, End, and Save.

- To paginate during a spelling check, choose Spell from the DisplayWrite 4 menu. Then choose Check Document from the Spell menu and set Paginate Document to Yes.

Note: You can also paginate during a merge operation. This process will be discussed in Part 3, "Producing Repetitive Documents."

Pagination is most frequently performed during a save operation. To paginate during a save,

press F2 and choose Paginate, End, and Save.

You will see the Paginate Document menu shown in Figure 5-1. There are several options to choose from.

Selecting the Starting Page

When you paginate, you usually want to do so for your entire file. In this case, you can skip over this option, since Paginate From Page 1 is the default. However, if you want to begin pagination partway through your file, specify the page of your choice.

Adjusting Line Endings

During pagination, line endings are adjusted, if necessary, to fit precisely within the left and right margins. If, however, you want each line to remain exactly as you typed it in the typing area, set Adjust Line Endings to No. (If you already set Adjust Line Endings to No when designing a format for your file, you do not have to do it again here. The lines will not be adjusted.)

Adjusting Page Endings

During pagination, your text will be evenly divided to fit within the selected top and bottom margins. But if you want to use CTRL-E to determine the page endings while still using the other features that pagination offers, set Adjust Page Endings to No. The pages will end only where you have pressed CTRL-E to insert a Page End code, but you will still be able to use the other pagination features.

Note: If you set Adjust Page Endings to No, Required Page End codes will be ignored; only regular Page End codes will be honored.

Avoiding Widows

In typography, a *widow* is a short last line of a paragraph sitting alone as the first text line on a page. Similarly, an *orphan* is the first line of a paragraph sitting alone as the last line of a page. DisplayWrite 4 will automatically avoid leaving widows and orphans even if it causes some pages to be slightly longer or shorter than others.

If you want each page of your text to have *exactly* the number of lines specified by your format, even if it means leaving widows and orphans, change Widow Lines from P (prevent) to A (allow).

Hyphenation

If you do not hyphenate ragged right text, some lines will be quite short and others quite long. Hyphenation gives ragged right text a straighter right margin. Figure 5-2 shows how

```
                   If you justify your right

          margin,    but     neglect    to

          hyphenate, your   printed  text

          may be quite unevenly  spaced.

          This    problem    is    more

          noticeable   if   you   use

          unusually large margins.
```

Figure 5-2. Justified text without hyphenation

justified text can look without hyphenation; this is a "worst case" because the margins are large. If you hyphenate justified text, the words will be spaced more evenly.

The Dictionary Hyphenation default is N (none), meaning that if you don't make any menu changes here your text will not be hyphenated. If you want to hyphenate, set Dictionary Hyphenation to P (Prompted mode) or to A (Automatic mode). In Automatic mode DisplayWrite 4 will look up words in its dictionary, make hyphenation decisions, and insert hyphens at the appropriate points. The system also looks up words in Prompted mode, but it only suggests places to hyphenate; you make the final decisions. Hyphenation takes place during the actual pagination process.

As when you used the Line Adjust key, the hyphens inserted during dictionary hyphenation are soft hyphens. These hyphens disappear if you later revise your text and the hyphenated words no longer fall at the end of the line.

Revision Marking

When you revise your text, DisplayWrite 4 lets you mark insertions and deletions with its Revision Marking feature. Insertions can be marked with bold and underlining; deletions can be marked with overstriking. This feature lets you keep track of the revisions you have made while you are working on your file. The process is explained in Chapter 4.

The Revision Marking choice on the Paginate Document menu lets you remove markings from inserted text and delete the text marked for deletion before you print the file. The first item, Remove Highlighting, removes the bold and underlining from inserted text; the second item, Delete Overstruck Text, deletes the text marked for deletion from your file. To remove highlighting or delete the text, change the default from No to Yes.

The Pagination Process

When you have completed all menu changes in the Paginate Document menu,

press ENTER.

What happens next depends on the choice you made for Hyphenation.

Note: To interrupt the pagination process at any point, press CTRL-BREAK.

Pagination Without Hyphenation

If you are not hyphenating, DisplayWrite 4 will proceed to paginate your file. When pagination is complete, you will see a message like this:

`"FILE.XYZ" is paginated.`

You will then be returned to the DisplayWrite 4 menu.

Pagination with Automatic Hyphenation

If you selected automatic hyphenation, DisplayWrite 4 will proceed to paginate your file, making hyphenation decisions as necessary. When you later return to your file, you will see words hyphenated that would, without hyphenation, cross the right margin.

Pagination with Prompted Hyphenation

If you selected prompted hyphenation, the program will halt at the first word that requires hyphenation. You will see your text on the screen with the cursor flashing at a suggested hyphenation spot. The message

`Cursor to hyphenation point and press Enter.`

appears on the screen. Now you have several options.

- To hyphenate the word at the suggested place, press ENTER.

- To hyphenate the word at another place, move the cursor to the spot where you want the hyphen to be and press ENTER.

- To move the entire word to the next line, move the cursor under the first letter of the word and press ENTER.

- To keep the whole word on the same line, move the cursor one space past the word and press ENTER.

The program will repeat the process for each word requiring hyphenation. When pagination and hyphenation are complete, a message tells you that your file is paginated, and you are returned to the DisplayWrite 4 menu.

Keeping Text Together with the Keep Function

You may want a specific number of lines of text to be printed on one page. Suppose, for example, that you are including a table in your file. You don't know where the page breaks will come, but you *do* know that you don't want the table split up.

You can use the Keep function to designate text that must be kept together. With Keep, your entire table will be printed on the current page if there is room; if not, the entire table will be printed on the following page.

Inserting Keep Codes

To insert Keep codes, start in the typing area. Move the cursor under the first character or code of the text you want kept together.

Press F8 (the Instructions key) and choose Begin.

Then, from the Begin menu,

choose Keep.

A Begin Keep code is inserted in your text.

Now move the cursor one space past the last character of the text to be kept together (again, make sure that you include all relevant codes).

Press F8 and choose End.

Then, from the End menu,

choose Keep.

An End Keep code is inserted into your text.
Now, when you paginate your file, the block of text between the Begin Keep and End Keep codes will be kept together.

When Keep Won't Work

The Keep function won't work if you have given DisplayWrite 4 conflicting instructions. Specifically, Keep won't work in the following situations:

- You have inserted a Required Page End code between the Begin Keep code and the End Keep code.
- You have set Adjust Page Endings to No.
- The text to be kept together is too long to fit on one page.

Deleting Page End, Required Page End, and Keep Codes

If you revise your text and the codes you inserted are no longer applicable, you can delete them:

Press CTRL-F5 and set Display All Codes to Yes.

When codes are displayed, move the cursor under the code you want to remove.

Press DEL, and then press ENTER.

Key	Function
F2	The Paginate, End, and Save choice saves and paginates your file
CTRL-F5	When Auto Page End is set to No in the Edit Options menu, the program will not begin a new page when you complete the last typing line on the current page
CTRL-F7	The Paginate choice in the Document Options menu lets you paginate while you are in the typing area
F8	The Begin choice, followed by Keep, designates the beginning of a text block to be kept on one page
	The End choice, followed by Keep, designates the end of a text block to be kept on one page
CTRL-E	During automatic pagination, ends the current page and begins a new page
CTRL-R	Inserts a Required Page End code, which forces a page to end at a designated place. Honored only during pagination, not during automatic pagination
CTRL-BREAK	Interrupts the pagination process

Table 5-1. Keys Used in Automatic Pagination and in Pagination

There is no need to delete Page End codes if you are going to paginate, as these codes will be ignored anyway.

Table 5-1 lists the keys involved in the Automatic Pagination and Pagination features and identifies their functions.

6

Designing Your Own Format

This chapter shows you how to customize the appearance of your writing by selecting margins, tabs, line spacing, and other format options. You will create a short text file using a new format.

Defaults

When you entered the EXAMPLE.1 letter, you didn't make any decisions about margins, tabs, or line spacing; yet when you printed the file, your letter looked acceptable.

This is because DisplayWrite 4 has predetermined, or default, settings that go into effect unless you tell them not to. There are default settings for almost every aspect of DisplayWrite 4's operation.

You change default settings for a file with the Document Options menu. If you don't make any changes, the defaults are in effect. In this case, "your" choices are actually DisplayWrite 4's choices. Figure 6-1 shows you some of DisplayWrite 4's formatting defaults.

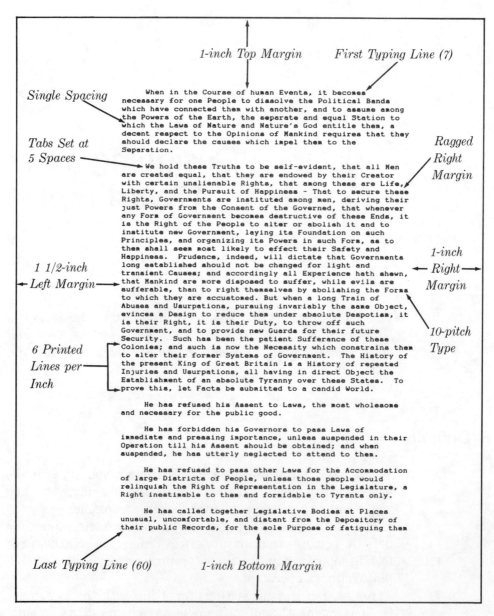

Figure 6-1. What a default page looks like

If you are using the default settings and the margins on your printed text look larger or smaller than they should, the paper guide or tractor feed on your printer may be creating an additional margin of its own. If the top margin appears larger than it should and the bottom margin appears smaller, the paper in your printer is probably advanced a few lines.

You may be at any location in your file when you design a format. However, unless you are at the beginning, you must paginate the file for the format to be in effect. To learn how to use several different formats in the same file, refer to Chapter 10.

> *Note:* If you want to create all future files using the format you design, you can change DisplayWrite 4's default settings. See Chapter 15 to learn how to do this.

Creating a Format

To design a format for a file, go to the typing area. Then

press CTRL-F7 (the Document Options key).

You will see the Document Options menu, as shown here:

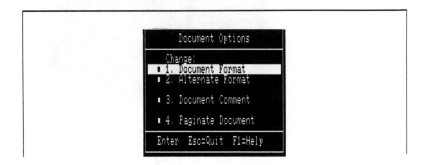

Choose Document Format. You will see the Change Document Format menu shown in Figure 6-2. (Note that you can also use the Document Options menu to change a document comment that you previously entered and to paginate your document during a working session.)

In this chapter, you will learn about the first four items in the Change Document Format menu: margin and tab changes, line spacing, typestyles, and page layout/paper options. All format changes that you make will be saved when you save the file. If you want to load the file at a later time to revise it, you will not have to design the format again unless you want to change it.

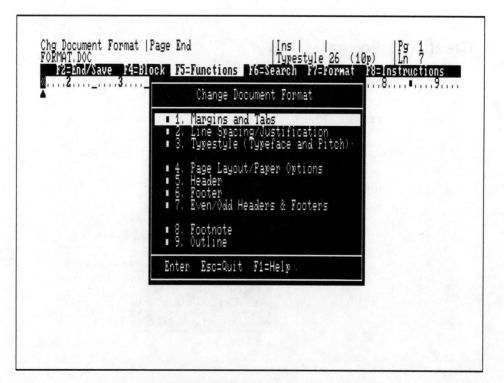

Figure 6-2.   The Change Document Format menu

Setting Margins and Tabs

To change margin and tab settings, select Change Margins and Tabs from the Change Document Format menu. You will see a scale line at the top of the screen and a set of instructions for changing margin and tab settings (see Figure 6-3).

Changing the Margins

Look at the scale line on your screen. The cursor will be over the << (the left-margin symbol). If you want a smaller margin, press the BACKSPACE key to move the margin symbol left

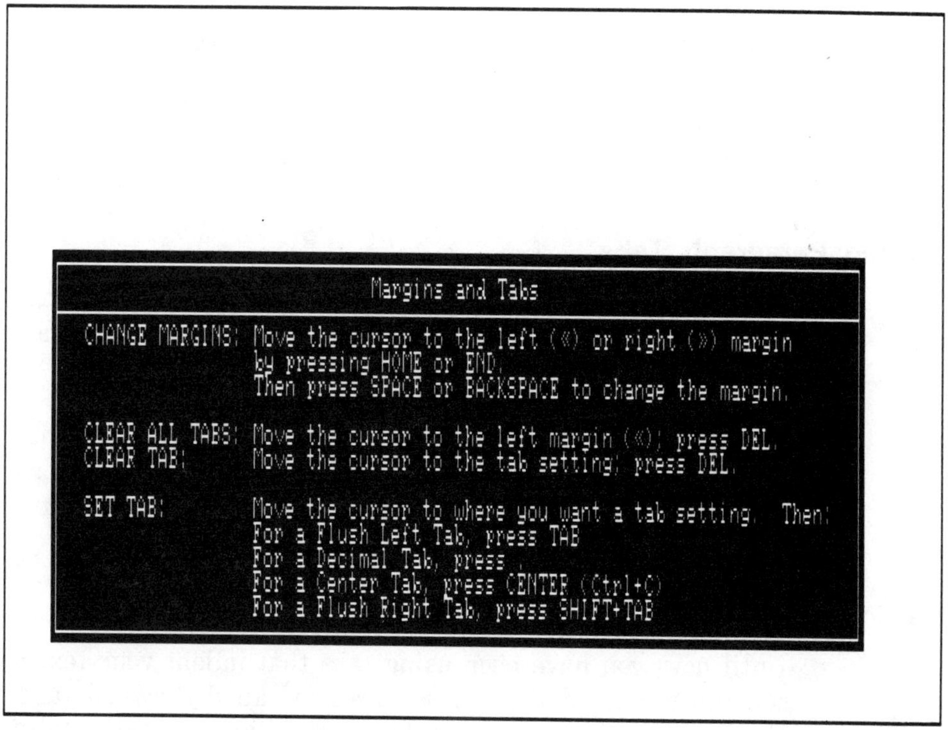

```
                        Margins and Tabs

CHANGE MARGINS: Move the cursor to the left («) or right (») margin
                by pressing HOME or END.
                Then press SPACE or BACKSPACE to change the margin.

CLEAR ALL TABS: Move the cursor to the left margin («); press DEL.
CLEAR TAB:      Move the cursor to the tab setting; press DEL.

SET TAB:        Move the cursor to where you want a tab setting.  Then:
                For a Flush Left Tab, press TAB
                For a Decimal Tab, press .
                For a Center Tab, press CENTER (Ctrl+C)
                For a Flush Right Tab, press SHIFT+TAB
```

Figure 6-3. The Margins and Tabs screen

to the desired position. If you want a larger margin, use the space bar to move the margin symbol right.

To set the right margin, use the END key to position the cursor over the >> (the right-margin symbol). Then use the space bar or the BACKSPACE key to move the margin symbol to the desired setting. (If you then want to reset the left margin, you can use the HOME key to reposition the cursor over the left-margin symbol.)

Clearing Tabs

To clear a single tab, use the LEFT or RIGHT ARROW key to move the cursor along the scale line until it is over the tab you wish to eliminate. Then

Press DEL.

To clear all tabs, use the HOME key to move the cursor to the left-margin symbol. Then

press DEL.

Setting Paragraph Tabs

Setting paragraph tabs with DisplayWrite 4 is easy. Use the LEFT or RIGHT ARROW key to move the cursor along the scale line to where you want a tab; then

press the TAB key.

The new tab appears on the scale line.

Setting Other Kinds of Tabs

Until now, you have been using tabs that indent your text a set number of spaces. These tabs are called *flush-left* tabs. DisplayWrite 4 can also produce other kinds of useful tabs;

```
LEFT        DECIMAL       COMMA       CENTER      RIGHT       COLON

1            .12345       ,12345        1           1         :12345
12          1.2345       1,2345        12          12        1:2345
123         12.345       12,345       123         123        12:345
1234        123.45       123,45       1234        1234       123:45
12345       1234.5       1234,5       12345       12345      1234:5
```

Figure 6-4. Types of tab settings available in DisplayWrite 4

Figure 6-4 shows the different kinds.

Decimal Tabs, Comma Tabs, and Colon Tabs   These tabs align a column of numbers on a decimal point, comma, or colon. To set these special tabs, move the cursor along the scale line to the desired spot and type . for decimal tabs, , for comma tabs, and : for colon tabs.

Center Tabs   This tab will automatically center text on a specified tab point. To set a center tab marker, move the cursor along the scale line to the desired point.

Press CTRL-C (the Center key).

Flush-Right Tabs   These tabs will right-align text at the selected tab setting. To set a flush-right tab, move the cursor along the scale line to the desired setting.

Press SHIFT-TAB.

When you are finished changing margins and tabs,

press ENTER

to save your changes and return to the Change Document Format menu.

Creating a Line Format

DisplayWrite 4 lets you select the number of spaces between printed lines, the type of right margin (straight or ragged), the number of lines per inch, and several other options.

To design a line format for your file, select Line Spacing/Justification from the Change Document Format menu. You will see the Line Spacing/Justification menu that is shown here:

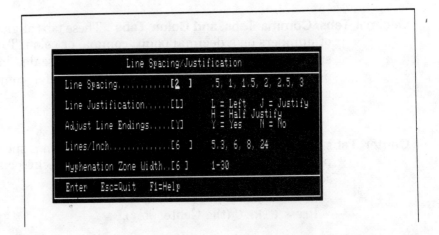

```
            Line Spacing/Justification

Line Spacing..........[2 ]    .5, 1, 1.5, 2, 2.5, 3

Line Justification......[L]   L = Left   J = Justify
                              H = Half Justify
Adjust Line Endings.....[Y]   Y = Yes    N = No

Lines/Inch............[6 ]    5.3, 6, 8, 24

Hyphenation Zone Width..[6 ]  1-30

Enter   Esc=Quit   F1=Help
```

Line Spacing

The default setting produces single-spaced text (as in your EXAMPLE.1 recommendation letter). The menu column on the right shows you what other selections you can make.

For example, to get double-spaced text, type 2 for Line Spacing. Your text will not look double-spaced on the screen, but it will be printed with double spacing. Notice that you can select half spacing as well as whole.

Straight and Ragged Margins

The margins on your EXAMPLE.1 recommendation letter resemble margins produced by a typewriter. The left margin is straight and the right margin is "ragged," which is called *ragged right*. However, DisplayWrite 4 provides two other options for margins. First, it can add tiny spaces between words to give you both a straight left *and* a straight right margin. These straight margins are said to be *justified*. You can also choose Half Justify. *Half-justified* margins are a compromise between ragged and justified margins. The right margin is straighter than a ragged right, but it is not fully justified.

All text is displayed on the screen as ragged right, but it will print out according to your choice. Figures 6-5*a*, 6-5*b*, and 6-5*c* illustrate the three possibilities.

To design a document that has a justified right margin, tab down to the Line Justification choice; then

type **j** to choose Justify.

Your printed text will have both a straight left *and* a straight right margin. (The terms on the menu are somewhat confusing because a ragged right margin is called "Left." Actually, all three choices give you a straight left margin.)

Adjusting Line Endings

Ordinarily, line endings will be slightly adjusted during pagination to fit more neatly within established margins. Line

```
        When in the Course of human Events, it becomes neces-
sary for one People to dissolve the Political Bands which
have connected them with another, and to assume among the
Powers of the Earth, the separate and equal Station to which
the Laws of Nature and Nature's God entitle them, a decent
respect to the Opinions of Mankind requires that they should
declare the causes which impel them to the Separation.
```

Figure 6-5a.   A ragged right margin

```
        When in the Course of  human Events, it becomes  neces-
sary for one  People to dissolve  the Political Bands  which
have connected them  with another, and  to assume among  the
Powers of the Earth, the separate and equal Station to which
the Laws of Nature and  Nature's God entitle them, a  decent
respect to the Opinions of Mankind requires that they should
declare the causes which impel them to the Separation.
```

Figure 6-5b.   A justified right margin

```
        When in the Course of human Events, it becomes   neces-
sary for one People to dissolve  the Political Bands which
have connected them with another, and  to assume among the
Powers of the Earth, the separate and equal Station to which
the Laws of Nature and Nature's God entitle them, a  decent
respect to the Opinions of Mankind requires that they should
declare the causes which impel them to the Separation.
```

Figure 6-5c.   A half-justified right margin

endings will also be changed by hyphenation, if you choose this option. However, you may want your lines of text to end exactly where you specify. If you set Adjust Line Endings to No, wordwrap will be off while you type in your file. Instead, a beep will warn you that you are approaching the right margin. However, you can type past the right margin if you want to. The line will not end until you press ENTER.

If you are typing lines of text that must print out exactly as they appear on your screen, set Adjust Line Endings to No.

Selecting the Number of Lines per Inch

This option lets you select the number of lines of text that will appear in each vertical inch of the printed version of your file. The default is 6 printed lines per inch.

You can use this option to give your text an expanded or a compressed look. Obviously, the fewer lines per inch, the airier your printed copy will look; the greater the number of lines per inch, the denser it will look. Of course, if you select many lines per inch (24, for example), you must use very small type or your printed lines will overlap.

To change the number of lines per inch from the default, tab down to Lines/Inch and type in the number of lines per inch that you want (it must be one of the choices shown in the column on the right). Your text will not look any different on the screen; but when you print it, the change will be in effect.

Adjusting the Zone Width

The *zone width* is the maximum number of blank spaces that DisplayWrite 4 will allow between the end of a line and the right margin before it prompts you for hyphenation. If you are not hyphenating, you will not be concerned with zone width. The default is 6 spaces.

If you select the largest zone width, your right margin will be very uneven, but you will almost never need to hyphenate. (Not many words are more than 30 characters long.) If you

select a small zone width you will have a tighter right margin, but you will frequently be prompted for hyphenation
decisions. Figures 6-6*a* and 6-6*b* show two paragraphs, one
with a zone width of 30 and the other with a zone width of 3.

To set a zone width of 15, tab down to Hyphenation Zone
Width on the menu. Then, to select the new zone width,

type **15**.

The zone width is now 15.

When you have completed all line format changes,

press ENTER

to save your changes and return to the Change Document
Format menu.

Selecting a Typestyle

DisplayWrite 4 lets you create printed text in a variety of
typestyles. To select a typestyle other than the default, which
is 26,

choose Typestyle from the Change Document Format
menu.

You will see the Typestyle menu that follows:

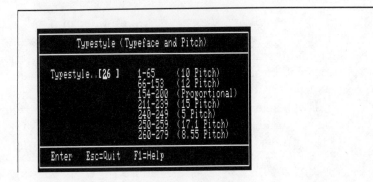

```
        When in the Course of human Events, it becomes
    necessary for one People to dissolve the Political Bands
    which have connected them with another, and to assume among
    the Powers of the Earth, the separate and equal Station to
    which the Laws of Nature and Nature's God entitle them, a
    decent respect to the Opinions of Mankind requires that they
    should declare the causes which impel them to the
    Separation.
```

Figure 6-6a.   A zone width of 30

```
            When in the Course of human Events, it becomes   neces-
        sary for one People to dissolve  the Political Bands which
        have connected them with another, and  to assume among the
        Powers of the Earth, the separate and equal Station to which
        the Laws of Nature and Nature's God entitle them, a  decent
        respect to the Opinions of Mankind requires that they should
        declare the causes which impel them to the Separation.
```

Figure 6-6b.   A zone width of 3

The available typestyles are grouped in the column on the right by *pitch.* For example, typestyles 1-65 are all 10 pitch. Pitch refers to the width of the type characters: the higher the pitch number the narrower the type. Figure 6-7 shows you some of the available pitches.

Note: The typestyle numbers represent IBM's printer element codes for the Wheelprinter, the Quietwriter, and the Pageprinter.

Your printer manual will let you know what typestyles and pitches your printer can produce. If you are using a dot matrix printer, you simply make your choice on the menu, and *if your printer has the capability,* it will print your text according to your specifications. If you are using a letter-

```
This line is 5 pitch.

This line is 8.55 pitch.

This line is 10 pitch.

This line is 17.1 pitch.
```

Figure 6-7. Some of the pitches you can produce with DisplayWrite 4

quality printer, you will have to insert the appropriate print element.

Let's say you want to print a table on a dot matrix printer in wider type than the default, which is 10 pitch. Type in a number from 260 to 279 to choose an 8.55-pitch typestyle. Your text will not look any different on the screen, but it will be printed in wider type. When you have finished typing the new typestyle number,

press ENTER

to save your changes and return to the Change Document Format menu.

Creating a Page Format

Use the Select Page Layout/Paper Options menu to select a paper size, to determine top and bottom margins, and to instruct DisplayWrite 4 how to feed paper to your printer and how to print headers and footers.

The defaults assume that you are using 8 1/2- by 11-inch paper, 1-inch top and bottom margins, and continuous-form paper. To make changes, select Page Layout/Paper Options from the Change Document Format menu. You will see a two-page menu, as shown next:

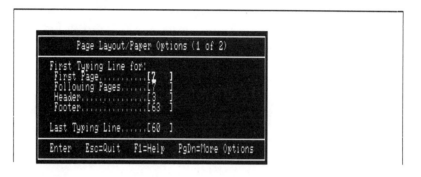

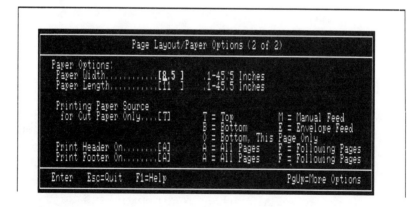

Setting the Top Margin

The first item, First Typing Line for:, lets you select the first typing line for the first page of your file, for the following pages, and for headers and footers (see Chapter 11). The default first typing line for the first page and for following pages is 7. This gives you a 1-inch top margin (there are 6 lines per vertical inch and your text begins on line 7).

Sometimes you may want to start the first page in a different place from the other pages. Perhaps you are writing a letter using company letterhead stationery for the first page and blank paper for the remaining pages. The letterhead may require a substantial top margin to prevent your printing over it. Another possibility is that you want the first page of a report or chapter to begin fairly far down the page but you want the remaining pages to begin higher on the page.

Notice that the Header and Footer choices set the header within the top margin and the footer within the bottom margin. You can change the first lines on which headers and footers print *as long as they print within these margins*. If you try to set a header or footer to print within the main text, you will get an error message.

To set a 2-inch margin for the first page of a file, change First Page to 13. (Since 6 lines equal 1 inch, you would need 12 lines for your 2-inch margin. Your text would begin on line 13.)

Setting the Bottom Margin

The Last Typing Line choice lets you set the bottom margin. The default is 60, which gives you a 1-inch bottom margin (there are 66 lines on a page). The smaller you set the Last Typing Line the larger the bottom margin. A Last Typing Line of 54 will produce a 2-inch bottom margin.

To set a 2-inch bottom margin, tab to Last Typing Line. Then

type 54.

Selecting the Paper Size

If you are printing on nonstandard-size paper (such as legal-size paper or envelopes), you will need to change the default paper size. Press PGDN to see page 2 of the Page Layout/Paper Options menu. Then type in the paper width and length you want. (Your choices range from one-tenth of an inch to 45 1/2 inches.)

Changing the Paper Source

This option is for users of multi-bin feeders only. If you are not using a multi-bin feeder, *make no changes in the Printing Paper Source.* Likewise, if you are printing from the top drawer of a sheet-feed paper handler, make no changes in this option, because you will be using the default Top.

The Bottom choice feeds paper from the bottom drawer of the sheet-feed paper handler. Bottom, This Page Only feeds the first page into the printer from the bottom drawer and the other pages from the top drawer (useful when you want to use letterhead for the first sheet). The Envelopes choice allows you to feed envelopes manually.

Printing Headers and Footers

The Print Header On and Print Footer On choices determine whether headers and footers are printed on the current page and all following pages or on following pages but not on the current page. Type **a** for All Pages and **f** for Following Pages.

When you have completed your Page Layout/Paper Options choices,

press ENTER

to save your changes and return to the Change Document Format menu.

Changing the Format of a Completed File

Suppose you design a format for a file—new margins, tabs, spacing, and so on. However, after you print a copy of the file, you decide that you don't like the way it looks. DisplayWrite 4 lets you redesign a format for your file at any time.

To redesign a format, you follow the exact steps outlined in this chapter, but you type in your new choices. Paginate your file when you are finished.

Practice Exercise

Now you are going to type in an exercise to give you practice with line changes, page changes, and margin and tab changes.

From the DisplayWrite 4 menu,

choose Create Document.

When prompted for a name,

type **example.2** and press ENTER.

When you enter the typing area,

press CTRL-7 and choose Document Format.

Then use what you have learned in this chapter to make the following changes:

- Change the left margin to 20
- Eliminate the tab at 25 and set a tab at 28
- Set triple spacing
- Set the first typing line to 15
- Set the last typing line to 51

When you are done making format changes, return to the Change Document Format menu. Then

press ESC

until you return to the typing area.

EXAMPLE.2 is a syllabus for a writing class. Enter it exactly as shown in Figure 6-8. You should see all your format changes on the screen except for triple spacing (which you can verify by looking at the second status line). When you are finished typing,

press F2

to save your text, and then print the file. Your printed copy will reflect all your formatting changes.

```
        SYLLABUS

    Clear Writing

            Getting started

            Writing clear sentences

            Writing clear business letters

    Correct Writing

            Run-together sentences and sentence fragments

            Subject-verb agreement

            Punctuation

            Pronoun reference

    Organizing Your Material

            Going from general to specific

            Making an outline
```

Figure 6-8. EXAMPLE.2

7

Printing

This chapter discusses the two methods of printing files: DisplayWrite 4 foreground printing and DisplayWrite 4 background printing. It discusses your printing options and shows you how to manage the print queue.

The Two Printing Methods

This chapter assumes that you have already selected your printer type. If not, read Chapter 1 and follow the instructions to install your printer for use with DisplayWrite 4.

DisplayWrite 4 provides two methods of printing files, so you can choose the method that best suits the tasks you are performing. In addition, you can stack up to ten printing jobs in the DisplayWrite 4 *print queue*—the line of files waiting to be printed—and you can arrange the printing job order so that a selected job gets printed first.

No matter which of the two printing methods you choose, DisplayWrite 4 will first convert your file to a form your printer can use and then print it. If you wish, you can save a copy of the converted file to your disk for printing at a later time. DisplayWrite 4 will give the converted file the extension .PRN if you don't specify any other.

In addition to printing DisplayWrite 4 files, DisplayWrite 4 can print DisplayWrite 3, final-form text, and print-ready ASCII files (files that you have saved to disk).

DisplayWrite 4 Foreground Printing

Use foreground printing when you just want to print files and you have no other immediate use for the computer. Foreground printing is the fastest printing method, but during the printing process you cannot perform nonprinting tasks. For example, you cannot create, edit, or paginate files. Foreground printing is the default.

DisplayWrite 4 Background Printing

With DisplayWrite 4 background printing, you can perform both printing and nonprinting tasks simultaneously. (After printing begins, the Print menu is displayed, but you can press ESC to return to the DisplayWrite 4 menu and pick another task.) However, both printing and nonprinting jobs may proceed more slowly than usual. If you select DOS Commands from the DisplayWrite 4 menu, printing will cease until you return to DisplayWrite 4.

DisplayWrite 4 background printing requires 64K more memory than foreground printing.

Note: The system defaults configure your system to use foreground printing *only.* If you plan to use background printing you must first change the Work Station defaults in the Revise Profile menu to permit both background and foreground printing. This process is explained in Chapter 15.

Printing the File

Before printing a file, check that your printer is turned on and properly loaded with paper. Then, from the Display-Write 4 menu,

choose Print.

You will see the Print menu.

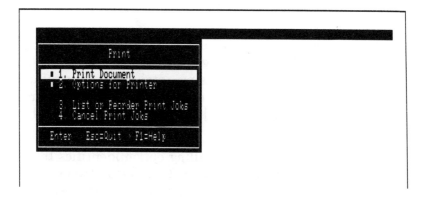

If you want to use all default settings, you can print the file quickly.

Choose Print Document.

Then type the name of your file in the Print Document menu and press ENTER. Your file will be printed.

Setting the Printer Options

DisplayWrite 4 provides many ways to customize a print job by letting you make choices from both the Options for Printer menu and the Print Document menu.

You must make the changes in the Options for Printer menu *before* you go to the Print Document menu to do the actual printing. To make these changes,

choose Options for Printer

from the Print menu. Then choose the printer you are planning to use for the job. You will see the Options for Printer menu as shown in Figure 7-1a. If you have a printer that uses ROM cartridges, you will also see Figure 7-1b.

The options and their uses are presented here:

- The Draft Mode option lets you specify the print quality if you are using a dot matrix printer. The default, Yes, gives you fast, single-strike printing suitable for rough drafts. The No choice gives you higher-quality printing because each character is struck twice—but, of course, printing is slower.

- The Paper Handling option identifies the way paper is fed to your printer. Continuous Paper is the default. If you are feeding sheets one by one, choose Manual Feed. The Prompted Manual Feed choice provides prompts for loading paper with manual-feed printers. If you have an automatic sheet feeder, choose Automatic Feed.

- The Collate Copies option lets you select the method for collating your printed copies. (Whether you can do this depends on the size of the print buffer. You can use the option with the Pageprinter and the Quietwriter.) By Document prints all the pages of the first copy of the file, then all the pages of the second copy, and so on. By Page prints all the copies of the first page, then all the copies of the second page, and so on.

- The Pause at Document Start option instructs the printer to pause before it starts printing your file. This lets you change fonts or insert a new print cartridge before printing begins.

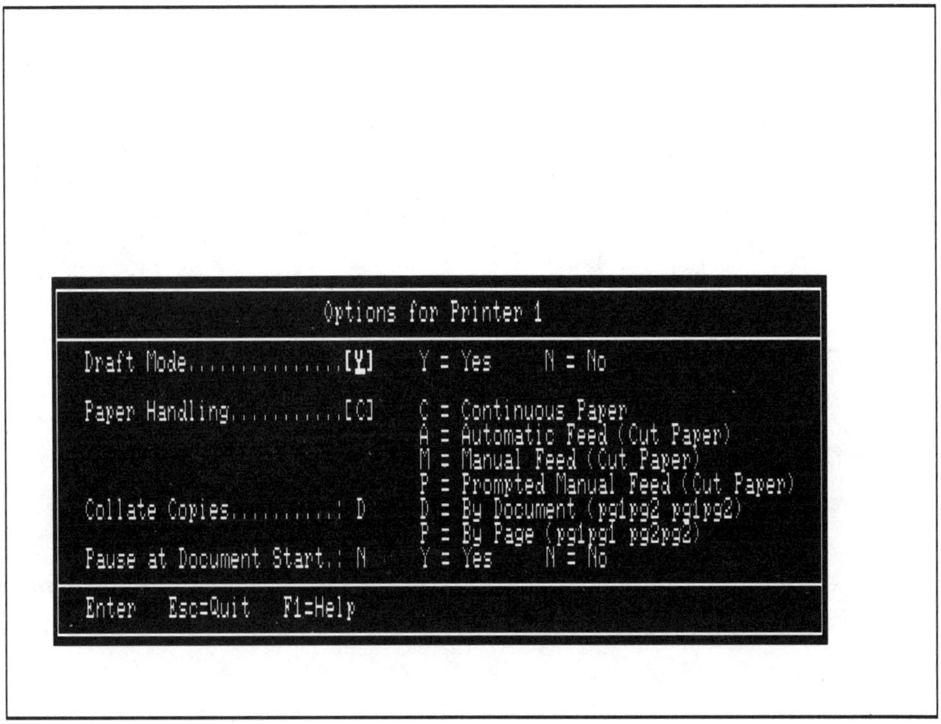

```
                  Options for Printer 1
Draft Mode..............[Y]    Y = Yes    N = No

Paper Handling..........[C]    C = Continuous Paper
                               A = Automatic Feed (Cut Paper)
                               M = Manual Feed (Cut Paper)
                               P = Prompted Manual Feed (Cut Paper)
Collate Copies.........: D     D = By Document (pg1pg2 pg1pg2)
                               P = By Page (pg1pg1 pg2pg2)
Pause at Document Start.: N     Y = Yes    N = No

Enter   Esc=Quit   F1=Help
```

Figure 7-1a.   The Options for Printer menu, page 1

- If you have a printer that uses ROM cartridges, you
  must list the cartridges that you are planning to use. All
  the information you need is on the cartridges themselves. For each of the three slots, list the typestyles that
  you will be using. You may list up to four typestyles per
  slot; separate typestyles by a space when you type them
  in. For the Printer Character Set choice, type the letter
  that identifies the character set. If there are certain cartridges that you use on a regular basis, you can list them
  in Profiles (see Chapter 15).

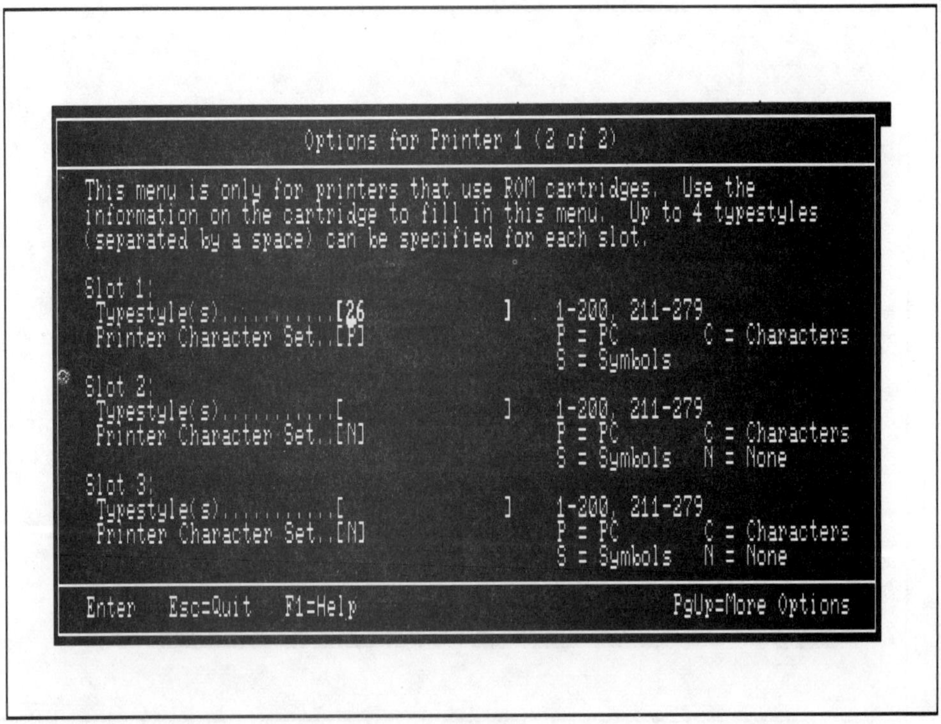

Figure 7-1b.   The Options for Printer menu, page 2

When you have completed all changes in the Options for Printer menu,

press ENTER.

Then

press ESC

to return to the Print menu.

Setting the Print Document Options

Now choose Print Document to make changes in the two-page Print Document menu (see Figures 7-2a and 7-2b). The

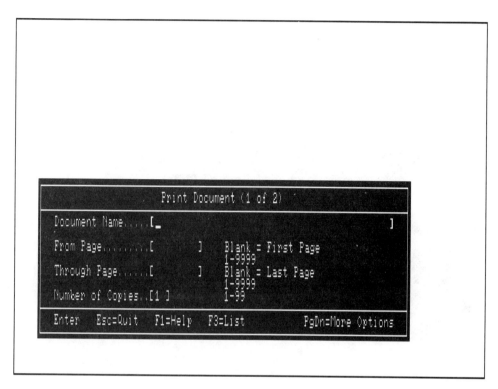

Figure 7-2a.   The Print Document menu, page 1

options you can choose from are explained here.

- For Document Name type the name of your file. If you are printing a DisplayWrite 3 final-form text or ASCII file, be sure to include the file extension.

- The From Page and Through Page options let you select a section of your file to be printed. If you want the entire file printed, skip these options.

- The Number of Copies option lets you select the number of copies to be printed (up to 99 copies).

- The Printer choice lets you select which printer you want to use to print the file. Printer 1 is the default.

```
            Print Document (2 of 2)

Printer........[1]    1 = Printer 1
                      2 = Printer 2
                      3 = Printer 3

Processing.....[B]    F = Foreground  B = Background

Output Device..[P]    P = Printer     D = Disk      B = Both

Document Type..[D]    D = Document or ASCII
                      F = Final-Form Text

Enter   Esc=Quit  F1=Help              PgUp=More Options
```

Figure 7-2b.   The Print Document menu, page 2

- The Processing option lets you select either foreground or background printing. Remember that you can select Background only if you have previously changed the Work Station defaults in the Revise Profile menu (see Chapter 15) to permit background printing.

- Output Device lets you save a converted file to disk without printing it. The file is saved with the extension .PRN (or .FFT if you choose Final-Form Text in the next option). The default setting Printer simply prints the document. The Disk setting saves the converted file but does not print it. If you choose Both, the file will be printed *and* the converted copy saved to disk.

- For Document Type, leave the default setting Document if you are printing a DisplayWrite 3 or DisplayWrite 4 file or a file that you have previously saved to disk with the extension .PRN (a print-ready ASCII file). Choose Final-Form Text if you are printing a final-form text document (extension .FFT).

Note: If you are printing a file that you have previously saved to disk, make sure that you print it on the same printer that you designated when you saved it.

After you have completed all menu changes,

press ENTER.

Printing will commence.

If you are using DisplayWrite 4 foreground printing, you will see the Foreground Processing for Print menu until printing is complete.

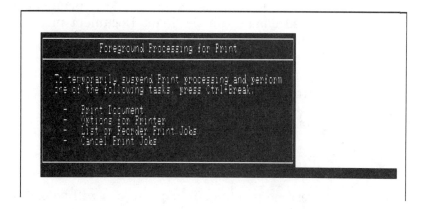

Then you will return to the DisplayWrite 4 menu.

If you are using DisplayWrite 4 background printing, you will see the Print menu during printing. You can continue with printing tasks or return to the DisplayWrite 4 menu for nonprinting tasks.

Making Changes During Printing

DisplayWrite 4 lets you queue up jobs to be printed. (During printing, the top status line displays the number of jobs in the queue.)

During the printing process, DisplayWrite 4 lets you add jobs to the print queue, cancel jobs, and change the job order. The last feature is particularly handy if a rush job comes in while routine jobs are being printed.

Adding Printing Jobs

If you are using foreground printing, press CTRL-BREAK to stop the printing process. Then, from the Print menu, choose Print Document.

If you are using DisplayWrite 4 background printing, choose Print Document from the Print menu to stop the printing process.

Enter the name of the new file to be printed and make any desired changes in the Print Document menu. (You cannot combine DisplayWrite 4 foreground printing with Display-Write 4 background printing.)

Press ENTER

to add the job to the print queue.

Press ESC

to resume printing. Your print jobs will be printed in order.

Note: If you need to make changes in the Options for Printer menu for the new print job, choose Options for Printer before you choose Print Document.

Displaying the Job Order
and Reordering Jobs

During the printing process, you can see what jobs are in your print queue and can move a print job to the top of the queue. If you are looking at the Foreground Processing for Print menu,

press CTRL-BREAK

to stop printing and display the Print menu. If you are using DisplayWrite 4 background printing, the Print menu will already be displayed.

Choose List or Reorder Print Jobs.

You will see your print jobs listed in order, with a # next to the job currently being processed:

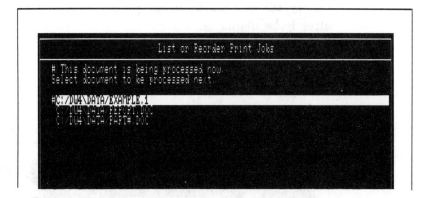

If you simply want to check that a file is in the queue, press ESC after checking the queue to resume printing.

If you want to change the order of the print jobs, select the job you want processed next (use the TAB key or the cursor movement keys to highlight the job). Then

press ENTER.

You will see the new job order. Note that printing will be completed for the file currently being processed *before* the file you select is printed. To resume printing,

press ESC.

Canceling a Print Job

During the printing process, you can remove any job from the print queue. If you are looking at the Foreground Processing for Print menu,

press CTRL-BREAK

to stop printing and display the Print menu. If you are using DisplayWrite 4 background printing, the Print menu will already be displayed.

From the print menu,

choose Cancel Print Jobs.

You will see your print jobs listed in order:

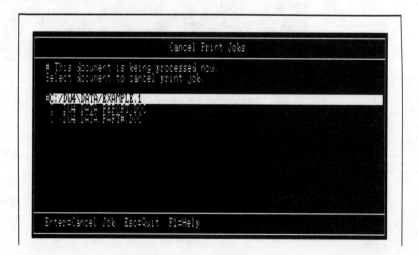

Select the print job you want to cancel (use the TAB key or cursor movement keys to highlight the job). Then

press ENTER.

The job is removed from the queue. You can cancel as many jobs as you want. When you are finished canceling jobs,

press ESC

and printing will resume.

8

Enhancing Text Appearance

This chapter shows you how to use centering, underlining, boldface, overstriking, and other techniques to enhance the appearance of your printed file. It teaches you how to use the Cursor Draw feature, which enables you to add simple charts and drawings to your text.

Centering

DisplayWrite 4 lets you center any line of text. Headings are frequently centered; you can also center a series of text lines to create special visual effects, as in Figure 8-1.

To center a line of text, move the cursor to the center of the line whose text you plan to center (don't type the text in yet). You can determine the center by looking at the ruler line at the top of the screen. The symbol that looks like a miniature house marks the center point.

You can actually center text around *any* point on your typing line or even around several points on one line. Just posi-

```
        A
       fun
      party
     Tuesday
    September
    8, at eight
   o'clock at my
   home - 1300
    Blair St.
    See you
      then.
       Joe
         .
```

Figure 8-1.   Centering text with DisplayWrite 4

tion the cursor at the point around which you want to center your text.

Note: The center point of the typing line is not necessarily the center of the printing paper; it is the center of the space between your margins.

To initiate centering,

press CTRL-C (the Center key).

Now type in the words you want centered. The words will automatically center themselves around the center point. To end centering, press ENTER to move to a new line or TAB to move to the next tab stop. You will achieve an effect like that shown here:

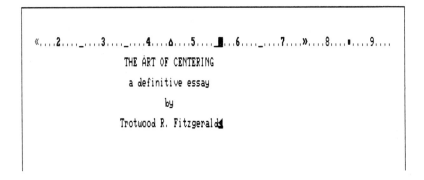

You can also center text that you have previously typed. To do this, you must be in Insert mode. Position the cursor under the first character of the words you want centered. Then, with the space bar or TAB key, move the text until the first character is at the point around which you want the text to center.

Press CTRL-C.

The text will center around the designated point.

Underlining

DisplayWrite 4 has a technique for underlining a single word and two techniques for underlining a group of words.

Underlining a Single Word

To underline one word, type the word you want underlined. Then, without typing a space,

press CTRL-W (the Word Underline key).

A Word Underline code is inserted into your text, and you will see the word underlined on the screen. (On color monitors you will see the word in a different color, rather than underlined. However, it will be underlined when it is printed.)

Underlining a Group of Words

To underline a group of words that you are about to type, move the cursor to where you want to begin underlining. Then

Press CTRL-U (the Underline key).

A Begin Underline code is inserted into your text. Now type all the words you want underlined.

Press CTRL-U again.

An End Underline code is inserted into your text and underlining ceases. When you print your file, the block of text between the Begin and End Underline codes will be underlined.

If you decide to underline text that you have already typed on your screen, you can follow the procedure just outlined to insert Begin and End Underline codes in the appropriate places.

You can also underline existing text by first defining the text to be underlined as a block. To use this method, move the cursor under the first character of the text you want underlined. Then

press F4 and from the Block menu choose Underline.

Following the prompt, move the cursor to the end of the block.

Press ENTER.

Begin and End Underline codes will be inserted at the appropriate places and the text block will print out underlined.

Note: Remember that if you are using a mouse, you define the text block first and then select the operation.

Boldface

When text marked for boldface is printed, the printer types the text and then types over it again; the second strike is offset from the first by a fraction of an inch. The result is that boldface text is darker and stands out from regular text:

Text that is **boldface** stands out from regular text.

Some printers cannot offset the second strike; however, simply printing the text twice produces a darker image. A few printers cannot do boldface at all.

To create boldface text, move the cursor to where you want the boldface to begin.

Press CTRL-B (the Bold key).

A Begin Bold code is inserted. Type in all the text that you want printed in boldface. (The text may appear highlighted on your screen.) Then, with the cursor one space past your last character,

press CTRL-B again.

An End Bold code is inserted into your text, and subsequent words are not highlighted. When you print your file, words between the Begin and End Bold codes will appear in boldface.

If you decide to boldface text that you have already typed on your monitor screen, follow the procedure just outlined to insert Begin and End Bold codes in the appropriate places.

You can also boldface text that already exists by using the Block menu. To use this method, move the cursor under the first character of the text you want boldfaced. Then

press F4 and choose Bold.

Following the prompt, move the cursor to the end of the block.

Press ENTER.

Begin and End Bold codes will be inserted at the appropriate places and the text block will print out in boldface.

Overstrike

When you overstrike a block of text, you mark over it with another character. Usually a hyphen or a slash is used for overstriking, but you can use any character you wish. Overstriking with the hyphen is shown here:

O̶v̶e̶r̶s̶t̶r̶i̶k̶i̶n̶g̶ ̶i̶s̶ ̶o̶f̶t̶e̶n̶ ̶u̶s̶e̶d̶ ̶w̶i̶t̶h̶ ̶l̶e̶g̶a̶l̶ ̶d̶o̶c̶u̶m̶e̶n̶t̶s̶

The default overstrike character is a slash (/). However, you can change to any character you wish. To select a different overstrike character, in the typing area,

press CTRL-F5 and tab to Overstrike Character.

Type in the desired overstrike character and

press ENTER.

While not a frequently used function, overstriking is used in the legal profession and at other times when it is necessary to show revisions. You might also want to over-strike a single character to create an accent over a word in a foreign language.

Overstriking a Single Character

To overstrike a single character, type the character. Then

press CTRL-BACKSPACE (the Required Backspace key).

Type the overstrike character. When you look at the screen, you will see the overstrike character but not your text. If you move the cursor back through the text or set Display All Codes to Yes, you will see the text but not the overstrike character. You *cannot* see both the text and the overstrike character on the screen at the same time; but when you print the file, the overstrike character will print over the text.

Overstriking a Group of Characters

To overstrike more than one character, type the text. Then move the cursor to where you want the overstriking to begin.

Press CTRL-S (the Overstrike key).

A Begin Overstrike code is inserted into your text. Then move the cursor one space past your last character, and

press CTRL-S again.

An End Overstrike code is inserted into your text.
You can also use the Block menu to overstrike text. To do so,

Press F4 and choose Overstrike.

Then, in response to the prompt, move the cursor under the last character you want to overstrike.

Press ENTER.

Begin and End Overstrike codes are inserted into your text and your text block will print out overstricken.

Removing Enhancements

If you decide you want to remove text enhancements such as underlining, bold, overstriking, and revision marking (see Chapter 4) from a section of text, use the Block menu: Move the cursor under the first character of the text from which you want to remove enhancements. Then

press F4 and choose Plain.

Following the prompt, move the cursor to the end of the block.

Press ENTER.

All Underline, Bold, Overstrike, and Mark codes will be stripped from the text block.

Superscripts and Subscripts

Superscripts print one-half line above the regular text line; subscripts print one-half line below it. Superscripts and subscripts are frequently used in scientific work. Figure 8-2 illustrates superscripts and subscripts produced by Display-Write 4.

Superscripts and subscripts are not displayed above or below the regular text line on the monitor screen; they are seen only when printed. Not every printer can produce these text enhancements, so check your printer manual.

If you are printing your text single-spaced, you may find that superscripts and subscripts run into the text on the lines directly above and below them. If this is the case, change the line spacing to 1.5 or 2 and print the document again.

Producing Superscripts

Move the cursor to the spot where the superscript is to begin.

Press CTRL-Y (the 1/2-Up key).

$$a^2 + b^2 = c^2$$

$$92^{\circ} \text{ centigrade}$$

$$E = mc^2$$

$$6 \times 10^{10}$$

$$H_2O$$

$$\log_b X$$

$$c(x_1 + y_1)$$

$$E_{max}$$

Figure 8-2. Superscripts and subscripts produced by DisplayWrite 4

A Half Index Up code is inserted into your text. Type the superscript.

Press CTRL-H (the 1/2-Down key).

A Half Index Down code is inserted into your text, and you are returned to your regular typing line.

Producing Subscripts

The procedure for producing subscripts is identical to that of producing superscripts except that you press CTRL-H first and CTRL-Y second.

Indenting Text

DisplayWrite 4 provides you with a quick way to indent an entire paragraph of text. Indenting is useful for typing lengthy quotations (called extracts), and for bulleted and numbered lists (see Figure 8-3). Of course, you could just use the TAB key to indent each line, but that is a slower and more tedious method.

To indent a paragraph, move the cursor to the beginning of the first line you want to indent.

Press CTRL-T (the Indent key).

Each time you press CTRL-T, the left margin will move one tab space to the right. For example, to move the left margin two tab spaces to the right,

press CTRL-T twice.

Then type the paragraph. As you type, each line of the paragraph will be aligned along the temporary left margin.

```
        Touchstone can prove that he has been a courtier not by
any good deed he has done but because:

        I have trod a measure.  I have flattered a lady.
        I have been politic with my friend, smooth with
        mine enemy.  I have undone three tailors.  I have
        had four quarrels, and like to have fought one.
```

Figure 8-3. Using the Indent function to indent a quotation

When you are done typing,

press ENTER.

This will terminate the Indent function and return the margin to its regular position for subsequent lines that you type.

You can also indent a paragraph that you have already typed. First, move the cursor to the beginning of the first line you want to indent.

Press CTRL-T.

Then move the cursor to any other line to reformat the paragraph.

Keeping Words Together

At times you may want certain groups of characters or words kept together on one line. For example, you probably prefer this —

```
Contact me at my office.  The telephone number is
(415) 555-1234.
```

to this—

```
Contact me at my office.  The telephone number is (415)
555-1234.
```

DisplayWrite 4 lets you insert a Required Space code between characters that you want kept together. When the system encounters characters connected with this code, it treats them like a single word and will not split them up.
To keep text together on a line,

type **(415),**

the first group of characters. Then enter the Required Space code:

Press CTRL-V (the Required Space key).

The code is inserted into your text. Type the remaining group of characters:

555-1234

The text will be treated as if it were a single word and will not be split. Note that the Required Space code works for only one space at a time, disabling itself immediately after that space.

Drawing with the Cursor

The DisplayWrite 4 Cursor Draw feature lets you use the four arrow keys to draw with the cursor. As the cursor moves around the screen, the character you have designated appears in each cursor position. (You cannot use a mouse for Cursor Draw.)

It takes a bit of practice to use Cursor Draw effectively, but after you get the hang of it, you will find this feature useful for drawing simple figures and charts directly in your file and for creating boxes around text (see Figures 8-4 and 8-5).

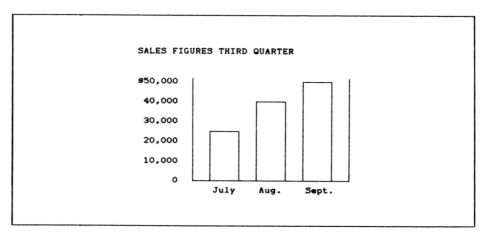

Figure 8-4. Drawing a graph with Cursor Draw

Figure 8-5. Drawing a box around text with Cursor Draw

Planning Your Drawing

Plan your drawing so it will fit on one page. You cannot draw over the page boundary.

If you want to draw a box around text, type the text *first*. Do *not* insert Center or Tab codes into your text as these will cause your drawing to misalign.

If you previously changed the default setting for Line Spacing, return the setting to 1 in the Line Spacing/ Justification menu. Also, if you want to draw past the right margin, set Adjust Line Endings to No in the same menu.

Creating the Drawing

Go to the typing area and move the cursor to the position where you want to start drawing.

Press ALT-1 or F11 (the Cursor Draw keys).

You will see the following:

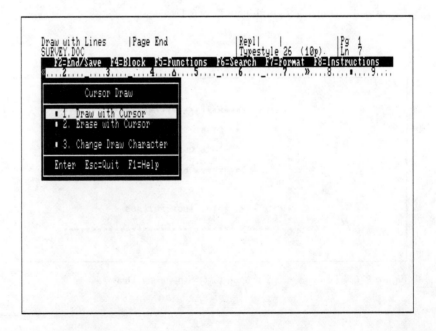

If you want to draw with connecting lines (the default character), simply press ENTER to select Draw with Cursor. You will see Draw with Lines on the status line. (The lines will be either horizontal or vertical; you cannot draw diagonal lines.)

If you want to choose another draw character, select Change Draw Character. Then, in response to the prompt, type the desired draw character.

Press ENTER, and then select Draw with Cursor.

You can now begin drawing. Use the four arrow keys to move the cursor around the screen and create your figure.

Look at the top status line, and you will see that you are in Replace mode even if you were in Insert mode previously. DisplayWrite 4 *automatically* puts you in Replace mode so that your drawing stays aligned. Also, Display All Codes is automatically set to No while you are using Cursor Draw.

While you are drawing, you can change your draw character at any time. Simply press ALT-1 or F11 and choose Change Draw Character.

You can also type in text. Just remember that the cursor will draw if you use the arrow keys to move the cursor to where you want to begin typing text. Use the space bar and the BACKSPACE key instead.

When you are finished drawing,

press ESC to end Cursor Draw.

Note: You can select, as a draw character, a character from the keyboard extensions (see Chapter 22). Just make sure that the character has been previously listed in the Edit Options menu (CTRL-F5).

Correcting Errors

You will undoubtedly make some mistakes (remember, Cursor Draw takes practice). You can erase your errors either after you leave Cursor Draw or while you are in it. (Of course, it is easier to position the cursor for error correction when you are *not* in Cursor Draw because the cursor is not drawing as you move it.)

To erase errors (while in or out of Cursor Draw), move the cursor to the place where you want to begin erasing.

Press ALT-1 or F11 and select Erase with Cursor.

Use the arrow keys to move the cursor under the characters you want to erase. The cursor will erase all characters in its path.

Did you erase a few characters that you wanted to keep? If so, press ALT-1 or F11, choose Draw with Cursor, and replace the deleted characters. When you are finished correcting errors,

press ESC

to resume normal typing.

If you want to edit your drawing or the text inside a box after you leave Cursor Draw, make sure you are in Replace mode before doing any editing. Use the space bar rather than the DEL key to erase characters.

The keys used for enhancing text appearance are listed in Table 8-1.

Note: The codes described in this chapter can be revised and deleted by the method described in Chapter 4. Remember to turn Display All Codes to Yes when revising codes.

Key	Function
ALT-1 or F11	Initiates the Cursor Draw feature
F4	Lets you define a block for underlining, bold, over-striking, or plain (remove all enhancements)
CTRL-F5	The Overstrike Character choice lets you select the overstrike character
CTRL-B	Inserts a Begin or End Bold code into your text, which begins or ends boldface
CTRL-C	Inserts a Center code into your text line around which text is centered as you type it in
CTRL-H	Inserts a Half Index Down code into your text to initiate a subscript or terminate a superscript
CTRL-S	Inserts a Begin or End Overstrike code into your text, which begins or ends overstriking
CTRL-T	Inserts an Indent code into your text, which sets a temporary left margin
CTRL-U	Inserts a Begin or End Underline code into your text, which begins or ends underlining
CTRL-V	Inserts a Required Space code into your text, which keeps words together on a line
CTRL-W	Inserts a Word Underline code into your text, causing the preceding word to be underlined
CTRL-Y	Inserts a Half Index Up code into your text to initiate a superscript or terminate a subscript
CTRL-BACKSPACE	Inserts a Required Backspace code into your text to overstrike a single character
ESC	Ends Draw with Cursor or Erase with Cursor

Table 8-1. Keys Used to Enhance Text Appearance

9

Text Searching

This chapter teaches you how to use the DisplayWrite 4 Find function and the Search/Replace function to search through your file for designated characters and, if you desire, to replace those characters with others.

What Searches Can Do

Let's say you worked many hours producing a sales report and created a file of over 50 pages. Unfortunately, when you got to the end, you discovered that one of your frequently used figures was incorrect. Your company sold only $47,000 worth of can openers in 1985, not $52,000, as you had believed.

Or perhaps you have been working on a research paper. As you type your final paragraph, you realize that the word "their" is not spelled "thier" and that you have misspelled the word throughout your report.

Without a word-processing program, these errors would cost time and correction fluid, but with DisplayWrite 4 you can make appropriate corrections in a matter of seconds. The system can search through your file for the characters you designate. (These characters are called a *string;* in the example just given, "$52,000" and "thier" are both strings.) Then, if you desire, the system can replace the characters in a string with others.

The DisplayWrite 4 Search feature contains two separate functions. The Find function searches your file for a designated string, and the Search/Replace function searches for a string and then replaces it with another string. The Search feature also contains a Go to Page function that moves the cursor to a designated page (see Chapter 3).

Finding Text

The DisplayWrite 4 Find function will search your file until it locates the string you are looking for. It will not replace text, however. Note that Find searches only in a forward direction; if you want your entire file searched, make sure the cursor is at the beginning of the file. (If you are in the middle, press F6, select Go to Page, type **1**, and press ENTER.)

Finding a Character String

To find a string of characters in your file,

press F6 (the Search key).

You will see the Search menu.

Choose Find.

Then, in response to the prompt, type in the characters you want to find. (You need type only enough to distinguish your string from the rest of the file. For example, if you are searching for the phrase "Four score and seven", the string "Four s" would probably be enough.)

Press ENTER.

DisplayWrite 4 starts searching your file for the first occurrence of the character string. When it finds it (in a fraction of a second), the cursor stops under the first character of the string.

To find the next occurrence of the string,

press F6 again,

but this time

choose Repeat.

Repeat this procedure until your entire file is searched.

When DisplayWrite 4 cannot find any more instances of your character string, you will see a screen message telling you that the specified characters are not found between the cursor position and the end of the document. Then move the cursor to the location where you want to continue working on your file.

Finding Codes

DisplayWrite 4 will find not only a character string for you, but also codes that you have previously inserted into your file. This feature can come in very handy during revisions. If, for example, you have centered a line of text but later decide that the line should be flush left, you can use Find to locate the Center code.

Finding codes is identical to finding character strings, except that when you see the Find What? prompt, you press the key that inserted the code. For example, to find a Center code,

press CTRL-C and then press ENTER.

When searching for codes, note the following:

- Pressing F8 and then ENTER will take you to the first occurrence of *any* code initiated by the F8 key.

- To find a Tab code, press CTRL-Q.

- To find a Format Change code (see Chapter 10), press F7.

- To find a Carrier Return code, press CTRL-ENTER.

- To find a Required Carrier Return code, press CTRL-L.

Searching and Replacing

The DisplayWrite 4 Search/Replace function will find characters in your file and replace them with other characters you select. Like Find, Search/Replace searches only in a forward direction; if you want your entire file searched, start by moving the cursor to the beginning of the file. You may replace up to three different strings each time you use Search/Replace.

Searching and Replacing Character Strings

To replace one set of characters in your file with another set, move the cursor to the place where you want the search to begin.

Press F6, and select Search/Replace.

You will see the first page of the two-page Search/Replace menu:

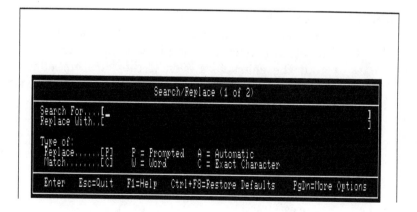

Fill in Search For by typing in the string that you want replaced. This can include any combination of uppercase and lowercase characters, symbols, codes, and spaces; however, DisplayWrite 4 will find only your *exact* string, as you typed it. If you type in "house", it will not find "House". Each Search For string can be a maximum of 60 characters.

Then fill in Replace With by typing in the replacement string. This string can also be up to 60 characters long.

Note: If you just want to delete the characters from your text, leave Replace With blank.

Prompted or Automatic Mode   There are two kinds of searches: Automatic and Prompted. Prompted is the default. If you choose Automatic, DisplayWrite 4 goes through your file and makes all changes without stopping. With Prompted, the system will stop at each occurrence of the specified string and ask whether you want to make the change or not.

Word or Character Match   DisplayWrite 4 can look for your string in two different ways: It will match by word or by exact character. The default setting is Exact Character; this choice will find the characters even if they are embedded in another word. For example, if you are searching for the string "can", Exact Character will stop at *can, can*cel, re*cant,* and *cante-* loupe. The Word choice will find the characters only when they compose a separate word.

If you want to Search/Replace two or three strings simultaneously,

press PGDN

to go to page 2 of the menu. Then complete the menu for the second and third Search/Replace strings.

Replacing Three Strings Simultaneously   After you have completed the menu,

> press ENTER

to begin the Search/Replace.

If you chose Automatic, the system will go through your file and make all changes. When the changes are complete, you will see the message

`Search/replace is completed. (#) phrases were changed.`

(The pound sign will be replaced by the number of changes made.)

If you chose Prompted, the system will stop when it comes to the first occurrence of your Search For string. (See the example in Figure 9-1.) You then have the following choices:

- Select Replace and Continue to replace the string and continue the search.

- Select Continue without Replacing to continue without replacing this instance of the string.

- Select Quit After Replacing to replace *only* this occurrence of the character string.

- Press ESC to quit *without* replacing the string.

Canceling an Automatic Search   To stop an automatic Search/Replace in progress,

> press CTRL-BREAK.

If you're not fast, it's too late.

Searching and Replacing Codes

DisplayWrite 4 lets you use Search/Replace on some codes, such as Format Change codes (you will learn about these in

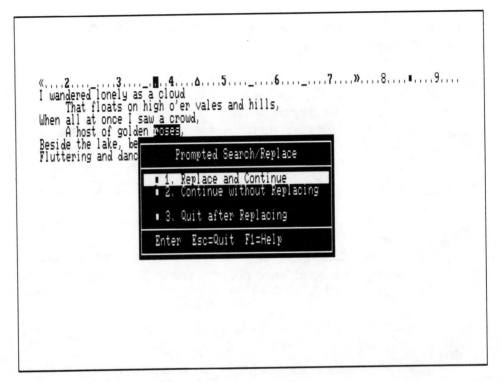

Figure 9-1. The system stops when it finds your string

the next chapter) and Required Carrier Return codes. You can Search/Replace to delete codes quickly from your text. To use Search/Replace to delete codes,

- Press CTRL-L at Search For to delete Required Carrier Return codes.

- Press F7 at Search For to delete Format Change codes.

- Leave Replace With blank.

- Leave Prompted as the mode if you want to delete only certain Format Change codes or Required Carrier Return codes and not others.

- Press ENTER.

Key	Function
F6	The Find choice initiates the Find function, which searches your file for designated characters. The Search/Replace choice initiates the Search/Replace function, which searches your file for designated characters and replaces them with others that you select
CTRL-BREAK	Stops an automatic Search/Replace in progress

Table 9-1. Keys Used in Global Searches

Table 9-1 identifies the keys used in Find and Search/Replace procedures.

10

Changing the Format in the Middle of a File

This chapter shows you how to change the format in part of a file—to use a different typestyle, to change line spacing or margins, or even to use a different paper size. You will also learn how to return to your starting format and how to revise format changes.

DisplayWrite 4 lets you change the format of an entire page or more, a line or more, or even part of a line. You can enhance the appearance of your printed document by using different typestyles and pitches within it, by switching from double spacing to single spacing for selected paragraphs, and by changing tab settings (see Figure 10-1).

You can make format changes within a file by using F7 (the Format key). After making format changes, you must paginate the file to ensure that all changes will be activated.

DisplayWrite 4 provides you with two separate methods for changing the format of a page or more: switching to an alternate format (which you design in advance) or making a

Minutes
FRIENDS OF THE LIBRARY Meeting

The FRIENDS OF THE LIBRARY met on Tuesday, October 8, at 8: p.m. at the home of Alice Skimpole, 45 Arington Drive. After an informal discussion about our goals for the coming year, Mr. Abe Bucket gave the following report on our fund-raising efforts over the past three months.

	July	August	Sept.
Book sales	100.50	75.00	135.00
Dues	38.75	95.00	145.50
Contributions	250.00	25.00	145.00
Total	389.25	195.00	425.50

It was proposed that we use the money for book repair. It was also suggested that each member do a minimum of five hours of volunteer work at the library each month.

Figure 10-1. Using different formats to enhance text appearance

page format change in your file. The alternate format method is particularly handy when you want to use the changed format in several places in your file. With a little practice, you will be able to determine which method is best in a particular case.

Using an Alternate Format

DisplayWrite 4 lets you design an alternate format along with your main format. Then, if several pages of your file need to have a different format, you can switch quickly to the alternate format. For example, you may be typing a double-spaced report with wide margins but want to include several pages of single-spaced tables with narrow margins. Or you may have typed a business letter and now want to type an envelope.

Designing an Alternate Format

Choose Create Document from the DisplayWrite 4 menu and type in the name of your file. (If you are performing this procedure on an already existing file, choose Revise Document.) Then

press ENTER.

You will be in the typing area.

Then press CTRL-F7 and choose Alternate Format from the Document Options menu.

"Chg Alternate Format" will appear on the top status line and you will see the Change Alternate Format menu shown in Figure 10-2.

Now you can select the appropriate items for making changes to the line format, margins and tabs, and page format as needed. Proceed *exactly* as you did when originally designing the format for your file (see Chapter 6), except, of course, that you must enter values for the alternate pages.

Notice that many of the alternate format defaults are different from those of the regular format. This is because the

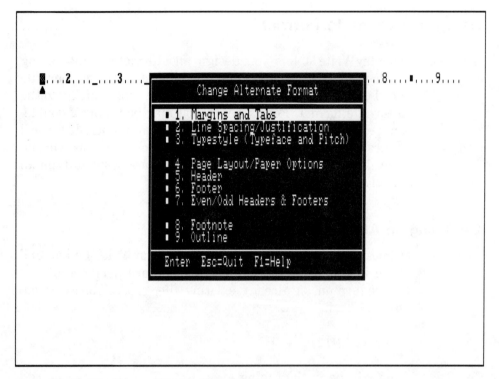

Figure 10-2. The Change Alternate Format menu

alternate format defaults have been designed for typing business envelopes, since this is one of the most common uses of an alternate format. Here are some important differences in the alternate format defaults:

- Adjust Line Endings is set to No. This turns wordwrap off, enabling you to end each line exactly where you wish.

- The first typing line is 13, rather than 7. This begins text two inches down the page and is suitable for typing a business envelope that has a printed return address. If you plan to type a return address yourself, you will have to change the first typing line to a much smaller number. But if you make the first typing line 3 or less, you may also want to change the first typing line for the header so it is a lower number than the first typing line for the text. (DisplayWrite 4 will let you proceed even if the first typing line is not greater than the first header line. For example, if you are printing labels, you will need to begin typing on line 1. Just don't include a header in your file.)

- The last typing line is 17 rather than 60.

- The footer begins on line 19. If you change the last typing line to 19 or greater, you must change the setting for the footer so it is farther down the page than the last typing line.

- The paper width is 9.5 inches and the paper length is 4.1 inches.

- The printing paper source is M, for Manual Feed.

When you are finished designing your alternate format,

press ESC

to return to the Document Options menu. Then

press ESC again

to return to the typing area.

Changing to the Alternate Format

Type the file using your regular format until you get to the place where you want an alternate format page to begin. Then

press CTRL-E

to begin a new page. (If you want to use an alternate format for a page you have already typed, just make sure that the cursor is at the upper left corner of the page. Pressing CTRL-HOME will get you there quickly.)

Press F7 and choose Reset Format from the Format menu.

You will see the Reset Format menu shown in Figure 10-3.

Select Alternate Format.

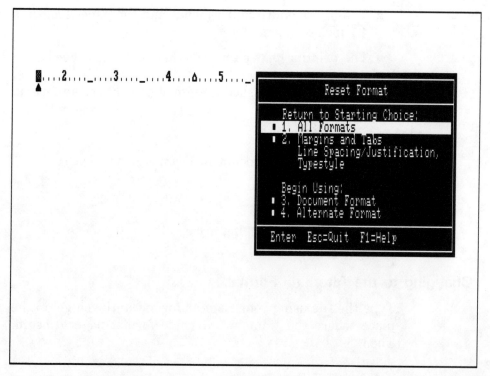

Figure 10-3.   The Reset Format menu

A Begin Alternate Format code is inserted into your text and you are returned to the typing area. Enter the text that you want to appear in the alternate format.

Returning to the Original Format

To return to the original format if you are typing the text for the first time,

press CTRL-E

to begin a new page. Then

press F7 and choose Reset Format.

If you are returning an already-existing page to the original format, make sure the cursor is in the upper left corner of the page. Then

press F7 and choose Reset Format.

When you see the Reset Format menu,

select Document Format.

Note: If your cursor is not correctly positioned, you will not be able to choose Document Format. If this happens, press ESC twice to get back to the typing area, and move the cursor to the upper left corner.

A Begin Document Format code is inserted into your file. You are returned to the typing area and can begin typing text in the regular format.

Paginate your file before you print it out. When you paginate, each Begin Alternate Format change and each Begin Document Format change will begin on a new page, even though you only inserted Page End codes (not Required Page End codes) into your file.

Note: If you use the same alternate format with different files, you will not want to redesign it each time you begin a new file. DisplayWrite 4 lets you change the alternate format defaults so you will not have to set them for each file. This process is explained in Chapter 15.

Using Page Format Change Codes

DisplayWrite 4 also lets you change the format of one or more pages by inserting Page Format Change codes into your text. This method is handy when you plan to use a particular format change only one time. You may change the format of pages you are about to create or of already-existing pages.

Making the Changes

To change the format for one or more pages you are about to create, type the file using either your regular format or the alternate format until you get to the place where you want to begin a new format. Then

press CTRL-E

to begin a new page. (If you want to use a different format for a page you have already typed, position the cursor at the upper left corner of the page.)

When the cursor is correctly positioned,

press F7.

You will see the Format menu. This menu looks similar to the Change Document Format menu and the Change Alternate Format menu. Since you are making the change for an entire page or more, *all* the menu options are available.

To make format changes, simply select the menu items you want and make format changes in the usual way. When all format changes are complete,

press ESC.

A Format Change code is inserted into your file, and you are returned to the typing area. Type in the text for the pages that are to appear in the new format, if they are not already typed in.

> *Note:* If you select only line format changes and margin and tab changes from the Format menu, your changes will take effect, but after pagination they will not begin on a new page. This is because only a Line Format Change code is inserted into your file, not a Page Format Change code.

Returning to the Original Page Format

To return to the original page format, move the cursor to the upper left corner of the first page that you want to appear in that format. (As you did before, use CTRL-E to get to the top of a blank page or CTRL-HOME to get to the top of an existing page.)

Press F7.

When you see the Format menu,

select Reset Format.

You will see the Reset Format menu. You choose All Formats to reset all formats to their original values. You choose Margins and Tabs, Line Spacing/Justification, Typestyle to reset only line format changes.

A Format Return code is inserted into your file and you are

returned to the typing area. Any text you type in now will be printed in the old format.

If, instead of returning to the original format, you want to change to another new format, just press F7 and select the desired line format, margins, tabs, and page format items from the menu. Another Format Change code will be inserted into your file instead of a Format Return code.

Note: If you are not at the beginning of the page when you press F7 to return to your old format, you will not be able to choose All Formats from the Reset Format menu.

Changing the Format of a Line or More

Suppose you have been typing a report, most of which is double-spaced, but which also includes sales figures in a special format. You would like the figures to be single-spaced and indented with special tab settings. You can do this easily because DisplayWrite 4 lets you change the format of a line or more of your file.

Making the Changes

To change the format of a line or more, move the cursor to the *beginning* of the line to be put in the new format. If you have already typed the text, move the cursor under the first character or code on the line.

Press F7.

You will see the Format menu, but not all the choices will be available to you. You can make changes in margins and tabs, line spacing and justification, and typestyles.

You can also "protect" a part of your file from having line

endings adjusted by selecting No for Adjust Line Endings in the Line Spacing/Justification menu. Then, even if you select Yes for Adjust Line Endings during pagination, line endings for the specified part of your file will not be adjusted.

When you have completed all changes,

press ESC

to return to the typing area. A Line Format Change code is inserted into your text. Type in the lines that are to appear in the new format, if they are not already typed.

Returning to the Original Line Format

Move the cursor to the beginning of the first line you want to appear in the old format.

Press F7 and choose Reset Format.

The only choice available to you is Margins and Tabs, Line Spacing/Justification, Typestyle. Make this choice. A Line Format Return code is inserted into your file and you are returned to the typing area.

Instead of returning to the original line format, you can change to a new line format. To do so, go to the beginning of the line where you want the new line format to begin and press F7. Then, instead of selecting Format Reset, simply make the changes you want.

Making Mid-Line Typestyle Changes

There is only one format change you can make in the middle of a line: you can change to a different typestyle. For instance, you might want several words in a text line to be printed in italics. *The new typestyle must be in the same pitch as the original.* If you want to change to a typestyle with a different pitch, make the change at the beginning of the line.

Making the Changes

To change typestyles in the middle of a line, move the cursor to the position where you want the new typestyle to begin.

Press CTRL-F (the Typeface key).

You will see the Change Typeface menu.

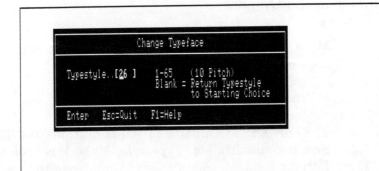

Notice that this menu is very abbreviated since you can only change to a typestyle of the same pitch.
Type the number of the typestyle you want and

press ENTER.

You are returned to the typing area. A Typestyle Change code is inserted into your text. Now type in the words that are to appear in the new typestyle.

Returning to the Original Typestyle

Make sure the cursor is positioned at the spot where you want to resume using the old typestyle.

Press CTRL-F again.

Then make the typestyle number blank. You can do this quickly by pressing ALT-8 (the Erase End of Line key), or you can use the space bar to blank out the item.

Then press ENTER

to return to the typing area. A Typestyle Return code is inserted into your text, and you are returned to the typing area to resume typing text with your original typestyle.

Revising Format Changes

Suppose that when you look at a printout with your newly designed format, you are not entirely pleased. Perhaps the new typestyles don't look as good as you had hoped, or the new margins look too wide. DisplayWrite 4 provides an easy way to revise your format changes. First, go to the typing area and move the cursor to the beginning of your file. Then follow these steps.

Press F6 and choose Find.

In response to the Find What? prompt,

press F7; then press ENTER.

Key	Function
CTRL-F7	Used to design the alternate format
CTRL-F7	Initiates mid-file format changes. These may be alternate format, page format, line format, or mid-line changes. Also used to return you to the original format
CTRL-F	Initiates mid-line typestyle changes
CTRL-F8	Used for revision of format changes

Table 10-1.   Keys Used for Mid-File Format Changes

The cursor will stop under the first Format Change code it encounters—either page, line, or typestyle.

If you want to revise the code,

press CTRL-F8 (the View/Revise key).

You will see either the Format Menu or the Change Typeface menu (depending on the code). Make the desired format changes using the techniques you have learned in this chapter. When you are finished, return to the typing area.

If you don't want to revise that code, press F6 and choose Repeat to locate the next Format Change code. Proceed through your file until you have made all desired changes.

Note: If you want to revise just one Format Change code, set Display All Codes to Yes and position the cursor under the code. Then press CTRL-F8 and make the desired changes.

Table 10-1 lists the keys used in creating and revising mid-file format changes.

11

Page Numbers, Headers, and Footers

This chapter shows you how to print a file with page numbers and with a text header and footer at the top and bottom of each page.

What Headers and Footers Are

A *header* is a text line (consisting of letters, numbers, or other characters) that appears at the top of each page of your printed file; a *footer* is a text line that appears at the bottom. The most common header or footer is a page number. Figure 11-1 shows a manuscript page with a text line ("first draft") for a header and a page number for a footer.

DisplayWrite 4 lets you create headers and footers that contain up to 512 characters each (including codes and spaces). You can select different headers and footers to appear on alternate pages of your printed file, begin page numbering with any number you specify, and have different

```
                                                            first draft

        SYLLABUS

        Clear Writing

                Getting started

                Writing clear sentences

                Writing clear business letters

        Correct Writing

                Run-together sentences and sentence fragments

                Subject-verb agreement

                Punctuation

                Pronoun reference

        Organizing Your Material

                Going from general to specific

                Making an outline

                              1
```

Figure 11-1. A right-aligned header and a centered footer

sections of the same file begin with the number 1 (for instance, for a report with several sections). Headers and footers print in the top and bottom margin areas.

Note: If you change typestyles within a file with F7 (rather than CTRL-F7), the header or footer will not print in the new typestyle. It will print in the typestyle of the original document format.

Creating Headers and Footers

You create headers and footers for your file the same way you design other aspects of the document format (see Chapter 6). To include a header or footer in a file you are creating or revising, go to the typing area.

Press CTRL-F7 and choose Document Format.

Note: Even if you are not at the beginning of your file when you create your header or footer, your header or footer will be in effect for the entire file after you paginate.

Selecting a Location for Your Headers and Footers

The default settings position your header beginning on line 3 and your footer beginning on line 63. Additionally, the defaults print your headers and footers on every page of your text. However, you can pick other beginning lines for your headers and footers and designate that headers and footers be printed on all pages *except the first page.* This option is useful if the first page of your file is a title page and you want it to appear without headers or footers.

If you need to change the settings for header and footer location,

choose Page Layout/Paper Options

from the Change Document Format menu. Under First Typing Line type the new choices for your header and footer. Remember, headers and footers *must always print outside the regular body of the text*, so pick a header number that is smaller than the first typing line for your text and a footer number that is larger than the last typing line.

If you are planning a header that is several lines long, make sure there is room for it in the top margin space. If there isn't, pick a *smaller* number for your first header line or a *larger* number for the first typing line of your text.

To designate that headers and footers print on all pages but the first page,

> press PGDN

to go to page 2 of the menu. For Print Header On and Print Footer On,

> type **F**

for Following Pages.

> Press ENTER

to save your changes and return to the Change Document Format menu.

Creating the Header

So far, you have used only the first four items on this menu. Now you are going to work with the next three.

From the Change Document Format menu,

> choose Header.

You will find yourself in a special typing area called the *header typing area*. It looks a lot like the regular typing area, but it has its own special rules:

- Line endings are not adjusted. What you type is what you get.

- There is no wordwrap.

- Spacing between lines is always single.

Now enter the header text you want. You can use the TAB key or the space bar to position your text the way you want it. Depending on how you position the characters, the text can be left-aligned,

```
A left-aligned header
```

right-aligned,

```
                                    A right-aligned header
```

both right- and left-aligned,

```
A left-aligned header              A right-aligned header
```

or centered (use CTRL-C or the space bar to center it).

```
                     A centered header
```

You can even have a header consisting of several lines *as long as you have room for them in the top margin area.* Here is a three-line header:

```
DisplayWrite 4 manuscript
Chapter 11
by Gail Todd
```

When you have typed your header text,

press F2 and choose Return and Save

to return to the Change Document Format menu.

Creating the Footer

To create a footer,

choose Footer

from the Change Document Format menu. You are taken to the footer typing area.

Following the same rules as for creating a header, type in the desired footer text. As with the header, your footer text may be placed anywhere you wish on the line and may contain several lines, *as long as they fit within the bottom margin.* When you are finished typing,

press F2 and choose Return and Save

to return to the Change Document Format menu. Then

press ESC

to return to the typing area.

Note: You may use boldfacing, underlining, centering, and other text enhancements in headers and footers. Just use the techniques that you have learned so far in this book to create the enhancements. You can press F4 while in the header or footer typing area and make menu choices from the Block menu.

Page Numbers

If you are typing a one-page business letter or memo, you will probably not want a page number on it. However, if you are working with longer files—reports, analyses, or research projects—you will want your printed file to contain page numbers, at either the top or bottom of each page. Page numbers can be part of other header or footer text or they can stand alone. For example, you can have either

```
DisplayWrite 4 manuscript, page 1
```

or

```
1
```

Note: Do not include headers and footers with page numbers in merged files (see Chapters 23 through 25).

To include page numbers in your manuscript, go to the header or footer typing area. Type any text that you want to appear before the page number. Then position the cursor where you want the number to appear.

Press F8 (the Instructions key).

You will see

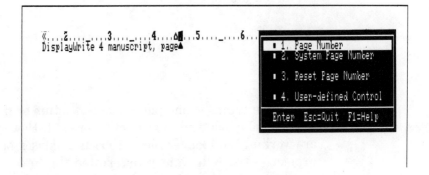

There are several menu choices.

Page Number

The Page Number choice creates ordinary whole page numbers. Numbering will begin at page 1. The Page Number choice also allows you to reset the page number later in your file.

To number your file with whole numbers,

select Page Number.

A Page Number code is inserted into your file and you are returned to the header or footer typing area.

System Page Number

If you want the page numbers in your header or footer to *exactly match* the page numbers in the top status line, select

System Page Number. Remember that if you have made revisions, these page numbers may contain decimals (such as Pg 1.1 or Pg 1.1.1).

However, even if you select System Page Number, you can eliminate decimals by paginating your file later. Numbers are reassigned during pagination as page lengths are equalized and decimal page numbers are eliminated.

When you select System Page Number from the Page Number menu, a System Page Number code is inserted into your file and you are returned to the header or footer typing area. You can now enter any header or footer text that follows the page number.

Resetting the Page Number

Let's say you are producing a lengthy report consisting of three sections. Each section is a separate file. You print the first file; it is 30 pages long. When you print the second one, you want the first page number to be 31, so that the complete report will be numbered consecutively.

To reset the page number, go to the header or footer typing area of the file for which you want to reset the page number.

Press F8 and choose Page Number

from the Instructions menu. Then

choose Reset Page Number.

When prompted, type the page number you want to start with; then

press ENTER

You are returned to the header or footer typing area to complete your header or footer.

Note: The Reset Page Number feature only works if you previously chose Page Number for your numbering system. The feature will not work if you chose System Page Number.

User-Defined Controls

The User-Defined Control choice inserts a user-defined control number into your header or footer that matches a control number in your printer function table. For information on creating and employing user-defined controls, see the section "User-defined Control" in the *DisplayWrite 4 Technical Reference* manual that came with your software.

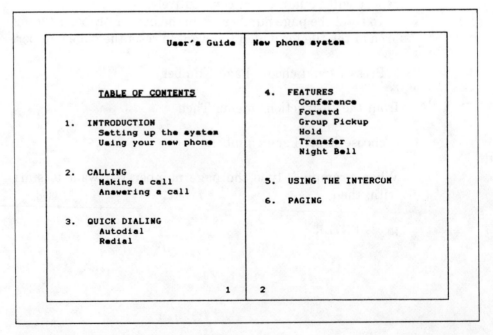

Figure 11-2. Alternating headers and footers

Creating Alternating Headers and Footers

DisplayWrite 4 lets you print one set of headers and footers on even pages and another set on odd pages. These are called *alternating* headers and footers. Alternating headers and footers are most frequently used with text that is printed on both sides of a page. If you open a book, you probably will see a header on each even-numbered page showing the book title and another header on each odd-numbered page showing the chapter title. Figure 11-2 shows two pages with alternating headers and footers. You can also create a header that prints *only* on even-numbered pages or one that prints *only* on odd-numbered pages.

To create alternating headers and footers you begin exactly as when you created ordinary headers and footers. (From the typing area, press CTRL-F7. From the Document Options menu, choose Document Format.) This time, instead of choosing Header or Footer from the Change Document Format menu, choose Even/Odd Headers & Footers. You will see the Even/Odd menu shown here:

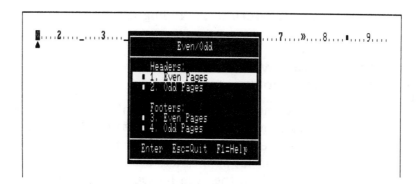

The Even/Odd Headers & Footers menu works the same way the Header and Footer menu did, except that there are *two* header typing areas and *two* footer typing areas. To enter an alternating header,

choose Even Pages.

When you get to the header typing area, type the text for the even-page headers. (In material printed on both sides of a page, the even-page header will appear on the left-hand page.) When you are finished,

press F2 and choose Return and Save.

You will see the Even/Odd menu again. This time

choose Odd Pages.

Now, when you get to the header typing area, type the text for the odd-page header. When you are finished,

press F2 and choose Return and Save.

You will be returned to the Even/Odd menu. Repeat the process with the footer part of the menu to create alternating footers, or

press ESC

until you return to the typing area.

Page Numbers with Alternating Headers and Footers

Page numbers can be part of alternating header and footer text, just as they can be part of regular headers and footers.

For example, to include ordinary page numbers as part of an alternating header, create the even header as just described. In the even header typing area,

press F8 and choose Page Number

at the location where you want the page number to print. Then do the same for the odd header. The pages of your printed file will be numbered consecutively.

Revising Headers and Footers

Revising headers and footers with DisplayWrite 4 is easy. You follow the *identical* procedure that you use to create a new header or footer. However, when you enter the header or footer typing area, you will see your *existing* header or footer text rather than an empty screen.

Revise the header or footer as desired. Then

press F2 and choose Return and Save

to save the new header or footer text.

Changing Headers and Footers in the Middle of a File

Perhaps you have a large report composed of different sections. You want each section to have its own header. Perhaps you also want page numbers to revert to 1 each time a new section begins. Or maybe you want to switch to a different header and footer in the middle of your file and later return to the originals. As you work with more complex files, you will undoubtedly come up with your own unique situations.

To switch to different headers and footers in the middle of a file, you will use the technique for changing the format of one or more pages that you learned in Chapter 10.

Creating the New Header or Footer

In the typing area, move the cursor to the upper left corner of the first page you want the new header or footer to appear on.

Press F7.

When you see the Format menu,

choose Header, Footer, or Even/Odd Headers & Footers.

You will enter the appropriate header or footer typing area and will see your existing header or footer on the screen. (In the case of Even/Odd Headers & Footers, you choose which one you want to revise before you enter the appropriate typing area.) Revise the existing header or footer or type in a new one.

If you wish, you can also reset the page number at this time (provided you have previously selected Page Number from the Instructions menu). To reset the page number,

press F8 and choose Reset Page Number.

Then type in the new number and

press ENTER.

When you have completed your new header or footer,

press F2, choose Return and Save, and press ESC.

A Page Format Change code is inserted into your text and you are returned to the regular typing area. The new header or footer will be in effect from the Page Format Change code until the end of your file or until the next Page Format Change or Page Format Return code.

Key	Function
CTRL-F7	Used to locate the header and footer on the page and to create the header and footer
F8	Used to insert page numbers into headers and footers and to reset page numbers in existing headers and footers
F7	Used to change to a different header or footer in the middle of a file

Table 11-1. Keys Used for Creating Headers and Footers

Returning to the Original Header or Footer

If you want to return to the original header or footer on a particular page, go to the typing area of that page and move the cursor to the upper left corner.

Press F7.

(If you are planning to return to the original header or footer, do not reset page numbering in the middle of the file.)

When you see the Format menu,

choose Reset Format.

Then

select Return All Formats to Starting Choice.

A Page Format Return code is inserted into your file, and you are returned to the typing area.

Table 11-1 identifies the keys used in creating headers and footers.

12

Combining and Separating Files

This chapter shows you how to combine and separate files. It teaches you how to save a file in ASCII notation so you can use it with other programs and how to insert an ASCII file into your current DisplayWrite 4 file.

How DisplayWrite 4 Stores Information

Many word-processing programs store information in *ASCII* notation. ASCII stands for the *American Standard Code for Information Interchange.* In ASCII notation each letter, numeral, or character is assigned a separate number. For example, an uppercase P is *always* assigned 80 and a lowercase s is always assigned 115; other numbers are assigned to such actions as backspace, line feed, and carriage return.

ASCII notation has become an industry standard. Most printers that work with personal computers use ASCII notation; communication programs convert information into ASCII to transmit it over telephone lines; and spreadsheet programs often have a print to disk option that converts spreadsheet information into an ASCII file.

DisplayWrite 4 does not store information in ASCII notation. Instead, it stores information in EBCDIC (Extended Binary-Coded Decimal Interchange Code). DisplayWrite 4, however, can "talk ASCII," so you are not limited in any way. If you are in Character mode, the system converts characters to ASCII before displaying them on your screen. (If you are in APA mode, you will see the EBCDIC characters.)

DisplayWrite 4 can save a text block as an ASCII file so you can use it whenever ASCII notation is required. It can also convert an ASCII file into EBCDIC and insert that converted file into a file you are working on. For example, if you want a spreadsheet report inserted into your DisplayWrite 4 file, you can print the report to disk with the spreadsheet program (thereby converting it into an ASCII file) and then insert the ASCII file into your DisplayWrite 4 text file.

Using the Notepad Function to Combine and Separate Files

In Chapter 4 you learned how to use the Notepad to store blocks of text and then to recall the text blocks to any file of your choice. This is the method used by DisplayWrite 4 to combine and separate files. You can also use Notepad to save a text block as an ASCII file. The system provides one Notepad, called the *System Notepad*, but you can also create as many of your own Notepads as you like. These are called *User-Named Notepads*.

Using the System Notepad to Save a Text Block

To save a block of text to a separate file, go to the typing area of the file you are working on and place the cursor under the first character or code of the block you want saved.

Press CTRL-F4.

You will see the Notepad menu.

Choose Move to Notepad

to eliminate the text block from the current file and save it in the Notepad.

Choose Copy to Notepad

to retain the text block in its current location and also copy the block to Notepad. Move the cursor to the end of the block you want defined and

press ENTER.

Your text block is saved in the Notepad.

To create a new file out of the saved block, just select Create Document from the DisplayWrite 4 menu and name the new file. When you enter the typing area,

press CTRL-F4 and choose Recall from Notepad.

The text saved in Notepad will now constitute a separate file with a name you have chosen.

Note: Remember that text will remain in Notepad *even if you turn off your computer.* Therefore, you can save the text in Notepad one day and create a new file out of it the next. However, each time you save text to the System Notepad, it will overwrite the text already there, so you can only save one block at a time in the System Notepad.

Creating Your Own Notepads

When you save text in the System Notepad, it is saved in a file called $NOTEPAD.DOC. However, you can also save text in Notepads you name yourself. The advantage of this is that you can have as many Notepads as you want. For example, if you want to save a paragraph of a letter, you can save it in a Notepad called PARA1.DOC. Then, if you want to save a second paragraph later on, you could save it in a separate Notepad called PARA2.DOC. If you had simply used the System Notepad, the second paragraph saved would have overwritten the first, and the first would have been lost.

To create and use your own Notepad, in the typing area

press CTRL-F5 and choose User-Named Notepads

for Notepad Choice. Then return to the typing area and save text to the Notepad as described in the previous section. However, before the text is saved, you will be prompted for the Notepad name. Type in the name you want for your User-Named Notepad (you can use any valid filename).

Your text will be saved in the Notepad you named. When you later choose Recall from Notepad, you will be prompted for the name of the Notepad from which you want to recall the text.

Saving a Text Block as an ASCII File

You can use Notepad to save a text block as an ASCII file. To save a DisplayWrite 4 text block as an ASCII file, in the typing area move the cursor to the start of the block. Then

press CTRL-F4 and choose ASCII Copy to File.

Then move the cursor to the end of the block.

Press ENTER.

You are prompted for a name for the ASCII file. If you don't specify an extension, DisplayWrite 4 will provide the extension. Type the filename and

press ENTER.

The text block is saved as an ASCII file.

> *Note:* In this case the file is saved as a separate file in the *same directory* as the Notepad, rather than in the Notepad itself. If you are saving your documents in a special subdirectory, you won't find your saved ASCII file there. You can specify a different Notepad Save Path with Profiles (see Chapter 15).

Inserting Another File into Your File

To insert a DisplayWrite 4 file into your file, first save, in Notepad, the file you want to insert. Then load the current file and position the cursor where you want the new block of text to appear (see Figure 12-1).

Press CTRL-F4 and select Recall from Notepad.

The block is retrieved from Notepad and inserted at the cursor location, as shown in Figure 12-2.

Combining Files with the Get Function

The Get function provides another method of combining files. Get involves more steps but has more options. In addition to inserting DisplayWrite 4 files into your file, Get lets you do the following:

- Insert DisplayWrite 3 files into your file
- Insert a standard ASCII file into your file

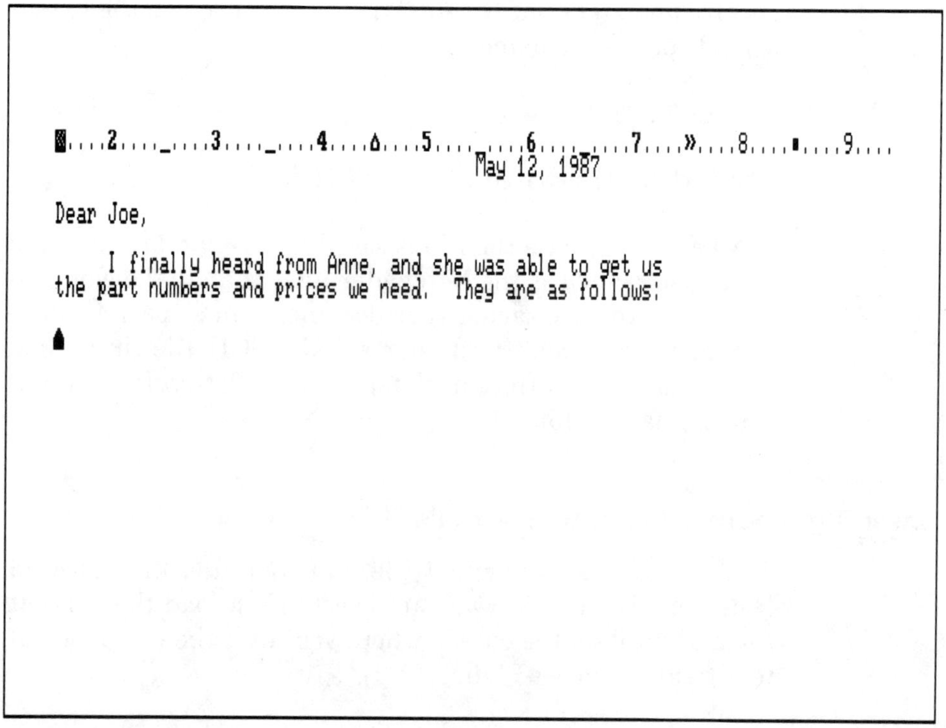

```
█....2...._....3...._....4....△....5...._....6...._....7....»....8....■....9....
                              May 12, 1987

Dear Joe,

     I finally heard from Anne, and she was able to get us
the part numbers and prices we need.  They are as follows:


█
```

Figure 12-1.   Preparing to use Recall from Notepad to move a file into the file you are working on

- Insert a 7-bit ASCII file (certain word-processing pro-grams create these) into your file

- Insert a revisable-form document into your file (see Chapter 14)

Additionally, if you are using Get to insert a DisplayWrite 4, DisplayWrite 3, or revisable-form document, you can select the specific pages you want to insert.

To use Get to insert another file into the file you are work-

```
█....2...._....3...._....4....△....5........6........7....»....8....■....9....
                                May 12, 1987

Dear Joe,

     I finally heard from Anne, and she was able to get us
the part numbers and prices we need.  They are as follows:

↕   PART #     PART NAME       SUPPLIER      PRICE
    764        7/8" bolt       Superior      0.20
    782        1/2" bolt       Superior      0.15
    723          1" bolt       Superior      0.30
    126        3/8" bolt       Anderson      0.15
    120        1/4" bolt       Anderson      0.15
```

Figure 12-2. Your file after using Recall from Notepad

ing on, move the cursor to the position where you want the new file inserted.

Press CTRL-F6.

You will see the Get menu shown in Figure 12-3.

Type in the name of the document you want inserted. Then, if you are retrieving a DisplayWrite 4, DisplayWrite 3, or revisable-form document and you want to retrieve only cer-

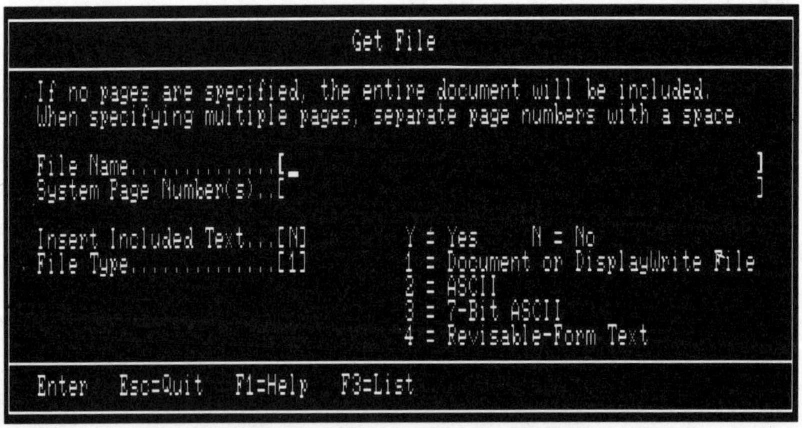

Figure 12-3. The Get Menu

tain pages, tab to the System Page Number(s) item and type the system page numbers of the pages you want inserted. Leave a space between each number.

If you are retrieving an ASCII, a 7-bit ASCII, or a revisable-form file, tab to File Type and type in the number representing your file type. When you have completed the menu,

press ENTER.

The file or designated pages will be inserted at the cursor location.

In Part Three of this book you will learn about the Insert Included Text menu item and how to use Get to create form letters.

Note: If you are using a floppy-disk system, have both the file you are retrieving and the file you are creating or revising on the same floppy disk.

ASCII to EBCDIC Conversions

When you use the Get function to insert an ASCII file into the file you are working on, the ASCII characters are converted to EBCDIC characters. In most situations this will have no effect on your work; an ASCII "a" becomes an EBCDIC "a", an ASCII "2" becomes an EBCDIC "2", and so on. As you can see in Figure 12-4, in only *a very few* situations will you be unable to convert an ASCII character to a similar EBCDIC character.

Note: When you insert an ASCII file into your file, you may have difficulty formatting the ASCII part. This is because an ASCII file has a required carriage return at the end of every line.

EBCDIC to ASCII Conversions

There are only 128 ASCII characters; EBCDIC has many more. Therefore, when you are using Notepad's ASCII Copy to File to convert a file from EBCDIC to ASCII, you may not be able to get some of the more unusual symbols. Of course, letters, numbers, and standard keyboard characters convert without any problem, but some of the symbols available as keyboard extension characters (see Chapter 22), such as copyright symbols, trademark symbols, and prescription symbols, are not available in ASCII. (Since many printers only print ASCII, however, you may not be losing anything.) Table 12-1 lists the keys used to combine and separate files.

ASCII Character	EBCDIC Character	EBCDIC Name
♦	™	Trademark symbol
	©	Copyright symbol
	≠	Not equal symbol
	ƀ	Substitute blank
	‖	Parallel symbol
	Ø	Zero slash
	□	Open square
	℞	Prescription symbol
	⟩	Right angle bracket superscript
	⟨	Left angle bracket superscript
	=	Double overline
∩	~	"Equivalent to" symbol
		Cycle symbol
–	®	Registered trademark symbol
∩	³	Superscript 3

From *DisplayWrite 3 User's Guide, Volume 2*, page 23-15. Copyright © 1985, 1986 by International Business Machines Corporation. Used with permission.

Figure 12-4.   ASCII characters that convert to dissimilar EBCDIC characters

Key	Function
CTRL-F4	The Move to Notepad or Copy to Notepad choice lets you save a text block in DisplayWrite 4's Notepad
	The ASCII Copy to File choice saves a text block as an ASCII file
	The Recall from Notepad choice inserts a file saved in Notepad into the file you are working on
CTRL-F6	Get inserts a DisplayWrite 4, DisplayWrite 3, revisable-form, standard ASCII, or 7-bit ASCII file into the file you are working on. Pages may be specified for DisplayWrite and revisable-form files

Table 12-1. Keys Used for Combining and Separating Files

13

Inserting
Voice Notes
into Your File

This chapter shows you how to insert spoken comments into your file and how to "play back" the comments later.

What Voice Notes Are

DisplayWrite 4 contains a Voice feature that lets you incorporate verbal comments into your file. You can insert special instructions or statements into a document, and another person can later listen to your verbal comments when working on the file.

Voice notes use approximately 2.4K of disk space *per second.* You can see that if you "chat" for several minutes, your file would become enormous. Therefore, use voice notes only for brief instructions or comments.

Preparing to Use the Voice Feature

To use the Voice feature, you must have the following equipment:

- A hard disk
- An IBM Voice Communications card
- The IBM Voice Communications Operating Subsystem program files stored in a directory called VCAPI
- A speaker and a microphone

If you intend to use voice notes during a work session, you must load the voice program files *before* you load Display-Write 4. When you see the DOS prompt,

type **audiohf** and press ENTER.

If the voice program files are not on the default drive C, then you must also specify the drive. In this case,

type **audiohf [d]** and press ENTER.

(The [d] represents the drive on which the voice program files can be found.)

Recording a Voice Note

To record a voice note, type your file in the usual way until you get to the place where you want to insert a verbal comment. Then

press F8 and select Voice Note.

Carefully plan what you want to say. Then

select Record.

At this point, you begin speaking and your voice note records. If you are speaking too softly, you will get a warning message on the screen.

If you need to pause during your recording (perhaps to clarify your thoughts), press the space bar. Press the space bar again to resume recording. When you have completed your voice note,

press ENTER

to stop recording. Then

press ESC

to return to the typing area.

You will see that a tiny musical note has been inserted into your file. (You will see this note even with Display All Codes set to No.) This is the Voice Note code.

Continue typing your file until you get to the next place where you want to insert a voice note, and repeat the procedure.

Note: If you transfer your file to DisplayWrite 3 format and then reconvert it to DisplayWrite 4, your voice note will be lost.

Playing the Voice Note

To play a voice note, you first load the file in the usual way. Then move the cursor directly under the Voice Note code.

Press CTRL-F8 and choose Play.

You will hear the voice note. Use the up and down arrow keys to adjust the volume if necessary. If you want to pause during voice note playback, press the space bar. Then press the space bar again to resume playback. If you want to terminate the playback entirely, press ENTER.

When the voice note has played back, you are returned to the typing area and can listen to another voice note or resume work on your file.

Re-recording a Voice Note

If you have recorded a voice note and later decide to change the information in it, you can re-record the note. To do so, load the file and, in the typing area, position the cursor under the Voice Note code. Then

press CTRL-F8 and choose Re-record.

Re-record the message. When you are finished,

press ENTER

to end the voice note.

Press ESC

to return to the typing area.

Deleting a Voice Note

To delete a voice note, you must delete the Voice Note code in your file. You delete this code exactly as you delete other codes. (Position the cursor under the code, press DEL, and then press ENTER.)

Because voice notes take up so much disk space, you should compress your file after you delete a number of voice note codes (see Chapter 14). This makes available to you the disk space formerly taken up by the voice notes.

Table 13-1 shows the keys used for voice notes.

Key	Function
F8	The Voice Note choice lets you create a voice note
CTRL-F8	The Play choice plays back the voice note
	The Re-record choice lets you re-record a previously recorded voice note

Table 13-1. Keys Used for Voice Notes

14

Managing
Your Files

This chapter teaches you how to use DisplayWrite 4 utilities to copy, rename, erase, recover, and compress text files. It also shows you how to convert files so they can be interchanged with other programs and how to issue DOS commands and return to DisplayWrite 4 without having to reload.

Why Your Files May Need Attention

In Chapter 2 we compared a disk to a file drawer, and the memos, reports, and letters that you produce to the separate folders that go into the drawer.

After a period of time, a file cabinet may become messy and overcrowded and need to be cleaned out. Maybe some files should be thrown away; others may need to be copied, with the copies placed elsewhere for safekeeping. Still others may need to be given new names.

In a similar manner, your data subdirectory or disk may become cluttered and inefficient after a while and need your attention. The system provides you with two methods for working on your files. First, DisplayWrite 4 provides a number of utilities (often called housekeeping utilities) that help you manage your files; second, you can choose DOS Commands from the DisplayWrite 4 menu. This choice enables you to leave DisplayWrite 4 temporarily, issue DOS commands, and return to DisplayWrite 4 without reloading.

Using DisplayWrite 4 Utilities

The DisplayWrite 4 utilities let you copy, rename, erase, compress, and recover files. A separate Document Conversion feature lets you interchange files between DisplayWrite 4 and other systems and programs (such as DisplayWrite/ 370, DisplayWrite/36, DisplayWrite 3, and DisplayWrite Assistant) for editing and printing.

To use the DisplayWrite 4 utilities,

choose Utilities

from the DisplayWrite 4 menu. You will see the Utilities menu shown here:

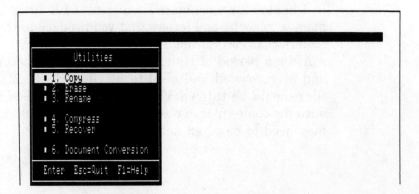

You may now select the utility you need. You will then be prompted for the name of the file.

Note: When prompted for the name of the file, you can press F3 (the List key) and select the file from the directory.

DOS Global Characters

When using DisplayWrite 4 utilities you may want to perform an operation on a group of files rather than on a single file. For example, to erase all files with the extension .JAN, you will find it less time-consuming to delete the files in one operation than to delete each file separately. DOS provides two characters called *global characters*, or *wildcard characters*, that let you perform a single operation on more than one file. You can use these global characters with the Copy, Erase, Compress, and Recover DisplayWrite 4 utilities.

When using any of these utilities, you will be prompted for the document name. You enter the global characters to represent characters in the filename or in the extension, as shown in the following two sections.

Using the Global Character * The global character * can represent any or all characters that follow in the filename or extension.

Say you want to copy, erase, compress, or rename all files with the extension .JAN. When prompted for the document name,

type ***.jan**

To use a utility on all files that have the filename SALES,

type **sales.***

To use a utility on all files whose filenames begin with MEMO,

type **memo*.***

To use a utility on all files in the directory,

type ***.***

Using the Global Character ?   The global character ? can stand for any single character. Say you want to erase the files MEMO1, MEMO2, MEMO3, and MEMO4. When prompted for the name of the file,

type **memo?**

Erasing a File

Whether you want to erase one file at a time or use the DOS global characters * and ? to erase a group of files, you can use the Erase utility on both DisplayWrite 4 files and DOS files.
   To erase a file, display the Utilities menu and

choose Erase.

Then, in response to the prompt, type the name of the file and

press ENTER.

You can use DOS global characters in the name to delete several files. You can also specify a directory or drive name to delete all the files on a directory or drive.

Press ENTER

to begin erasing files. If you need to stop the process,

press CTRL-BREAK.

(If you're not fast, it's too late.) When the specified files are erased, you are returned to the Utilities menu.

Renaming a File

You can use Rename to rename either a DisplayWrite 4 file or a DOS file. To rename a file, display the Utilities menu and

choose Rename.

The Rename Document menu will appear.
Type the current name of the file. Then type the new name and

press ENTER.

The completed menu will look like this:

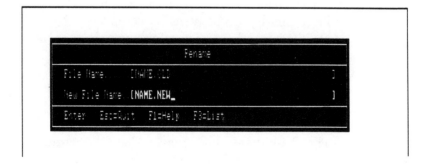

Press ENTER again

to begin renaming. The file is renamed and you are returned
to the Utilities menu.

Copying a File

You should periodically make backup copies of all your data
files in case the originals get damaged or destroyed. Important files should always be copied to a floppy disk and kept in
a separate location.

The Copy utility also comes in handy when you want to
write the same letter or memo to several people. You can
write the letter once, copy the file for each person who will
receive it, and then, for each copy, go to the typing area to
correct the name, address, and any other information that
must be personalized.

The Copy utility lets you copy a DisplayWrite 4, Display-
Write 3, DisplayWrite Assistant, or DOS file. You may copy
the file to either the same directory or disk or to a different
one. If you copy the file to the same directory, you must pick
a new name for it, since you cannot have two files with the
same name on one directory. If you are using a floppy-disk
system, make sure that you have room on your disk for both
the original file and the copy.

Because files that have been greatly revised use disk space
inefficiently, the Copy utility compresses DisplayWrite 4 files
as it copies them. Therefore, you may find that the copy
occupies less disk space than the original.

To copy a file, display the Utilities menu and

choose Copy.

The Copy menu will appear. Type the name of the file to be
copied. Use DOS global characters to copy several files or
specify a directory name to copy all the files in a directory.
Then tab to New File Name.

To copy the file to the same directory, type the new name and

press ENTER.

To copy the file to a different directory, type a new name or the old name, whichever you prefer, and

press ENTER.

If you need to stop the copying process,

press CTRL-BREAK.

When the specified files are copied, you are returned to the Utilities menu.

Compressing a File

As you revise your files by moving and deleting text, a certain amount of unused disk space becomes "locked up" and unavailable to receive new work. You can use the Compress utility to free this disk space. It is a good idea to compress a file after several revisions.

While a file is being compressed, DisplayWrite 4 contains both the original file and the compressed copy. If you are using a floppy-disk system, check beforehand that you have enough free disk space for both copies. When compression is complete, the original file is deleted and only the compressed file remains.

To compress a file, display the Utilities menu and

choose Compress.

Type the name of the file you want to compress. Use DOS

global characters to compress several files. To compress all the files on a directory, type the directory name.

To begin compression,

press ENTER.

If you need to stop the compression process,

press CTRL-BREAK.

When the specified files are compressed, you are returned to the Utilities menu.

Recovering a File

The Recover utility allows you to recover files that were not properly saved to disk. Such a mishap can occur because of a power outage, because you removed your disk without pressing F2, or because your disk is damaged in some way. (The Recover utility will not work on DOS files.)

When you type a file, DisplayWrite 4 temporarily creates a file with the same name as your file, but with the extension .$$C. When you save your file, the .$$C file is deleted. However, if your file is not properly saved to disk, the .$$C file is not deleted and you will be unable to access your file. Recover deletes the .$$C file after it properly saves your file. Anytime you try to access a file and you get the message "FILE.XYZ is already in use" and, in fact, the file is not being used, you must recover the file.

The Recover utility may not be able to restore all of your text. Therefore, after recovering the file, go to the typing area and check for lost data.

Before you attempt to recover the file, use the Rename utility to rename .$$C file. *Do not delete this file, since it contains the data you want recovered.* Then use the Erase utility to delete the .$$T file if it exists (this file contains any block deletes). You are now ready to begin the recovery.

To recover a file, display the Utilities menu and

choose Recover.

Type the name of the renamed .$$C file. To begin recovery,

press ENTER.

If you need to stop the recovery process,

press CTRL-BREAK.

When the specified files are recovered, you are returned to the Utilities menu.

Converting a File

The Document Conversion utility can convert revisable-form or final-form files produced by other programs into Display-Write 4 files. It can also convert DisplayWrite 4 files into either final-form or revisable-form files. The Document Conversion feature lets DisplayWrite 4 use files produced by other programs that support these two text forms; it also lets these other programs use DisplayWrite 4 files.

Revisable-Form Text

Use the Document Conversion utility to convert a Display-Write 4 text file to a revisable-form file when you want another system or program to edit it. Some systems and programs that can use revisable-form text are DisplayWrite 3, DisplayWrite/36, DisplayWrite/370, and DisplayWrite Assistant. The default extension .RFT is appended to revisable-form files if you don't specify any other.

You can also use the Document Conversion utility to convert a revisable-form file generated by another system or program to a DisplayWrite 4 text file, so DisplayWrite 4 can edit it.

In addition to the Document Conversion utility, DisplayWrite 4 provides other methods of working with revisable-form documents:

- You can use Get to insert (and convert to DisplayWrite 4) all or part of a revisable-form document into the document you are working with.

- When you are creating or revising a document, you can specify a revisable-form document when prompted for the document name. Then, when you press F2 to save the file, you will see additional menu choices, providing you with the option of saving the file as a revisable-form document.

- You can change the system defaults (see Chapter 15) to *always* provide you with additional choices in the End/Save menu, so you can save any file in revisable form. (It is a good idea to make this change if you frequently work with revisable-form files.)

Final-Form Text

Use the Document Conversion utility to convert a file produced by another system or program to final-form text when you want DisplayWrite 4 to print it, or to convert a DisplayWrite 4 file to final-form text so it can be printed by another system or program. You must then convert the file back to DisplayWrite 4 before DisplayWrite 4 can edit it. The default extension .FFT is appended to final-form text files if you don't specify any other.

You can also print final-form text documents *without converting them* by selecting Final Form Text as the document type in the Print Document menu.

The Conversion Process

When you convert a file, the original file is not deleted from your disk. Therefore, if you have a floppy-disk system, make sure you have sufficient disk space to hold both the original and the converted file.

To convert a file, display the Utilities menu and

choose Document Conversion.

You will see

Type the name of the file to be converted. Then type the name you want for the converted file. Finally, choose the number representing the type of conversion:

- Choose Document to Revisable-Form Text to send a DisplayWrite 4 text file to another system or program for editing.

- Choose Revisable-Form Text to Document to receive a file from another system or program so you can edit it with DisplayWrite 4.

- Choose Document to Final-Form Text to send a DisplayWrite 4 file to be printed by another system or program.

- Choose Final-Form Text to Document to enable DisplayWrite 4 to edit a file it has previously converted to final form for printing by another system or program. (DisplayWrite 4 can print final-form files but not edit them.)

To begin the conversion process,

press ENTER.

When the file is converted, you are returned to the Utilities menu.

Issuing a DOS Command from DisplayWrite 4

The DOS Command choice on the DisplayWrite 4 menu lets you issue a DOS command while using DisplayWrite 4. It lets you leave DisplayWrite 4 momentarily, execute the DOS command, and then return to DisplayWrite 4.

If you are printing files with DisplayWrite 4 background print, printing will cease as soon as you select DOS Command Task and will resume when you return to DisplayWrite 4.

To issue a DOS command, display the DisplayWrite 4 menu and

choose DOS Commands.

The screen will display the DOS prompt:

```
The IBM Personal Computer DOS
Version 3.20 (C)Copyright International Business Machines Corp 1981, 1986
              (C)Copyright Microsoft Corp 1981, 1986

DOS Commands
Type EXIT to Return to DisplayWrite 4
(C) Type Command:_
```

When you are finished issuing DOS commands,

type **exit** and press ENTER.

You will be returned to the DisplayWrite 4 menu.

Issuing DOS Commands with a Floppy-Disk System

Commands like ERASE, RENAME, and COPY are *internal* commands: they are loaded into your computer's memory when you boot your system. You do *not* need to insert your DOS disk to use these commands. When the prompt is displayed, simply type, in the standard DOS format, the command you wish to execute. Note that drive B is still the default drive, so if you don't specify any drive, the commands you issue will be executed on your data files in drive B.

Commands such as FORMAT and DISKCOPY are *external* commands: they are not loaded when you boot your system. Before you can use these commands, you will have to insert your DOS disk in drive A.

When the DOS prompt is displayed, remove your program disk from drive A and insert the DOS disk. Close the drive door. Type the name of the command. For example, to format a blank disk in drive B,

type **a:format b:**

(Since drive B is still the default drive, you need the a: to tell DOS to look for the format program in drive A.)

Then proceed in the usual way. When you are finished issuing external DOS commands, remove the DOS disk from drive A and replace it with your program disk. Then

type **exit** and press ENTER.

You will be returned to the DisplayWrite 4 menu.

15

Changing
the Defaults

*This chapter shows you how to change the DisplayWrite 4
default settings to suit your own needs. It also shows you how to
create several sets of defaults for different types of work and
how to switch from one set of defaults to another.*

Personalizing DisplayWrite 4

You have already seen that DisplayWrite 4 has default settings that govern every detail of the system's operation and of
the printed document. The system was given these defaults
because they are frequently used settings. For example, since
people usually print one copy of a file at a time, 1 is the Print
Document default for Number of Copies; similarly, since
people frequently use single spacing for their writing, single
spacing is the default.

However, the DisplayWrite 4 default settings may not be
suitable for your work. You may customarily need to have
several copies of each file printed and find it time-consuming
to make changes in the Print Document menu each time you

print a file. Or you may generally write double-spaced research papers and not want to change Line Spacing on the Line Spacing/Justification menu for each document. DisplayWrite 4 lets you change the default settings to personalize them for your work.

In the DisplayWrite 4 system, a set of defaults is called a *profile*. With this system, you can create several different profiles in order to have a separate set of defaults for each type of work that you do. For example, suppose you often write business letters, which are single-spaced with a justified right margin and a large top margin to accommodate your company's letterhead; they also require envelopes. However, you also produce research papers, which are double-spaced with a ragged right margin and a small top margin. For these two different outputs, you need two different profiles.

As you may have suspected, there is a default set of defaults. It is contained in the PROFILE.PRF profile. The profile you are using at any time is called the *active* profile. When you load DisplayWrite 4, PROFILE.PRF is the active profile.

Revising the Default Profile

If you generally produce one type of writing, you may need only one profile. Of course, as you work, you can always make changes in individual menus to accommodate occasional variations.

To change the DisplayWrite 4 default profile,

choose Profiles

from the DisplayWrite 4 menu.

You will see the Profiles menu as shown in Figure 15-1.

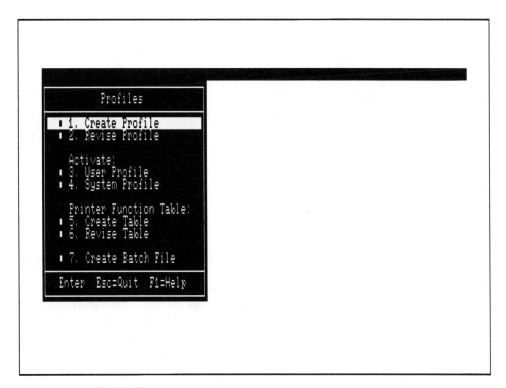

Figure 15-1. The Profiles menu

Choose Revise Profile,

and you will be prompted for a profile name.
    Notice that the name of the default profile, PROFILE.PRF,
is entered for you. Since you want to revise this profile,

    press ENTER.

You will see the Revise Profile menu.

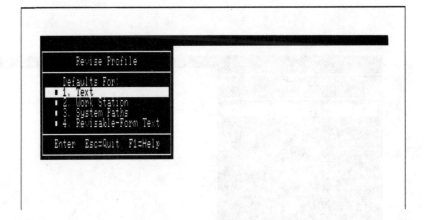

(Later you may want to revise profiles that you have created yourself. Follow the procedure just given, but type in the name of your own profile.) The default settings in the Revise Profile menu are divided into four basic groups: text defaults, work station defaults, system path defaults, and revisable-form text defaults.

Text Defaults

You can change text defaults by choosing from the following menu options:

- Document Format
- Alternate Format
- Edit Defaults
- Math Format
- Paginate

■ Spell

■ Merge Tasks

Work Station Defaults

You can change work station defaults by choosing from the following options:

■ Options for printers

■ Print Document options

■ Keyboard/Mouse options

■ Revise keyboard extensions

■ Display options (lets you select the colors for both Character and APA modes)

■ Unit of measure within menus (lets you specify whether units of measure for page length and width and for line density will be in inches or in centimeters)

System Paths

You can change the default drive and system path for these choices:

■ Keystroke programs

■ Notepad

■ Revisable-form text

■ Temporary merged documents

Providing Additional Support
for Revisable-Form Text

You can change the defaults to provide additional support for revisable-form text, enabling you to:

- Include revisable-form text options in the End/Save menu

- Erase or keep the revisable-form text version of a document after it has been converted to a DisplayWrite 4 document for revision

- Erase the DisplayWrite 4 document after it has been converted to a revisable-form text document

Making the Changes

To actually change the default settings, choose Text, Work Station, System Paths, or Revisable-Form Text from the Revise Profile menu. From there, read through the menus and make the changes that you want. Most of the menus will look familiar to you because they are the same menus you have been using all along. The difference is that the changes you make now will affect all the files you work on in the future, not just the file you are working on at the moment. (Remember, you can always make individual changes to a file at the time you are working on it.)

Some menus deal with aspects of DisplayWrite 4 that you have not yet learned about. These topics will be explained in later chapters, with the exception of two subjects that are introduced later in this chapter: determining the colors used in your display (applicable only to color monitors) and turning wordwrap off.

When you have made all the changes you want,

press ESC

until you return to the End/Save menu.

Choose End and Save

to save your revisions. Then press ESC to return to the DisplayWrite 4 menu. Your revised profile will already be in effect.

Creating a New Profile

Once you have revised the PROFILE.PRF profile to your satisfaction, you may still want to create one or more additional profiles in order to have different sets of defaults for different types of writing.

To create a new profile from scratch,

choose Create Profile

from the Profiles menu. Type in the drive, path, and name you want for your new profile. If you don't specify a file extension, DisplayWrite 4 will append the extension .PRF to your profile name.

Note: If you have created a default directory for your data files, *do not* save your new profile there. Instead, save it in the DW4 directory, where the rest of the program files are. You must be sure to specify exactly where you want your profile to be saved by including a drive and path in addition to the profile name. On a hard-disk system, you specify **C:\dw4\newprof**. On a floppy-disk system, you specify **a:newprof**.

The Create Profile menu will be displayed. Proceed exactly as you did when revising your PROFILE.PRF profile. Go through the menus, entering the new defaults that you want. (Until you change them, the default settings will be the ones in your PROFILE.PRF profile.)

When you have made all the desired changes,

press ESC

until you return to the End/Save menu.

Choose End and Save

to save the new profile. You will be returned to the Profile menu and will see a message telling you that your new profile has been created:

```
> "C:\DW4\NEWPROF.PRF" is created.
```

With a hard-disk system, you can create as many profiles as you want to. With a floppy-disk system, you can create only as many as you have room for.

Your new profile is not yet in effect. To put it into effect, you must *activate* it.

Activating a Profile

The default profile PROFILE.PRF is the active profile until you specify a different one. To activate a different profile, display the Profiles menu and

choose User Profile.

You will be prompted for the profile name. Type it in (don't forget the drive and path) and

press ENTER.

You will see a message telling you that your new profile has been activated:

```
> "C:\DW4\NEWPROF.PRF" is activated.
```

To use the newly activated profile,

press ESC

to return to the DisplayWrite 4 menu.

You may now proceed with DisplayWrite 4 tasks. The defaults determined by your new profile will be in effect. The profile will remain active until you return to the Profiles menu and activate a different profile or until you leave DisplayWrite 4.

If you want your new profile, rather than PROFILE.PRF, to be automatically active, you will have to modify the batch file that loads DisplayWrite 4. This process is explained in Appendix D.

Activating the Original Defaults

The default settings that come with the DisplayWrite 4 program are always available to you no matter how many profiles you create or how many times you revise PROFILE. PRF. These original defaults are called the *system profile.*

To activate the system profile, display the Profiles menu and

choose System Profile.

You will see the message

> "System Profile" is activated.

The original DisplayWrite 4 default settings are now in effect.

Changing the Color Display

If you have a color monitor, you can change the colors of your display with the Display Options choice on the Work Station Defaults menu.

To select the colors of your display,

choose Display Options.

You will see

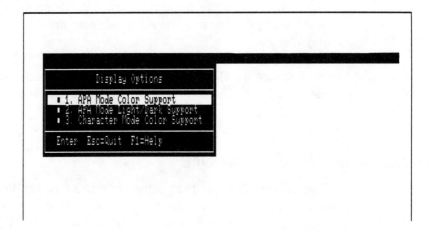

Then, from the Display Options menu, choose the correct display, depending upon whether you are in Character mode or APA mode. If you are using APA mode, you can also choose Light/Dark Support, which lets you specify either light characters on a dark background or the reverse. For now, assume you have chosen Character Mode Color Support. You will see the screen in Figure 15-2.

Notice that you have eight choices identifying the colors used in every aspect of DisplayWrite 4. For each item that you want to change, type two digits: the first digit selects the foreground color and the second digit selects the background color.

For example, the current main color of the Text Task area is black on white; you can see that choice represented on the menu by the two digits 07. To change the color of the display, tab to the item you want and type the two-digit number representing your choice of foreground and background colors for that item. When you are finished changing colors,

Press ENTER.

You will see a display showing you how the new colors will look. If you like what you see and want to make the change,

press ENTER.

If you don't like what you see,

press ESC

and start over.

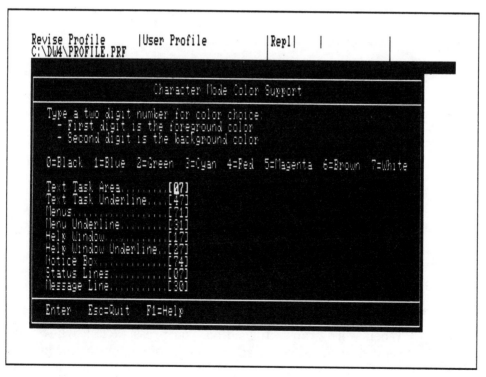

Figure 15-2. Selecting colors

Turning Wordwrap Off

You can change the default settings so that wordwrap is turned off, letting your computer keyboard work more like the keyboard of an ordinary typewriter. When you turn wordwrap off, you must also turn Adjust Line Endings on the Line Spacing/Justification menu off so that your line endings are not adjusted and you can make all line-ending decisions yourself.

When you are typing a file with wordwrap turned off, the system will beep to warn you when you approach the right margin. If you don't end the line, you can type right through the margin.

To change the defaults so that wordwrap is turned off, display the Text Defaults menu and

choose Edit Defaults.

Then set Auto Carrier Return to No. This will turn wordwrap off.

Now, to turn Adjust Line Endings to Off, display the Text Defaults menu and

choose Document Format; then choose Line Spacing/ Jusitification,

and set Adjust Line Endings to No.

Now when you are in the typing area and want to end a line you must press CTRL-ENTER.

Redefining the Carriage Return Key

When wordwrap is turned on, you press ENTER when you want a hard, or required, carriage return. With wordwrap turned off, you still must press ENTER for a hard carriage return, but now you must press CTRL-ENTER for a soft carriage return since the system will no longer do it for you.

DisplayWrite 4 lets you redefine the carriage return (ENTER) key so that, when you turn wordwrap off, you can press ENTER to end a line with a soft carriage return. Then, if you want a required carriage return (for instance, at the end of the paragraph), you will have to press CTRL-ENTER.

Note: Although there is no functional difference between a hard carriage return and a soft carriage return when wordwrap is turned off, if someone later works on the file with wordwrap turned on, there will be the usual difference between the soft carriage return and the hard carriage return.

To redefine your carriage return key so that pressing ENTER inserts a soft Carrier Return code into your text and pressing CTRL-ENTER inserts a Required Carrier Return code, display the Work Station Defaults menu. Then

choose Keyboard/Mouse Options.

You will see

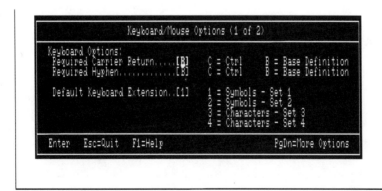

Change the Required Carrier Return choice to Ctrl. You will now have to press CTRL-ENTER when typing in order to insert a required carrier return into your text.

Redefining the HYPHEN Key

When wordwrap is on, you press HYPHEN to insert a hard hyphen only; the system inserts soft (syllable) hyphens for you (if you are hyphenating). With wordwrap turned off, however, you still press HYPHEN for a hard hyphen, but you now must press CTRL-HYPHEN to insert a soft hyphen since the system no longer does this automatically.

You can redefine your HYPHEN key so that, with wordwrap off, pressing HYPHEN puts a soft hyphen into your text. If you want a hard hyphen, you will then have to press CTRL-HYPHEN.

To redefine your HYPHEN key so that pressing HYPHEN produces a soft hyphen and pressing CTRL-HYPHEN produces a hard hyphen, display the Keyboard/Mouse Options menu and change the Required Hyphen choice to Ctrl. You will now have to press CTRL-HYPHEN when you want to insert a hard hyphen into your text.

16

The Spelling Checker

This chapter shows you how to check the spelling of a single word, of all the words on a page, or of your entire file. You will also learn how to create and use special supplements—lists of words that you use frequently but that are not in the DisplayWrite 4 dictionary. And you will find out how to use medical and legal dictionaries.

What a Spelling Checker Can and Cannot Do

All that any spelling checker can do is to compare the words in your file with its own list of correctly spelled words and mark any differences.

No spelling checker can make the kinds of intelligent decisions about spelling—or about grammar, syntax, or usage—that the human mind can. If a word in your file is in the spelling checker's dictionary, the spelling checker considers it *right;* if it isn't, the spelling checker marks it for correction. Thus, a spelling checker would highlight for correction not only a word like "thier", but also a word like "DisplayWrite", since this word is not in the spelling checker's dictionary. On the other hand, the words in the sentence, "I went two the library too meat my sister" would be considered correct because each word *is* in the dictionary.

Making the Checker More Useful— The Supplement

Since it would be annoying to have words like your company's name constantly marked for correction, DisplayWrite 4 lets you create a special supplement in which you place the correct spellings of words that are not in the dictionary. The system then checks the supplement (which can hold up to 4500 characters at any time) along with the dictionary. You can add words to the supplement *temporarily* so that they will not be marked for correction while your current file is being checked, or you can add words to the supplement *permanently* so that they will not be marked for correction while *any* file is being checked.

The U.S. English Dictionary

The dictionary that comes with the DisplayWrite 4 program is the U.S. English dictionary, a list of the correct American spellings of English words. This dictionary is used for spelling checks unless you specify another. Other dictionary programs can be purchased separately.

Two Ways of Checking Spelling

DisplayWrite 4 provides two ways of checking the spelling of a file: with F10 (the Spell key) and from the DisplayWrite 4 menu. With F10 you can quickly check the spelling of a word, a page, or even all the words in a file you are working on. From the DisplayWrite 4 menu, you have different spell options. You can choose either Prompted or Automatic mode, change dictionaries and supplements, check a section of a file, and paginate.

Checking Your Spelling from the DisplayWrite 4 Menu

To check the spelling of a file from the DisplayWrite 4 menu,

choose Spell and select Check Document.

You will see the two-page Check Document menu in Figures 16-1*a* and 16-1*b*. The last file you worked on is entered in as the Document Name. Notice that this menu includes an option that lets you paginate your document while spelling is being checked.

Checking Specified Pages

If you want only a section of your file checked for spelling, fill in the From Page and Through Page choices with the first and last pages you want checked. If you leave these items blank, the entire file will be checked.

Paginating During the Spelling Check

You have the option of paginating your file while spelling is being checked. If you paginate now, you will not have to do it before printing. If you choose to paginate, you can make changes in the pagination defaults on page 2 of this menu.

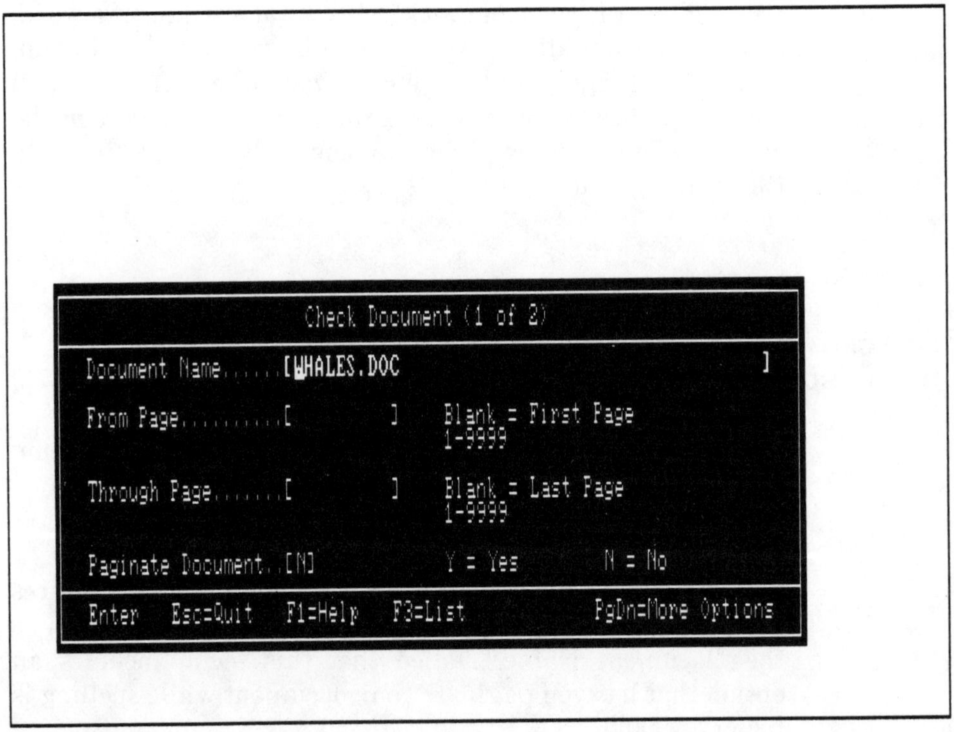

```
                    Check Document (1 of 2)

 Document Name......[WHALES.DOC                                    ]

 From Page.........[         ]    Blank = First Page
                                  1-9999

 Through Page......[         ]    Blank = Last Page
                                  1-9999

 Paginate Document..[N]           Y = Yes         N = No

 Enter   Esc=Quit   F1=Help   F3=List              PgDn=More Options
```

Figure 16-1a. The Check Document menu, page 1

Checking Spelling in Prompted Mode

Prompted mode is the default. In Prompted mode, the system stops each time it comes to a word in your file not found in the dictionary; you then correct the word if necessary.

To begin a prompted spelling check, complete any menu changes; then

press ENTER.

Figure 16-1*b*.   The Check Document menu, page 2

DisplayWrite 4 will stop as soon as it comes to a word not found in the dictionary or supplement. You will see your file on the screen with the word highlighted and the Prompted Spell menu below it (see Figure 16-2).

You have several options:

- Choose List Possible Words if you want the system to prompt you with possible choices. If you want one of the

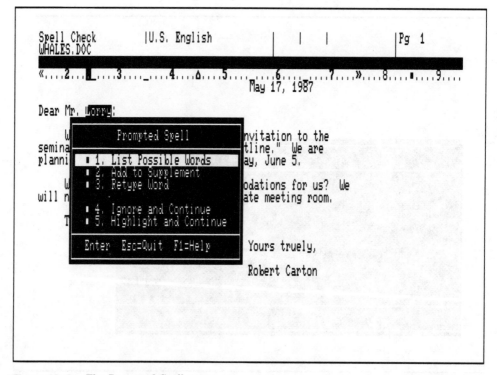

Figure 16-2. The Prompted Spell menu

suggested words, select it and press ENTER. If you don't want any of the suggested words, press ESC and make another prompt line choice.

- Choose Add to Supplement if the word is correctly spelled and you don't want it highlighted again during this session.

- Choose Retype Word if the word needs correction. Type the word correctly and press ENTER. If the retyped word still does not match a word in the dictionary or supplement, you will be prompted to repeat the procedure.

- Choose Ignore and Continue if you want the word accepted for this single occasion only.

- Choose Highlight and Continue if you want to correct the word in the typing area later on.

DisplayWrite 4 will proceed word by word in this manner until all of your file is checked. When checking is complete, you will see

> Spelling check is complete. Words marked: #.

You are returned to the Spell menu.

Note: To cancel the prompted spelling check, press ESC if the system is stopped. Otherwise, press CTRL-BREAK.

Checking Spelling in Automatic Mode

In Automatic mode, the system checks the spelling of your entire file without stopping. Then, when you go to the typing area, every word not found in the dictionary or supplement is highlighted for your correction (see Figure 16-3). If you want an automatic spelling check, choose Automatic in the Check Document menu. Then make any other menu changes you want. To begin the spelling check,

press ENTER.

When the spelling check is complete, you will see

> Spelling check is complete. Words marked: #.

and the Spell menu will be displayed.

Note: To stop an automatic spelling check in progress, press CTRL-BREAK.

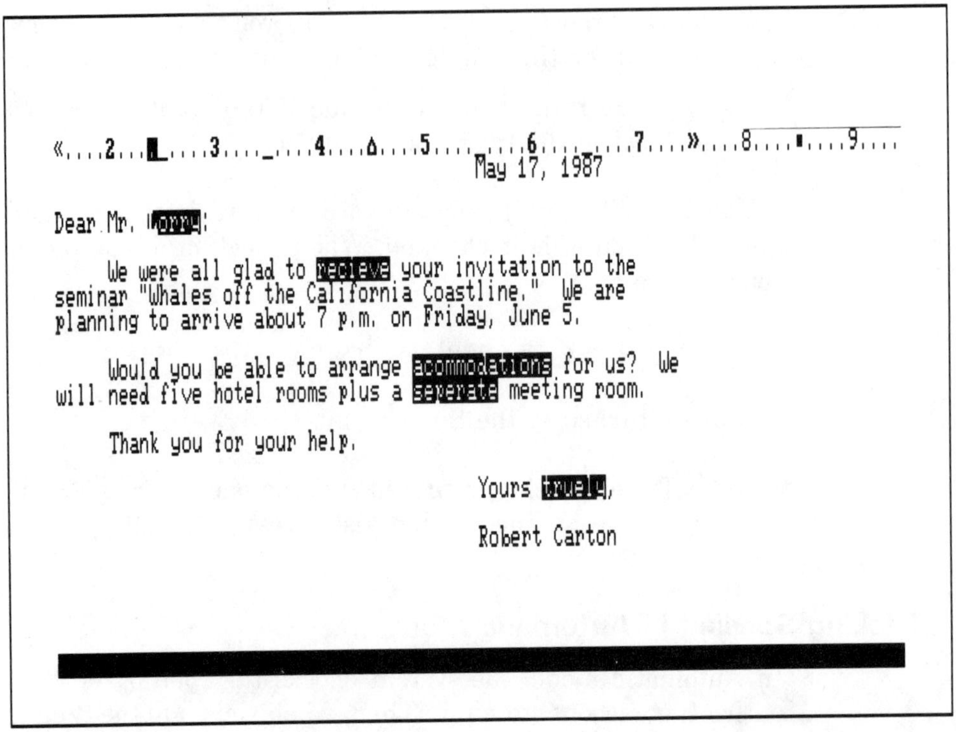

«....2....█....3...._....4....△....5........6........7....»....8....■....9....

                              May 17, 1987

Dear Mr. ▮orry▮:

     We were all glad to ▮recieve▮ your invitation to the
seminar "Whales off the California Coastline." We are
planning to arrive about 7 p.m. on Friday, June 5.

     Would you be able to arrange ▮acommodations▮ for us? We
will need five hotel rooms plus a ▮seperate▮ meeting room.

     Thank you for your help.

                              Yours ▮truely▮,

                              Robert Carton

Figure 16-3.   All words not found in the dictionary or supplement are highlighted

Making Corrections in Automatic Mode

To make corrections, you must select Revise Document from
the DisplayWrite 4 menu and return to the typing area. As
you view your file, you will see highlighted all the words not
found in the dictionary or supplement.

Move the cursor under the first letter of the first highlighted word. To remove the highlighting,

press ESC.

Then retype the word, if desired.

In the screen example, Mr. Lorry's name is highlighted because it is not in the dictionary. However, since it is spelled correctly, you would not need to retype it.

Move the cursor under the next highlighted word and repeat the process, correcting the spelling if necessary. (A quick way to move the cursor to the second highlighted word is to press F6 and choose Find. Then, in response to the Find What? prompt, press F10 and then ENTER. To move to each highlighted word after that one, just press F6 and choose Repeat.)

You can use the Spell Word feature to suggest alternative spellings whenever the cursor is under a highlighted word. Simply press F10 and choose Word to see a list of alternative spellings (see "Checking a Single Word" later in this chapter).

Storing the Supplement on Disk

If you used Prompted mode, you may have added a number of words to the supplement as you proceeded through your file. At this point the words are only in the "memory" supplement; they are not stored on disk. If you commonly use these words in your work, you can store them permanently so they will not be highlighted for correction when you check the spelling of other files in the future.

To save the words in the supplement,

press ESC

to exit the Spell menu. You will see the following screen:

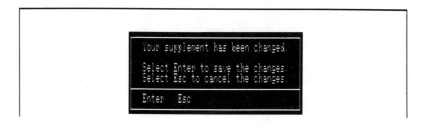

Press ENTER to store the words permanently in the supplement or press ESC to abandon the changes.

Note: If you are using a floppy-disk system, problems can occur easily because DisplayWrite 4 stores the supplement on your data disk in drive B, not on your program disk in drive A. If you use a different data disk, your supplement is not there. To solve this problem, you must change the name of the default supplement dictionary program from USENGL.SUP to A:USENGL.SUP so DisplayWrite 4 will store and look for the program on your program disk. Make this change through the Profiles menu (see Chapter 15).

Excluding Parts of Your File from the Spelling Check

DisplayWrite 4 has a feature that lets you exclude sections of your file from a spelling check. This feature comes in handy if your file contains a large list of people's names or a lengthy quotation in a foreign language.

To eliminate sections of a file from the spelling check, you must be in the typing area of the file you want marked. Move the cursor to the point where you want the spelling check to cease.

Press F8 and choose End.

Then, from the End menu,

choose Spell Check.

An End Spell Check code is inserted into the text.

Next, move the cursor to the place where you want the spelling check to begin again.

Press F8 and choose Begin.

Then, from the Begin menu,

choose Spell Check.

A Begin Spell Check code is inserted into your file. When you check the spelling of the file, the marked section will be skipped.

Checking Spelling from the Typing Area

DisplayWrite 4 lets you quickly check the spelling of a single word, all the words on a page, or an entire file while you are still in the typing area.

Checking a Single Word

To check the spelling of a single word in your file, place the cursor under any letter of the word.

Press F10 (the Spell key) and choose Word

from the Spell menu shown here:

DisplayWrite 4 will look up your word in the U.S. English dictionary and in the supplement. If the word is spelled correctly, you will see

```
> Word spelled correctly.
```

If the word is not spelled correctly, you will see a list of possible substitutions displayed in a window under your word (see Figure 16-4). Choose the appropriate replacement and press ENTER. The incorrectly spelled word will be replaced with your choice. If you don't want to replace the word, press ESC.

If DisplayWrite 4 can't find the word in the dictionary or supplement and there are no reasonable substitutions, you will see

```
> No possible words were found.
```

In this case you will have to look up the spelling in another dictionary.

Checking a Page

To check the spelling of an entire page while you are in the typing area, you must first go to the beginning of the page. To do so,

press CTRL-HOME.

Then

press CTRL-F10 and choose Page.

DisplayWrite 4 looks up every word on your page (but not numbers and graphic symbols) in the dictionary and supplement. When checking is complete, you will see all words not found highlighted and a message telling you how many words are highlighted. The cursor will be positioned under the first letter of the first highlighted word.

Press ESC

to remove the highlighting.
Correct or accept each of the highlighted words, and then
proceed with your file.

Note: The spelling check of a single page is *always* done in

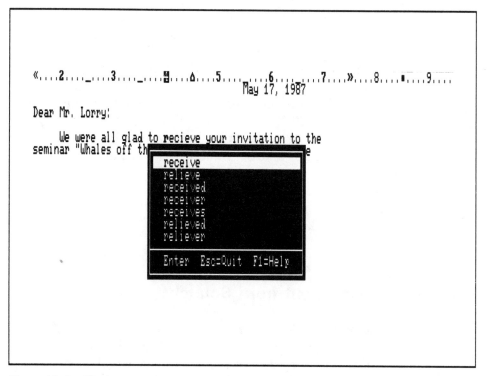

Figure 16-4. The box contains a list of possible substitutes

Automatic mode, even if you have changed the default to Prompted in the Profiles menu (see Chapter 15).

Checking an Entire File from the Typing Area

You can check the spelling of an entire file from anywhere in the typing area. To check the spelling of a file,

press F10 and choose Document.

The spelling checker will pause at the first misspelled word. It will be highlighted, and you will see the Prompted Spell menu. (Spelling will be in Prompted mode unless you have changed the defaults through the Profiles menu.)

If the word is actually correctly spelled, choose Ignore and Continue or, if you want the system to skip over other occurrences of the word, choose Add to Supplement. If the word is incorrectly spelled, choose List Possible Words or Retype Word, depending on whether you need help. You can also choose Highlight and Continue if you want to make the corrections later.

After you have made your choice, the system will pause at the next misspelled word and repeat the process until the spelling check is complete.

Creating a Supplement from Scratch

So far you have learned how to add words to the supplement during prompted spelling checks and then how to save them to disk. You can also create additional supplements from scratch, composed of nondictionary words that occur in your writing. You can save these words in the default supplement dictionary program USENGL.SUP, or you can save them under another name. You may want to have several supplements—one for each type of writing that you do.

Listing the Words

To create a supplement from scratch, you begin by creating an ordinary file into which you enter the words that you want in your supplement. Note the following:

- You can put each word on a separate line or put several words on a line with a space between words.

- Type both uppercase and lowercase versions of the word if you want both to be considered correct. Some words may need to be typed twice—once all in lowercase and once with an initial capital letter (in case the word occurs at the beginning of a sentence).

- If you plan to hyphenate, indicate hyphenation points by pressing CTRL-HYPHEN between syllables. You will not see the hyphens when the word is completely typed. *Do not simply type an ordinary hyphen between the syllables.*

```
«....2..▮._....3....._....4....Δ...5....._....6....._....7...»....8....▪..
Susan
Robert
Amy
Jonathan▲
```

When you have typed all the words that you want included in your supplement,

press F2

to save the file and

choose Spell

from the DisplayWrite 4 menu.

Saving Your New Supplement on Disk

If you want to add the words to the default supplement, just choose Add Words to Supplement from the Spell menu and enter the name of the file in which you listed the words. Then

press ESC

to exit the Spell menu and

ENTER

to save the newly added words on your disk.
If you want to create an entirely different supplement,

select Dictionary Change

from the Spell menu. Then, in the Dictionary Change menu, tab to Supplement Name and type in the name you want for the new supplement (remember that the supplement will be stored on the default drive and in the default directory unless you specify otherwise).

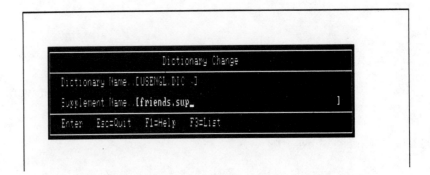

Press ENTER.

Now, from the Spell menu, choose Remove All Words from Supplement. (This erases any words currently in the memory supplement.) Then choose Add Words to Supplement and enter the name of the file containing the list of words. (It probably is entered already for you.)

friends.doc

Any word in the file that is not in the dictionary is added to the new supplement in memory. A message at the bottom of the screen lets you know how many words have been added.

The next step is to save the supplement permanently on disk.

Press ESC

to exit the Spell menu. Then

press ENTER

to save the new supplement to disk.

Your new supplement will be stored under the name you selected in the Dictionary Change menu. Now, when you check the spelling of a file, the list of words you just entered will not be highlighted for correction.

In the future, when you want to use the new supplement to check the spelling of a file, you need only go to the Dictionary Change menu and change the Supplement Name from USENGL.SUP to the supplement you created. If you saved the words in the USENGL.SUP, they are automatically available when you do a spelling check.

Revising a Supplement

You may want to revise a supplement from time to time in order to add or delete words. To make a revision, you must reconvert the supplement into an ordinary text file. The process is essentially the reverse of the process you went through to create the supplement.

Making the Revisions

If the supplement you want to revise is *not* the default USENGL.SUP, first

choose Dictionary Change

from the Spell menu. You will see the Dictionary Change menu.

Choose Supplement Name.

In response to the prompt, type the name of the supplement you want to revise:

friends.sup

Press ENTER.

You are returned to the Spell menu. The words from the supplement you just named are loaded into memory.
To proceed,

choose Store Supplement to Document.

In response to the prompt, type in the name of the text file you want to use to revise your list:

friends1.doc

Press ENTER.

You will see the message

```
> Supplement words are stored in "FRIENDS1.DOC".
```

Return to the DisplayWrite menu and then revise the text file by the usual method.

Note: You can retain the name of the original text file if you want to (FRIENDS.DOC, in this case).

Saving the Revised Supplement

After you revise the text file containing the words in the supplement, save the file with F2, and then return to the Spell menu. Now use the process described in "Saving Your New Supplement on Disk" to replace the old supplement with the revised one. *Make sure to include the step in which you choose "Remove All Words from Supplement," or you will just be saving the old supplement over again.*

Using Specialized Dictionaries

The U.S. English dictionary comes with the DisplayWrite 4 program, but IBM DisplayWrite Medical and IBM Display-Write Legal dictionaries are also available on disk for those who do specialized work. These programs must be purchased separately.

Checking a File with a Specialized Dictionary

Before you can use your specialized dictionary, you will need to know its exact file name. From DOS you can use the DIR command, and from DisplayWrite 4 the F3 key, to view the directory of the disk containing the specialized dictionary. The file will have the extension .DIC.

Choose Spell from the DisplayWrite 4 menu and then select Dictionary Change. In the Dictionary Change menu, type the file name of the dictionary you want to use.

If you want to save supplement words in a specialized supplement, or if you have already created a specialized supplement to go with your specialized dictionary, tab to Sup-

Key	Function
F6	Initiates the Find function. When you choose Find, and insert F10 as the Find string, the cursor will jump to each word highlighted for correction
F8	The End choice followed by Spell Check indicates the start of a text block that will *not* be checked for spelling
	The Begin choice followed by Spell Check indicates the end of a text block that will *not* be checked for spelling
F10	Lets you check the spelling of a single word, a page, or of your entire file while you are in the typing area
CTRL-HYPHEN	Lets you indicate hyphenation points when you are creating a supplement dictionary program

Table 16-1. Keys Used in Spelling Checks

plement Name and type the name of the specialized supplement.
When you are finished making menu changes, press ENTER to return to the Spell menu. You may now use the specialized dictionary to check your file.

Note: If you check your file from the typing area, with F10, the system will *not* use the specialized dictionary; it will use the default U.S. English dictionary.

If you are consistently using the specialized dictionary instead of the U.S. English dictionary, go to the Profiles menu and make the specialized dictionary the default. That way you will not have to enter the name of your specialized dictionary each time you do a spelling check on a file.
Table 16-1 lists the keys used for spelling checks.

ADVANCED
WORD-PROCESSING
FEATURES

17

Creating Footnotes

This chapter shows you how to use DisplayWrite 4 to create and revise footnotes for your text files. It also teaches you how to store frequently used footnotes in a footnote "library."

The DisplayWrite 4 Footnote Feature

If you have ever used a typewriter to type a manuscript with footnotes, you know how difficult it is to calculate the space required at the bottom of each page. The same problem occurs with many word-processing programs. An even more annoying situation arises if you try to add a footnote to or delete one from a completed manuscript, since you then must renumber by hand each footnote that follows the change. And if you don't have room on a page to add a footnote, you may also have considerable retyping to do.

DisplayWrite 4 eliminates all these problems. The system *automatically* calculates the space your footnotes need and inserts each one, under a separator line, on the correct page.

Best of all, it numbers them all, and it will renumber and reposition them for you if you add or delete a footnote later on.

The footnotes are formatted, numbered, and positioned during the DisplayWrite 4 pagination process, so you must always paginate if you create footnotes, even if your file is very short. When you paginate, Adjust Page Endings and Adjust Line Endings must not be changed from Yes, the default setting. If you make any changes to footnoted text or to the footnotes (adding, deleting, or revising), you must go through the pagination process again to incorporate your changes.

Creating a Footnote

Figure 17-1 shows you how your footnoted text will look if you use the footnote defaults. Notice the *footnote reference number* in the body text that signals a footnote. The same reference number appears below the separator line, in front of the footnote itself. Footnotes are single-spaced even if your body text is double-spaced.

To create a footnote, type your file in the usual way until you get to the spot where you want a footnote reference, as in the following example. *Do not type any reference number or symbol.*

```
«....2...._...3...._.█.4....Δ....5...._...6...........7....»....8.....■....9....
article "No Clock in the Forest" that the name de Boys was
from the French de Bois, meaning woods, and that Roland de
Bois personified some of the qualities of nature in his
honest, direct person.▲
```

Press F8 and choose Footnote.

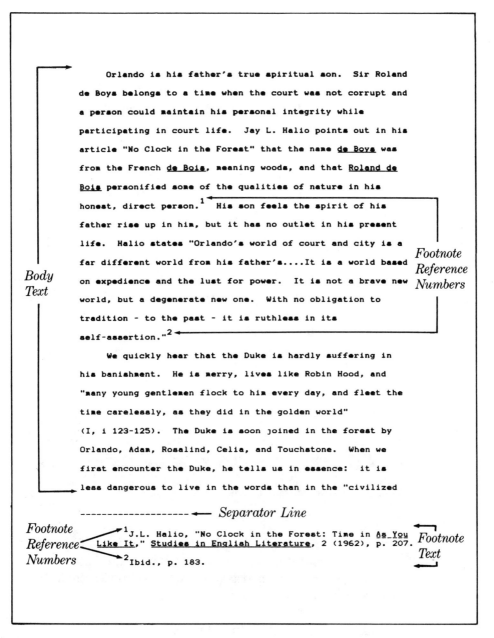

Body Text

Orlando is his father's true spiritual son. Sir Roland de Boys belongs to a time when the court was not corrupt and a person could maintain his personal integrity while participating in court life. Jay L. Halio points out in his article "No Clock in the Forest" that the name de Boys was from the French de Bois, meaning woods, and that Roland de Bois personified some of the qualities of nature in his honest, direct person.¹ His son feels the spirit of his father rise up in him, but it has no outlet in his present life. Halio states "Orlando's world of court and city is a far different world from his father's....It is a world based on expedience and the lust for power. It is not a brave new world, but a degenerate new one. With no obligation to tradition - to the past - it is ruthless in its self-assertion."²

Footnote Reference Numbers

We quickly hear that the Duke is hardly suffering in his banishment. He is merry, lives like Robin Hood, and "many young gentlemen flock to him every day, and fleet the time carelessly, as they did in the golden world" (I, i 123-125). The Duke is soon joined in the forest by Orlando, Adam, Rosalind, Celia, and Touchstone. When we first encounter the Duke, he tells us in essence: it is less dangerous to live in the woods than in the "civilized

Separator Line

Footnote Reference Numbers

¹J.L. Halio, "No Clock in the Forest: Time in As You Like It," Studies in English Literature, 2 (1962), p. 207.
²Ibid., p. 183.

Footnote Text

Figure 17-1. DisplayWrite 4 can footnote your text

You will see the two-page Footnote menu shown in Figures 17-2*a* and 17-2*b*.

If, instead of using numbers for your footnotes, you would like another reference character (for example, an asterisk),

tab to Reset Footnote Number or Character.

Then type the character you want. This step will change the footnote reference character *for that footnote only*, so you must make the change for each footnote.

Don't make any other menu changes at this time. To go to the footnote typing area,

press ENTER.

Then type your footnote. (You can use underlining or boldface if you desire.) Do not type in the footnote number or footnote symbol, because the system will supply it for you. Do not press ENTER for a carriage return.

Notice that the top status line shows that you are on a page numbered 9000 or higher:

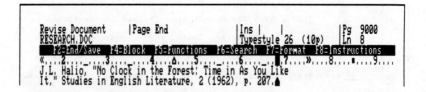

This is not an error; DisplayWrite 4 stores each of your footnotes on a separate page beginning with page 9000.

When you are finished typing your footnote, return to the regular typing area:

press F2 and select Return and Save.

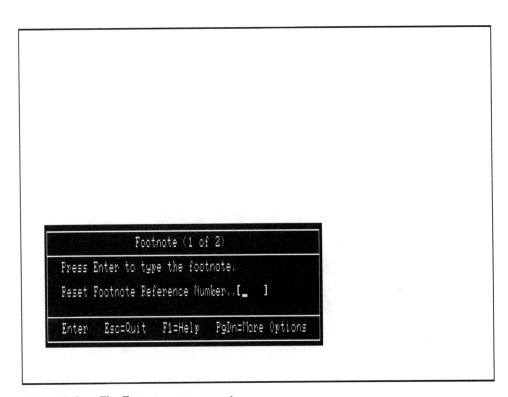

Figure 7-2a. The Footnote menu, page 1

You will see the appropriate reference number or symbol inserted into your body text. When you print your file, the number or symbol will print as a superscript. At this point you will not see any footnote text at the bottom of the page.

If you set Display All Codes to Yes in the Edit Options menu, you will see a jumble of codes and symbols at the footnote reference point. They tell the system to begin the footnote in the correct format, to insert the number or symbol as

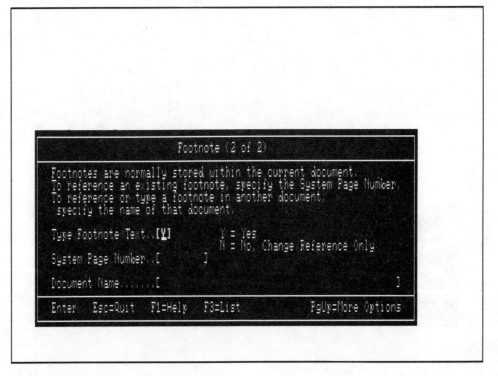

Figure 17-2*b*.   The Footnote menu, page 2

a superscript, and to return to ordinary text (see Figure 17-3).

Type your text until you get to the next place you want a footnote, and repeat the entire process. When you are finished with your file,

press F2 and choose Paginate, End, and Save.

Then print your file. You will see each footnote correctly numbered and positioned at the bottom of the appropriate page.

Note: After pagination, your footnotes will appear on the screen display at the bottom of each page.

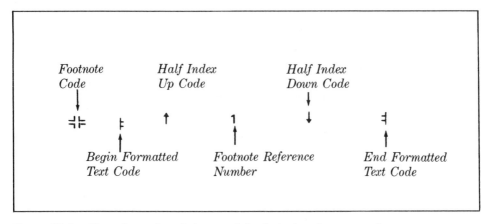

Figure 17-3. The codes and symbols around the footnote reference number

Revising a Footnote

You can revise a footnote even after paginating and printing your file. To revise a footnote, return to the typing area and move your cursor under its Footnote code in the body text. The top status line will read "Footnote" when you are under the correct code:

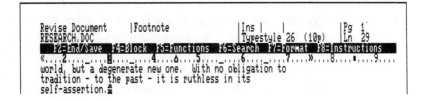

Press CTRL-F8 (the View/Revise key).

When the Footnote menu is displayed,

press ENTER

to go to the footnote typing area. Revise the footnote as desired. To return to the regular typing area,

press F2.

Be sure to paginate to incorporate your revisions.

Note: If you simply revise the footnote as it appears on the bottom of the page after pagination, your revision will be deleted when you paginate again.

Adding a Footnote to a Footnoted File

If you decide to add another footnote after you have completed your file, you can do so easily. Return to the typing area and position the cursor in the body text where you want the new footnote reference. Then follow the same steps you used to create the original footnotes.

After the file is repaginated and reprinted, you will see the new footnote included and the following footnotes renumbered.

Adding Body Text to a Footnoted File

You can also add body text to a footnoted file even if you have already paginated and printed it. Return to the typing area and, if the text falls in the middle of the page, just type it in. If the text comes directly after a footnote reference, make sure the cursor is past all the footnoting codes before you start typing. (Codes will be displayed above the cursor when you are under them.)

If you are adding text at the end of a footnoted page (but before the separator line), you must position your cursor *directly under* the Begin Formatted Text code at the end of the body text. (Set Display All Codes to Yes and look up at the status line to ensure that you are under the right code.) Then type the new text. If you position the cursor *after* the Begin Formatted Text code instead of *under* it, your additions will disappear when you paginate.

To move body text with footnote references, move the text with a block move in the usual way. Do not try to move any actual footnotes. They will be correctly repositioned during pagination.

Deleting a Footnote from a Footnoted File

To delete a footnote, go to the typing area and place the cursor under the Footnote code in the body text of the footnote you want removed. You will see the footnote symbol above the cursor and the word "Footnote" on the top status line. To delete the code,

press DEL and then press ENTER.

Do not delete or change any other codes.

When you are finished deleting footnotes, save your file. The footnotes will be deleted and the remaining footnotes repositioned and renumbered during pagination.

Checking the Spelling of Footnoted Text

If you paginate the file during a spelling check, the system *will not* check the spelling of your footnotes. Therefore, if you want the system to check spelling in your footnotes, you must paginate either through CTRL-F7 (the Document Options key) or by choosing Paginate, End, and Save when you press F2 to save a file. Then choose Spell from the DisplayWrite 4 menu.

Creating a Footnote Library

If you use some of your footnotes repeatedly, you can store them in a footnote "library"—a file made up exclusively of footnotes, each on a separate page. When you want to use a footnote from the library, you can simply call it into the file you are working on without having to retype and reedit it.

Storing a Footnote in the Library

The following process both creates a footnote for the text you are working on and stores the footnote in the footnote library for future use.

Type the text of your file in the usual way. When you come to the place where you want a footnote reference,

press F8 and choose Footnote.

When you see the Footnote menu,

press PGDN

to go to page 2 and

tab to Document Name.

Type the file name you want for your footnote library (this should not be the same as the name of the file you are working on):

footnote.lib

DisplayWrite 4 will store your footnote on the next available page in the footnote library. To go to the footnote typing area,

press ENTER.

Type the footnote in the usual way. When you are finished, to return to the regular typing area,

press F2 and choose Return and Save.

After pagination, your footnote will appear at the bottom of the page. However, the footnote is *not* stored on page 9000 of your file. It is stored in the file you named in the Footnote menu. This file is your footnote library.

The next time you press F8 and choose Footnote, the name of the footnote library file is already entered for you next to Document Name. If you don't want to store this footnote in the footnote library, tab to Document Name and press ALT-8 to erase the name.

Printing a Reference Copy of the Library

Whenever you add footnotes to your footnote library, print a copy of the footnote library file for your own reference. You can then look at the reference copy to know which footnote you want to call into your current file. In order to use each footnote, you will need to know the number of the system page that it is stored on. Since system page numbers aren't printed, write the page number of each footnote by hand, as shown in Figure 17-4.

When printing a reference copy of your footnote library, remember that each footnote must remain on a *separate page.* If you use pagination before printing your reference copy, your footnotes will no longer be stored one to a page; you then will no longer be able to call in a particular footnote from the library. Therefore, use one of the following two methods when printing your reference copy:

- Print the footnote library file *without using pagination.* Each footnote will be printed on a separate page. Write the system page number of each footnote by hand.

---

① All visitors must obtain a pass from security before coming
   to your office.

② The fourth-floor cafeteria is reserved for employees.

③ See Joe if you have any questions about vacation or
   sick-leave policies. Requests for vacation time must be
   submitted two months prior to the time of the desired
   vacation.

④ See Anne if you have any questions about deductions on your
   check.

Figure 17-4. A copy of the footnote library with system page numbers handwritten in

- Make a copy of the footnote library file (using the DOS
  or DisplayWrite 4 Copy utility). Next, using the copy (not
  the original), go to the typing area and press ENTER a
  few times after each footnote to create blank lines (for
  increased readability). Then paginate the copy. This will
  group several footnotes per page, giving you a more con-
  cise reference copy. Write the system page numbers by
  hand. Make sure you use the *original file* when you want
  to call a footnote from the library into your current file.

Note: If you have a floppy-disk system, the footnote library
is stored on your data disk in drive B, not on your program
disk. You can't store it on your program disk very easily
because there isn't much room. When you call a footnote
from the footnote library into another file, make sure both
files are on your data disk during the pagination process.

Using a Footnote from the Footnote Library

In the typing area, type your text until you get to the place where you want the footnote reference.

Press F8 and choose Footnote.

When the Footnote menu appears, make the following changes:

- Set Type Footnote Text to No.
- For Document Name, type in the name of the footnote library.
- For System Page Number, type in the system page number of the desired footnote. (Use your printed reference copy to determine the correct system page number.)

Your completed menu might look like Figure 17-5.
When you are finished making menu changes,

press ENTER.

You will be returned to the regular typing area. A footnote reference number appears in your text.
Repeat this process for each footnote you want called in from the footnote library. If some of your footnotes are being written to page 9000 of your file and some are being called in from a footnote library, the footnote reference numbers in your file will not be sequential, but they will be renumbered during pagination.

Revising a Footnote in the Library

You revise a footnote in the footnote library the same way you would revise any text file. Just make sure that you do not change the system page numbers during revision.

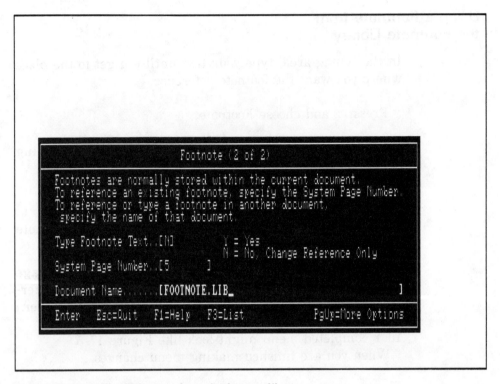

Figure 17-5. Calling a footnote from the footnote library

To find a particular footnote quickly, enter the typing area of the footnote library file.

Press F6 and choose Go to Page.

Then type the number of the page (obtained from your reference copy) that contains the footnote you want to revise, and

press ENTER.

Revise the footnote as you would revise ordinary text. When you are finished revising all footnotes,

press F2 and choose End and Save.

Resetting the Footnote Number

You may want to create several small files that you plan to print to look like one large document. When the final document is printed, you will want all your footnotes numbered sequentially, not file-by-file. To accomplish this, you must reset the footnote reference number, since the system automatically starts each file with footnote number 1.

To reset the footnote number, type your file until you come to the footnote reference you want to reset. Then, if you are revising an existing footnote, position your cursor under the Footnote code and

press CTRL-F8.

If the footnote has not been created yet,

press F8 and choose Footnote.

You will see the Footnote menu.

For Reset Footnote Reference Number, type in the reference number you want that footnote to have. All footnotes that follow that footnote will be numbered sequentially from its number.

Press ENTER.

You will be in the footnote typing area. Type the footnote in the usual way, or make any necessary revisions if the footnote already exists. Then, to return to the regular typing area,

press F2.

Paginate to number your footnotes correctly.

> *Note:* Your footnote will always have the number you reset it to, even if earlier footnotes are added or deleted. Therefore, if you revise footnotes in the early part of your document, you may have to reset the number again.

Designing a Footnote Format

You can change the appearance of your footnotes by designing your own footnote format instead of using the default settings.

Among the options you can change are the typestyle of the footnote, the appearance of the line that separates the footnotes from the text, and the amount of footnote text on a page.

Before and after each footnote reference number in both the body text and the footnote are *leading and trailing characters*. The default leading character is a Half Index Up code and the default trailing character is a Half Index Down code. These two codes cause the footnote reference number to be printed as a superscript. (The footnote reference number in the footnote text also has a Tab code as a leading character.)

You can, however, select other characters or codes for leading or trailing characters (up to eight leading and eight trailing characters). For example, you might want your footnote reference in the body text to look like this:

footnote reference (1)

Changes like these are made through the Footnote Format menu.

Changing the Footnote Format

To design your own footnote format for a file, go to the typing area. Then

press CTRL-F7 and choose Document Format.

(If you are also using an alternate format that contains footnotes, you will have to change the settings in the alternate format as well.) From the Change Document Format menu,

choose Footnote.

You will see the two-page Footnote Format menu shown in Figures 17-6*a* and 17-6*b*.
The menu selections offer these formatting choices:

- *Typestyle*. Lets you select a typestyle for your footnotes that is different from the typestyle used in the rest of your text.

- *Separator Line Character*. Lets you select the character used in the line that separates the body text from the footnotes.

- *Separator Line Length*. Lets you select the number of characters in the separator line. (The default setting is 20.)

- *Maximum Number of Footnote Lines per Page*. Lets you select how many footnote text lines can appear on a page. (The default setting is 48.)

- *Maximum Number of Lines Between Footnotes*. Lets you select how many blank lines are placed between footnotes. (The default setting is 1.)

- *Reference Number in Text: Leading Characters and Trailing Characters*. These two items let you select leading and trailing characters for footnote reference numbers in the body text.

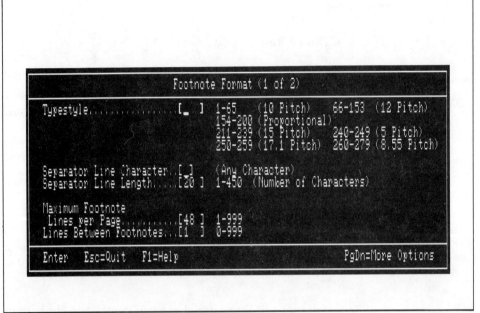

Figure 17-6a. The Footnote Format menu, page 1

- *Footnote Number: Leading Characters and Trailing Characters.* These two items let you select leading and trailing characters for footnote reference numbers in the footnote text.

- *Continuation Text for Footnote.* Lets you choose the message that tells readers that a footnote is continued on a subsequent page. (The default message is "(Footnote Continued).")

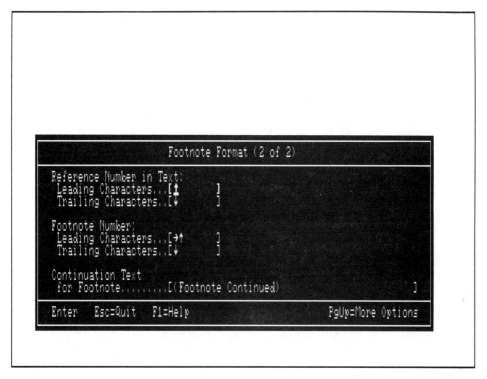

Figure 17-6*b*.   The Footnote Format menu, page 2

When you have completed all your menu changes,

press ENTER

to return to the Change Document Format menu.
Table 17-1 shows the keys used in footnoting.

Key	Function
F2	Returns you to the regular typing area from the foot-note typing area
F8	The Footnote choice takes you to the Footnote menu so you can create footnotes
CTRL-F8	When you are revising footnotes, takes you to the foot-note typing area

Table 17-1. Keys Used When Creating Footnotes

18

Creating Outlines

This chapter teaches you how to create and revise outlines with DisplayWrite 4.

When you write a sizeable file, such as a report or presentation, you probably first make an outline to guide you. You may want to include the outline as part of your file (perhaps as a table of contents) or you may want to discard it when you are finished typing in the file.

The DisplayWrite 4 Outline feature helps you create outlines like the one shown in Figure 18-1 by inserting the *outline character* (either a letter or a number) for each outline entry and by indenting the entry the specified amount. If you later add or delete entries, DisplayWrite 4 will renumber or reletter the remaining entries for you.

DisplayWrite 4 lets you create outlines with up to eight levels. You will find this more than sufficient since very few outlines are more than four levels deep. A default outline character is assigned to each outline level except level eight; level one uses uppercase Roman numerals, level two uses capital letters, and so on. Before and after each outline char-

```
        I.    Getting started with the product

              A.    Installation

                    1.    Unpacking

                    2.    Checking the wiring

                    3.    Providing a stable surface

       II.    Features of the product

              A.    Durability

              B.    Ease of use

      III.    Maintaining the product

              A.    Cleaning

                    1.    Cleaning products to use

                    2.    Cleaning products to avoid

                    3.    Frequency

              B.    Monthly checkout

       IV.    Repair and service

              A.    What to do before you call

              B.    The "troubleshooting" phone number
```

Figure 18-1. An outline produced by DisplayWrite 4

acter, except in level eight, are leading characters and trailing characters. These are the codes and characters that determine the indentation and punctuation of the outline character. You will learn how to select your own characters for level eight later in this chapter, when you are shown how to change the outline defaults. Figure 18-2 shows you the default outline and leading and trailing characters for the first seven levels.

Outlines are formatted and numbered during pagination, so you must always paginate your file after you create an outline. During pagination, Adjust Page Endings and Adjust Line Endings must be left at the default, Yes. (Use a Required Page End code if you want a page to end at a particular place.) If you make any changes to your outline (adding or deleting items), you must paginate again to incorporate your changes.

Making the Outline

To make an outline, choose Create Document from the DisplayWrite 4 menu, and go to the typing area. If you want

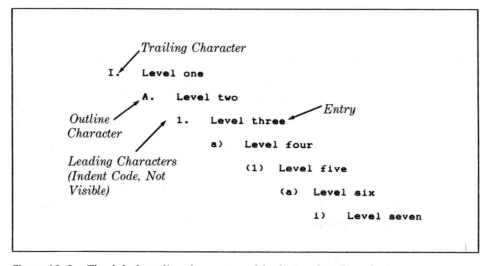

Figure 18-2.   The default outline characters and leading and trailing characters

your outline double- or triple-spaced, make the change with CTRL-F7. Do not type any text yet.

Press CTRL-O (the Outline key).

Look on the left of the top status line. It will tell you that you are at outline level one. Notice that the default outline character and the End Formatted Text code are visible on the screen (see Figure 18-3). At the bottom of the screen is a long prompt line. You are concerned only with the part that says

```
> Press Outline (Ctrl+O) to increment level...
```

If you want to begin your outline at level one, simply begin typing the entry; or you can press CTRL-O again to get to the next level.

Note: If your entry is more than one line long, your text will wrap at the temporary left margin created by the Outline feature.

Assuming you want to begin your outline at level one, type the first entry for your outline, like this one:

```
«....2...._....3...._....4....Δ....5...._▌..6...._...._...7....»....8....▪..
      I.   Getting started with the product▲
```

Do *not* type the actual outline character since this is already typed in for you. You can underline or boldface your text. When you are finished typing your entry,

press ENTER.

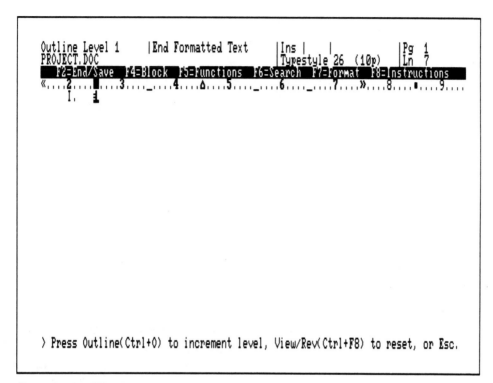

Figure 18-3. What you see when you press CTRL-O

(You can press ENTER a second time to add a blank line between entries.) The cursor will jump down a line to the left margin. To type the second entry,

press CTRL-O.

You will be at outline level one again, with an uppercase Roman numeral two on the screen. Suppose, however, you want to make a level two outline entry at this point. In this case, press CTRL-O again.

The II disappears and instead you will see a capital A, the first level two outline character. Notice that it is correctly indented for your level two entry.

Type the entry:

```
«....2.........3.........4.. △...5......6......7....».....8.... ■..
      I.  Getting started with the product
      A.  Installation▲
```

Press ENTER.

Repeat this process for each entry you want to make. (If you press CTRL-O too many times and go past the level you want, you can keep pressing CTRL-O until the system eventually returns to your level, or you can press ESC and start over.)

When you have completed your outline, paginate and save your file.

Revising the Outline

You can revise an outline to change outline text or to add, delete, copy, and move entries. After revision, DisplayWrite 4 will renumber and reletter your outline during pagination.

Changing Outline Text

Before you revise the text of an entry, set Display All Codes to Yes. You will see a mass of codes and symbols before each text entry. As you move your cursor under the codes, you will see them identified on the top status line. The second code on each typing line is the Begin Formatted Text code; the last code before text begins is the End Formatted Text code. *Do not position the cursor between these two codes when you revise text.* If you do, when you start revising, you will see the message

```
> These text changes will be removed by Pagination or Merge.
```

and all your changes will be temporary. Instead, position the cursor in the body of the text and use the usual techniques to retype your entry.

Deleting, Moving, and Copying Entries

You can use the F4 Block functions to delete, move, and copy entries. Just make sure that you have highlighted *all* codes connected with each entry, as shown in Figure 18-4.

Adding an Entry

There are several methods of adding an entry. The method described here is the simplest. To add an outline entry, move the cursor to the line *above* where you want to add an entry and position the cursor at the right end of the line. The cursor should be under the Required Carrier Return code.

Press ENTER.

This step creates a blank line for the new entry and positions the cursor at the left margin.

Press CTRL-O

until you get to the desired outline level.

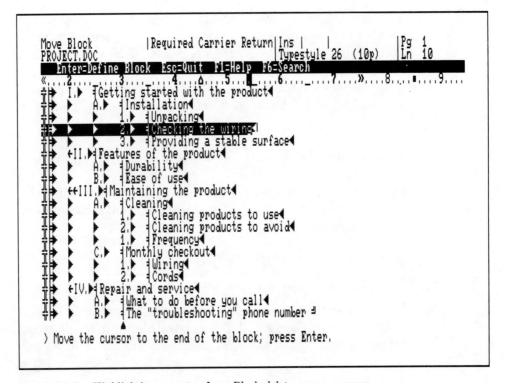

Figure 18-4. Highlighting an entry for a Block delete, move, or copy

Type in the entry. Do *not* press ENTER after typing the entry. Paginate and save the file to renumber or reletter the entries.

Changing an Outline Level

To change the level of an existing entry (for example, to make a level two entry into a level three entry), position the cursor under the Outline Level code for the entry you want to change.

Press CTRL-F8. Then press CTRL-O

until you are at the desired level. If desired, revise the entry. Paginate to reorder the remaining entries.

Resetting the Outline Character

You may not always want your outlines numbered or lettered sequentially from beginning to end. For instance, an outline may consist of several parts and you may want the level one headings in each part to begin with an uppercase Roman numeral one. Conversely, if you plan to combine several small outline files into one large printed document, you may *not* want the first level one character in each file to be Roman numeral one. Instead, you probably want the outline characters in the final document to be in sequence from beginning to end.

To reset the outline character if you have not yet typed the entry,

press CTRL-O

until you reach the outline level you want. If the entry already exists, move the cursor under the Outline Level code for that entry and

press CTRL-F8.

(Refer to the top status line to make sure you are under the right code.)

Then, in response to the prompt,

press CTRL-F8.

You will see the Reset Outline Level menu:

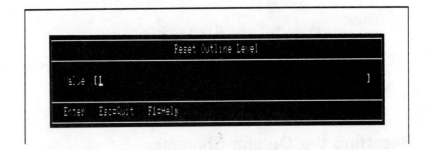

If the default character in the menu is not what you want, type in the desired character. Do *not* type any leading or trailing characters, because the system will supply them. Your replacement character must be the same kind as the one you are replacing—for example, a level one uppercase Roman numeral must be replaced with another uppercase Roman numeral.

Press ENTER.

You will see that the new character you chose has replaced the original in your outline. Paginate to relabel the remaining entries in sequence.

Note: If you later add or delete entries before your selected character, your new character may no longer be correct. However, pagination will *not* resequence a character that you have reset. You will have to return to the typing area and reset the character again. If you want to undo the reset process totally, return to the Reset Outline Level menu and, for Value, press ALT-F8. Then press ENTER.

Combining Outline Levels

You can combine outline level identifiers so that the outline character from the previous level or levels is displayed along with the character for the current level. Outlines used in scientific writing frequently use combined outline characters. Figure 18-5 shows you the outline in Figure 18-1 with outline level characters combined.

You can combine outline characters for an outline you are about to create or for one already created. In the typing area,

press CTRL-F7 and choose Document Format. Then select Outline.

You will see the Outline Format menu, which lists all the outline levels.

Select the first level that you want to combine with a previous level, and

press ENTER.

For example, if you choose level two, you will be able to display both outline level one and level two characters at outline level two. You can choose more than one level, but you have to proceed one level at a time. (Do not choose level one since there is no previous level to combine it with.) You will see the Outline Level Format menu, as shown in Figure 18-6. In the menu,

set Combine with Previous Levels to Yes and press ENTER.

You will be returned to the Outline Format menu to select

```
        I.      Getting started with the product

                I.A.    Installation

                        I.A.1.      Unpacking

                        I.A.2.      Checking the wiring

                        I.A.3.      Providing a stable surface

       II.      Features of the product

                II.A.   Durability

                II.B.   Ease of use

      III.      Maintaining the product

                III.A.  Cleaning

                        III.A.1.    Cleaning products to use

                        III.A.2.    Cleaning products to avoid

                        III.A.3.    Frequency

                III.B.  Monthly checkout

                        III.B.1.    Wiring

                        III.B.2.    Cords

       IV.      Repair and service

                IV.A.   What to do before you call

                IV.B.   The "troubleshooting" phone number
```

Figure 18-5. Combining outline levels

another level for combining. When you are finished combining levels,

press ESC

until you return to the typing area.

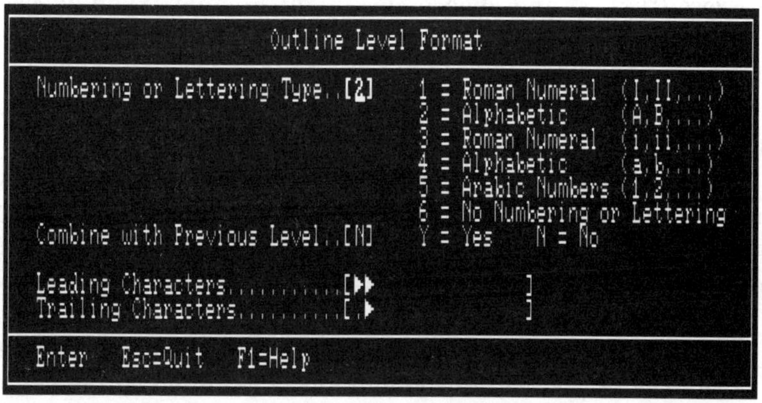

```
                    Outline Level Format

Numbering or Lettering Type..[2]    1 = Roman Numeral   (I,II,...)
                                    2 = Alphabetic      (A,B,...)
                                    3 = Roman Numeral   (i,ii,...)
                                    4 = Alphabetic      (a,b,...)
                                    5 = Arabic Numbers  (1,2,...)
                                    6 = No Numbering or Lettering
Combine with Previous Level..[N]    Y = Yes    N = No

Leading Characters...........[▶▶                   ]
Trailing Characters..........[.▶                   ]

 Enter   Esc=Quit   F1=Help
```

Figure 18-6. The Outline Level Format menu

Note: The number of characters in the combined outline levels may be so great that your tab settings are not sufficiently far apart to accommodate them all. To solve this problem, set your tabs farther apart.

Designing an Outline Format

Until now you have been using the default outline characters and leading and trailing characters. However, you can select different characters if you wish. You can also choose an outline character and leading and trailing characters for level eight, which has no default settings. It is possible to have up to 16 leading characters and 16 trailing characters at *each* level, although it is unlikely you would ever need that many.

To design your own outline format, go to the typing area.

Press CTRL-F7 and choose Document Format. Then choose Outline.

You will see the Outline Format menu listing all the outline levels.

Choose the outline level you want to change. You will then see the Outline Level Format menu. In addition to combining outline levels (discussed in the previous section), you can make the following changes:

- *Numbering or Lettering Type.* Lets you choose the outline character you want. You can also choose No Numbering or Lettering if you don't want any outline character.

- *Leading Characters.* Lets you choose the characters and codes that come before the outline character.

- *Trailing Characters.* Lets you choose the characters and codes that come after the outline character.

The default leading and trailing characters that you see on the menu (the small sideways triangles) are the Indent codes that set up a temporary left margin. Outlines with combined outline characters frequently do not have indentations.

To change the leading and trailing characters for a certain level,

tab to Leading Characters or Trailing Characters.

Then type the characters and codes you want. Press CTRL-T once for each level of indentation you require. Each time you press CTRL-T, the left margin of that outline level will be indented one tab stop. You may combine Indent codes with punctuation and with other codes.

To erase all leading or trailing characters for a particular level,

press ALT-8

for that item. When you have designed the outline characters for that level,

press ENTER.

Then repeat the process for the next level. When you have redesigned all the levels you wish to,

press ESC

until you return to the typing area.

Table 18-1 lists the keys used in creating outlines.

Key	Function
ALT-8	In the Reset Outline Level menu, lets you undo a reset of the outline level character
CTRL-F8	Lets you change the level of an outline entry or reset the outline level character
CTRL-O	Takes you to outline levels one through eight so you can create outlines
CTRL-T	Inserts into your text an Indent code that sets up a temporary left margin. (Indent codes are frequently used leading and trailing characters in outlines)

Table 18-1. Keys Used in Creating Outlines

19

Creating Tables

This chapter teaches you how to use DisplayWrite 4 to create tables. It shows you how to lay out the columns and type in text; it also shows you how to revise and rearrange columns.

If you type a table in the regular typing area, you face many problems. For one, you have to calculate where to place each column and how much space to leave between columns; if you later decide to add or delete a column, all your calculations will be incorrect, and you will have to do the work over. Another problem occurs if you want to delete a line of text in one of several columns. You can easily delete the text (by using the space bar to move the cursor over the text while in Replace mode, for example), but you can't close up the empty line in that column without eliminating the line, still containing text, in all the other columns. Conversely, you can easily add a line or two of text to a single column, but that causes all the other columns to show blank space on those lines.

The DisplayWrite 4 Column feature solves all these problems for you. The system calculates exactly how much space you need between columns and then inserts that amount of space for you. If you want to add, delete, move, or copy columns, it will perform the operation and recalculate the space. During the revision process, you isolate the column temporarily, making it, in effect, a separate page. In this way, you can make any changes you want to that column without affecting other columns. When you are finished, you reinsert the revised column into the table.

There are basically two types of tables that DisplayWrite 4 creates—text tables and tabular tables. Text tables are essentially columns of text such as you see in a newsletter or magazine (see Figure 19-1). Tabular tables are usually composed of rows and columns of numbers, although they may contain text as well (see Figure 19-2).

Often the column farthest left and the top row or rows of a table contain headings for the table, as in Figure 19-2. DisplayWrite 4 lets you designate these areas as *reference areas* so that you can view your headings when you isolate a column and revise it.

As you work through this chapter and produce your own tables, you will be using typing areas that you have not used before. The Layout Table typing area is where you design your table, set up reference areas, and redesign your table after revisions. The Create Table typing area is where you type a tabular table. The Revise Column typing area is where you create text columns and isolate both text and tabular columns for revision.

Creating tables with DisplayWrite 4 takes a little bit of practice. However, after you gain some proficiency with the Table feature, you will enjoy the ease and accuracy with which you can create complex tables.

MADISON H.S. NEWSLETTER

CAREERS

Madison is planning
two conferences in
June to help students
plan their careers.
Both conferences will
be held on Saturdays
so that students and
parents can attend.

The first, "Careers
in Science," will be
held in the auditorium
on June 15, at 1:00
p.m.   Representatives
from firms in the
area will be present.

The second, "Preparing
for College," will be
held in the library
on June 22, at 3:00
p.m.   Representatives
from local colleges
will discuss the re-
quirements for enroll-
ment in various col-
lege programs.

COUNSELING

Madison has a new drug
education and counsel-
ing program available
to students.   A licen-
sed clinical social
worker, Mr. Jeffrey
Star, will be present
on the campus on Thurs-
days.

Mr. Star will conduct
seminars with small
groups of students
from each grade.   In
addition students may
request a private
counseling session by
leaving a note in Mr.
Star's box in the
office.

Mr. Star will also
visit individual
classrooms and give
brief lectures on
topics of interest to
students.

Figure 19-1. A text table

```
                         FAMILY BUDGET


                  JAN      FEB     MAR     APRIL      MAY    JUNE


food              450      370     390      410       460    385

rent              400      400     400      400       400    400

clothing          140       35       0       45        80      0

transportation     40       85      50       65       130    150

entertainment     130       15      25       10        85     40
```

Figure 19-2.   A tabular table

Making a Tabular Table

Create a file in the usual fashion. Plan ahead for your table
by selecting a suitable format for your file. For example, you
may need unusually small margins to allow room for all your
columns. Even though DisplayWrite 4 does the actual calculations, you must provide sufficient space. You may want your
table in a special typeface or pitch, or you may want double
or triple spacing. You may be planning to use a special paper
size to print your table. (Make sure that your margins are
compatible with your paper-size selection.) Do *not* make any
tab changes for your table; you will do that during the layout
process.

   After selecting a suitable format, enter the typing area and
move the cursor to the line where you want your table to
begin. Check that Display All Codes is set to No because the

codes will cause your table to appear misaligned.

Press F9 (the Table key) and select Layout New Table.

You will enter the Layout Table typing area, as shown in Figure 19-3. Notice that instructions are displayed on the screen.

Count the number of characters contained in the longest entry in your first column. Then type that many characters, setting the appropriate tab for positioning either before or

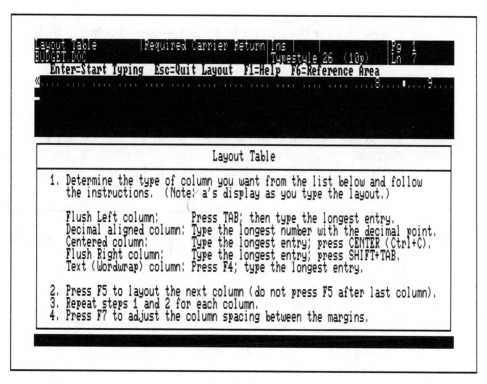

Figure 19-3. The Layout Table typing area

after you type, as indicated here:

- *Flush left.* Press TAB and type the characters.
- *Flush right.* Type the characters and press SHIFT-TAB.
- *Center.* Type the characters and press CTRL-C.
- *Decimal.* Type the characters, inserting a period where you want the decimal point.

Instead of the characters you type, you will see a line of lowercase a's on the screen and a tab marker. The a's are used as placemarkers while you lay out your column.

When you have typed the longest entry for your first column,

press F5.

This separates one column from the next. Then type enough characters for the longest entry in the second column, including the appropriate tab marker, and

press F5 again.

Repeat this process for each column in your table, but after you type the last column, *do not press F5 and do not press ENTER.*

Your line should now look something like this:

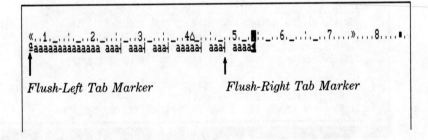

Flush-Left Tab Marker   *Flush-Right Tab Marker*

In the screen display, the first column has a flush-left tab marker and the remaining columns have flush-right tab markers.

Press F7.

You will see

```
█.,.1.,._.,!._.,.2._.,.!._.,.3._.,.!._.,4△.,.!._,.5._.,.!._.,.6._,.!._,.7.,.,.,.».,.,.8.,.,.█.
█aaaaaaaaaaaaaa    aaa┤ ‾  aaa┤ ‾  aaa┤ ‾  aaaaa┤ ‾  aaa┤ ‾  aaaa┤
```

Your line of a's will be spread out evenly between your margins.

Press ENTER.

As the left corner of the top status line indicates, you are now in another typing area, the Create Table typing area. You can start typing your entries.

If your first column is supposed to be left-aligned, you are already in the correct position; just type your entry. If not, press TAB to get to the desired position and then type the entry. When you are finished, press TAB to move to the next position and type that entry. As you type, your entries will be aligned according to the tab settings you have chosen. Continue until you have completed all of the entries on the line, as shown here:

```
«.,1.,.,.,!.,.,.2.,.,.,!.,.,┤.,.,.,!┤4△.,.,┤.,5.,.,.,┤.,6.,.,┤.,.,7.,█».,.,.8.,.,.█.
clothing            140        35        0        45        80        0█
```

To get to the next line

press ENTER,

and repeat the entire process. Do not press ENTER when you have completed your table. Instead

press F2.

You are returned to the regular typing area and can type any text that you want below your table.

Aligning Text Entries

If the first line of a tabular table consists of text headings (as in Figure 19-2), these headings are aligned according to the tab settings you chose for the columns. If you want your headings aligned differently, you can use one of two approaches. The first method is to leave a few blank lines in the typing area for your headings before you begin your table. When you have completed your table and returned to the regular typing area, just type your headings in the reserved space as ordinary text, positioning them wherever you like.

The second method is to return to the typing area after completing your table. Turn Display All Codes to Yes, position your cursor under the space to the right of the Begin Table code, and create a blank line or lines *between* the code and the beginning of your table. Type your headings in these lines and then set Display All Codes to Off again. The advantage of the second method is that your headings are part of the table, so you can define them as a top reference area if you need to. However, do *not* try to rearrange your columns after you have inserted headings in this manner.

Making a Text Table

A table of text columns is created in much the same way as a tabular table is created, except that the text is actually typed in the Revise Column typing area, not in the Create Table typing area.

Create a file in the usual way and select an appropriate format for your table. Make sure the margins are sufficiently wide apart to accommodate your text columns, and make any other changes (line spacing, justification, and so on) that you want. Then, with the cursor on the line where you want your table to begin,

press F9 and choose Layout New Table.

You will be in the Layout Table Typing area.

Press F4

to let the system know you are creating a text column. A flush-left tab marker will be displayed on the screen.

Figure out the maximum number of characters you need in your column and type that many characters. You will see a's on the screen instead of the characters you type. Then

press F5

to separate that column from the next column. Press F4 again to designate a text column and repeat the process for each column in the table, except that when you complete the last column, do *not* press F5 and do *not* press ENTER. Instead,

press F7.

You will see your columns become evenly distributed between the margins.

Press ENTER; then press F2.

You will be returned to the regular typing area. Now

set Display All Codes to Yes

and position your cursor under the Begin Table code. Then

set Display All Codes to No again and press F9.

This time you will see the Revise Table menu shown in Figure 19-4.

Choose Revise Column.

You will be in the Revise Column typing area. Type your entire column. As you type, the column will appear in the correct width.

If you want to adjust the line endings of your column and hyphenate, do it now using F12 or ALT-2. Hyphenation is particularly important in columns because uneven line endings appear more prominent in a narrow column than in a wider text line. You *cannot* hyphenate table columns during pagination or spelling checks as you can ordinary text.

To adjust line endings, move the cursor to the left edge of the first line you want to adjust and press F12 or ALT-2, making hyphenation decisions as described in the section "Adjusting Line Endings" in Chapter 4. Continue down the column.

When you are finished typing the column,

press F2 and select Return and Save

to return to the regular typing area. You will see your

column appropriately placed. To create the second column, move the cursor to the line that the Begin Table code is on; then move the cursor to the right until it is under the tab setting for the second column. The scale line will show you when the cursor is correctly positioned. Then

press F9 and choose Revise Column.

Repeat the entire process to create the second and all subsequent columns.

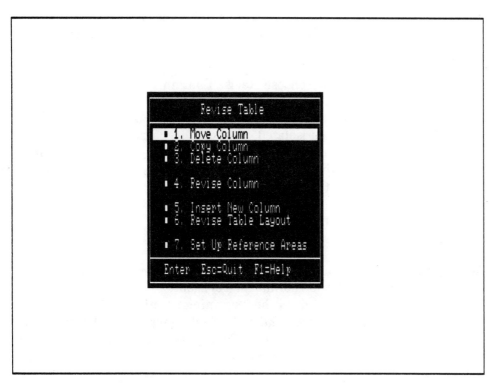

Figure 19-4. The Revise Table menu

Revising a Table

After you complete a table, you may want to revise it. Perhaps you want to rewrite text in a text table, add or delete entries in a tabular table, or alter margins and column widths to create a more pleasing appearance.

Isolating a Column for Revision

The advantage of isolating a column in order to revise it is that no changes you make to that column will affect the format of the rest of the table.

To isolate a column for revision, you must be in the regular typing area. Move the cursor to the line containing the Begin Table code and position the cursor under any character in the column you want to revise.

Press F9 and choose Revise Column.

The Revise Column typing area will be displayed and your column will be isolated, as shown in Figure 19-5.

Type any revisions that you want. If you are typing text columns, adjust the line endings after revision. To return to the regular typing area,

press F2 and choose Return and Save.

Adding an Item to a Tabular Column   To add an item to a tabular table, first isolate the column for revision.

To add an item to the beginning or middle of the column, position the cursor under the first character of the item that will follow the new item. Type in the new item. Both items will now be on the same line.

Press ENTER,

```
Revise Column          |                |Ins |     |       |Pg  1
TABLE.DOC              |                |Typestyle 26  (10p)  |Ln  13

█.2.....:...Δ.3.....:...»4.....:....5.....:....6.....:....7.....:....8....■....9.....:..
CAREERS

Madison is planning
two conferences in
June to help students
plan their careers.
Both conferences will
be held on Saturdays
so that students and
parents can attend.

The first, "Careers
in Science," will be
held in the auditorium
on June 15, at 1:00
p.m. Representatives
from firms in the
area will be present.

The second, "Preparing
```

Figure 19-5. The column is isolated on the left side of the screen

and the original item will jump down to the next line. If the original item is not correctly aligned, press TAB.
   To add an item at the end of the column,

   press CTRL-END and then press ENTER

to create a blank line for the new item. Type the new item.

Deleting an Item from a Tabular Column   To remove an item from a tabular table, isolate the column for revision.

Set Display All Codes to Yes.

Then delete the item with F4, making sure that you delete all codes associated with the item. Some of the codes may be quite far in front of the item you are deleting, as shown here:

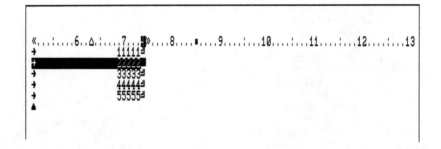

Set Display All Codes to No.

Changing the Table Format

When you view the completed table on the screen, you may decide to make the margins wider or narrower. Or you may make other line format changes (such as changing from single to double spacing or selecting a different typestyle). After making these changes, you may need to change the width of one or more columns.

Changing the Margin   If you want to change the left and right margins of your table you *cannot* simply change the margins of your file in the Document Format menu, *even if the table is the only thing in your file*. The reason is that the Line Format Change code that precedes the Begin Table code has locked in the format for your table.

To change the margins and make other format changes, position the cursor under the Line Format Change code (directly to the left of the Begin Table code).

Press CTRL-F8.

You will see the Format menu. Make any desired changes. When you choose Margins and Tabs, you will be warned:

```
> A table follows.  Tabs should not be changed.
```

This reminds you that table tabs are set in the Layout Table typing area, so you should not change them here.

When you are finished making format changes,

press ENTER and then ESC

to return to the typing area. Your new margins are visible on the scale line, but your table will not have changed to accommodate them. That is because you now need to go back to the Layout Table typing area to adjust your columns to the new margins.

Fitting Columns to New Margins and Changing Column Width To adjust your columns to the new margins and to change the width of any of the columns, position the cursor to the line containing the Begin Table code.

Press F9 and choose Revise Table Layout.

You will be in the Layout Table typing area.

If you want to make a column wider or narrower, you add characters to or delete characters from the line of a's representing the column. Then

press F7.

The columns will be evenly spaced between your margins. To return to the regular typing area,

press ENTER.

If you adjusted the width of any text column, you will see now that your text has *not* been rearranged to fit the new column width. To rearrange your text, you must isolate the column in the Revise Column typing area and use Line Adjust to adjust line endings. At this time you can also make new hyphenation decisions.

Inserting, Deleting, Moving, and Copying Columns

DisplayWrite 4 lets you rearrange columns in both text and tabular tables. You can insert or delete entire columns, move a column from one location to another, and copy a column so that it appears in two locations at once.

Inserting a Column

To insert a new column into your table, move the cursor to the line that the Begin Table code is on and position the cursor under the *first* character the new column is to precede. If you want to add your new column to the right of the last column, place the cursor on or to the right of the right margin symbol.

Press F9 and choose Insert New Column.

Type as many characters as required for your new column, including the tab setting. (Tab instructions are displayed on the screen to help you.) Notice that instead of a's your new entry is represented by o's:

```
«,.1.........,2.......:....|.......|.4.△....|.5.......|6.......|.7......:.|».8....■.|
ºaaaaaaaaaaaaaaa      aaa| oooo|     aaa|     aaa|     aaaaa|      aaa|     aaaa|
                     JAN      FEB       MAR      APRIL       MAY      JUNE

food                 450      370       390      410        460      385
```

When you are finished,

press F7.

This will adjust the spacing.

Press ENTER.

You will be in the Create Table typing area. Type the new column. Then

press F2 and choose Return and Save

to return to the regular typing area. The new column is now included in your table.

Deleting a Column

To delete a column, move the cursor to the line that the Begin Table code is on and position the cursor under a character in the column you want to delete.

Press F9 and choose Delete Column.

You will see your column highlighted, as shown in Figure 19-6.

Press ENTER

to delete the column. You are returned to the regular typing area with your column deleted.

To realign the remaining columns, position the cursor under the Begin Table code.

Press F9 and choose Revise Table Layout.

You will be in the Table Layout area.

Press F7.

The columns will be adjusted. To return to the regular typing area,

press ENTER.

	JAN	FEB	MAR	APRIL	MAY	JUNE
food	450	370	390	410	460	355
rent	400	400	400	400	400	400
clothing	140	35	0	45	80	0
transportation	40	85	50	65	130	150
entertainment	130	15	25	10	85	40

Figure 19-6. The column you want to delete is highlighted

Moving or Copying a Column

Move the cursor to the line where the Begin Table code is located and position it under a character in the column you want to move or copy.

Press F9 and choose either Move Column or Copy Column.

You will see the selected column highlighted.
In response to the prompt, move the cursor under the first character that will follow the moved or copied column. If you want to move or copy the column to the right of the last column in your table, position the cursor on or to the right of the right margin symbol.

Press ENTER.

You will be returned to the regular typing area and will see your column in its new location.
To realign the remaining columns, position the cursor under the Begin Table code.

Press F9 and choose Revise Table Layout.

You will be in the Table Layout area.

Press F7.

The columns will be adjusted. To return to the regular typing area,

press ENTER.

Making Regular Text into a Table

If you typed columns in the regular typing area (without using the Table feature), you can later define these columns as a table. You can then use the DisplayWrite 4 Table feature to isolate a column for revision instead of having to retype the entire table.

To define existing columns as a table, move the cursor to the first line of the columns you want defined as a table.

Press F9 and choose Define Existing Text as a Table.

Lay out the columns exactly as you did when laying out a new table. Be sure to make each column wide enough to accommodate the longest entry to fit in that column.

Press F7

to adjust the columns, and then

press ENTER

to exit the Table Layout screen.

Following the prompt, move the cursor to the last line of text you want included in the table.

Press ENTER to return to the typing area.

Creating Reference Areas

While you are revising a column, you may want to view the headings in the first row or first column of the table. DisplayWrite 4 lets you set up a side reference area, a top reference area, or both, so you can view these headings while you have a column isolated for revision.

The side reference area shows the left column (unless you are revising the left column, in which case the side reference area shows the columns to the right of the column you are revising). The top reference area consists of as many rows as you designate from the top of your table.

Setting Up Reference Areas

You can set up your reference area from the Layout Table typing area at the time you are laying out your table. After you have pressed F7 to space your column evenly,

press F6.

You will see the Set Up Reference Areas menu:

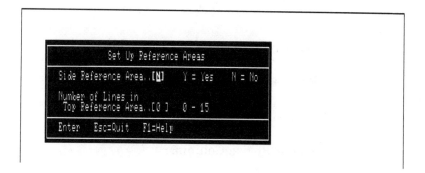

To set up a side reference area, set Side Reference Area to Yes.

To set up a top reference area, tab to Number of Lines in Top Reference Area, and type in the number of lines your top headings will occupy.

When you are finished making choices,

press ENTER

to return to the Layout Table typing area. Then

press ENTER again

to return to the Create Table typing area.

Revising a Column Using Reference Areas

To use reference areas, you isolate the column for revision in the usual way. In the regular typing area, move the cursor to the line that the Begin Table code is on and position the cursor under any character in the column you want to revise.

Press F9.

If you did *not* set up your reference areas when you created your table, or if you want to change your reference area designations, you may do so now: From the menu,

choose Set Up Reference Areas.

Make any desired changes or additions.

Press ENTER

to return to the Revise Table menu. Then

choose Revise Column.

You will see the column you selected for revision. To its left will be your side reference area, separated from the column by a thick line. The line or lines on top of your column that you designated as a top reference area are also separated from the column (see Figure 19-7).

Revise the column in the usual way. When you are finished, to return to the regular typing area,

press F2 and choose Return and Save.

Revising the Reference Areas

You revise a column that has been designated as a side reference area exactly as you revise any other column. You posi-

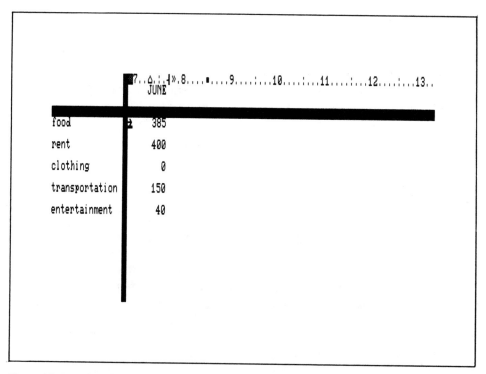

Figure 19-7.   You will see your side and top reference areas separated from the column you are revising

tion the cursor under a character on the first line of the column, press F9, and choose Revise Column from the Revise Table menu.

Revising text that has been designated as part of a top reference area is different because the cursor will not move into the top reference area. Therefore, you revise such text in the regular typing area.

Table 19-1 lists the keys used in creating tables.

Key	Function
F2	Returns you to the regular typing area after you create or revise a table
F4	Lets the system know you are laying out a text column
F5	Separates one column from another while you are laying out your table
F6	While in the Layout Table typing area, displays the Set Up Reference Areas menu so you can set up reference areas for your revision process
F7	Adjusts the spaces between your columns to fit the specified margins
CTRL-F8	With cursor under the Line Format Change code in the regular typing area, takes you to the Format menu so you can change your table format
F9	Takes you to the Layout Table typing area to lay out your table or to the Revise Table menu so you can revise your table
F12 or ALT-2	Used to adjust and hyphenate text columns

Table 19-1. Keys Used in Making Tables

20

Performing
Calculations

This chapter shows you how to use the DisplayWrite 4 Math function to perform arithmetic computations on numbers in your file.

The DisplayWrite 4 Math Function

The DisplayWrite 4 Math function lets you quickly add a row or column of numbers in a table you have made. You can also add, subtract, multiply, and divide numbers that appear anywhere in your file. The results of your calculations will be displayed on the second status line. You can then insert these results at a designated location in your file.

You can also use the system to find the average of a series of numbers and to perform calculations using a constant that you previously entered into the system.

Some Hints for Using the Math Function

If you are typing a lot of numbers, you may find it helpful to press the NUM LOCK key. This key enables you to use the numeric key pad on the right side of your keyboard without having to press the SHIFT key to type the numerals. Press NUM LOCK again to "toggle off" — to return the numeric key pad to its usual functions.

Fifteen is the maximum number of digits you can have in any one number or in the total. If you try to use numbers with more than 15 digits or if your computations produce a total of more than 15 digits, you will get the message

```
> Math operation is cancelled.  Number is too large.
```

The simplest way to indicate a negative number is to type a hyphen (a minus sign) in front of the number. You can also show that a number is negative in any of the ways listed in Table 20-1.

To save your file when the item count and total appear at the top of the screen, you must always clear the total by pressing CTRL-F9 (the Math key) and selecting Clear Total. This resets the item count and total to zero. You then press ESC to exit from the Math feature. You cannot create or revise your file while the status lines display an item count and total.

What You Do	How the Number Looks
Type a hyphen or a hyphen and a space before the number	-10.30 or - 10.30
Type a hyphen directly after the number	10.30-
Enclose the number in parentheses	(10.30)

Table 20-1. How to Indicate a Negative Number

A Quick Way to Add a Column or Row

You can use the DisplayWrite 4 Math function to add a row or column in a table quickly *as long as the numbers in the table are aligned at a decimal tab.* You may use the DisplayWrite 4 table feature to create the table, or you may set your tabs in the Margins and Tabs menu and make the table by hand.

Adding a Column

Look at the six-month household budget found in Chapter 19. Notice that decimal places have been added to some of the numbers to represent cents.

Let's say you want to calculate your total expenses for the month of January, as displayed here:

	JAN	FEB	MAR	APRIL	MAY	JUNE
food	450.80	370.15	390.30	410.20	460.05	385.50
rent	400	400	400	400	400	400
clothing	140	35	0	45.50	80.80	0
transportation	40.50	85.85	50.50	65.80	130.90	150.10
entertainment	130.95	15.20	25.95	10	85.30	40.65

With Display All Codes set to No, position your cursor anywhere under the first number in the JAN column; then

press CTRL-F9 (the Math key).

You will see the Math menu shown in Figure 20-1.

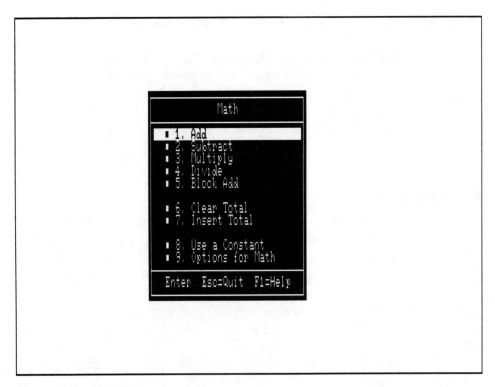

Figure 20-1.   The Math menu

Choose Block Add.

Notice that the cursor is now under the decimal point.
Move the cursor to the last number in the column. The cursor
will automatically move under the decimal point, and the
numbers in the column will be highlighted. A number does
not have to contain a decimal, but it must be aligned at a
decimal tab.

```
«,:.....1.........:...2....▯....3.....:..•...4...△..:..•..5.....:....•..6........•.7.....:....•..
              JAN      FEB      MAR     APRIL     MAY      JUNE

food          ▮▮▮▮▮   370.15   390.30   410.20   460.05   385.50

rent          ▮▮▮     400      400      400      400      400

clothing      ▮▮▮     35       0        45.50    80.80    0

transportation ▮▮▮▮▮  85.85    50.50    65.80    130.90   150.10

entertainment ▮▮▮▮▮   15.20    25.95    10       85.30    40.65
```

Note: You don't have to start your addition with the first number in the column or row or end with the last, but you can't choose to add only some of the numbers between the first and last numbers you are adding. As you move the cursor down the column or across the row, *all* numbers between the first number chosen and the last number chosen will be highlighted.

Press ENTER.

Your column is added. The number of items added and the total are displayed on the left side of the status lines.

```
Item Count = 5

Total = 1,162.25
```

To bring the item count and total back to zero so you can add another column,

press CTRL-F9 and choose Clear Total.

Repeat the entire process to add the next column. When you are finished adding columns,

press CTRL-F9 and choose Clear Total. Then press ESC.

The total and item count display are erased from the status lines, and you can continue to create or revise your file.

Adding a Row

The process of adding a row is identical to that of adding a column, except that you move the cursor horizontally across the screen rather than vertically.

Performing Calculations on Numbers in Your File

The DisplayWrite 4 Math function will add, subtract, multiply, and divide numbers that appear in your file even if they are not consecutive numbers in a row or column. These numbers can be in text or in a table. They do not have to be aligned by any sort of tab.

To use this feature, move your cursor under any digit in the first number that you want to include in the procedure:

```
«▌..2...._....3...._....4....Δ....5...._....6...._....7....».,..8....▪....9....

Dear Mr. Jorkins:

     As I will indicate at our annual meeting next week, we
had a very successful first quarter.  Our store took in over
$300,000.  Our expenses for rent during this period came to
$6,200 and labor costs to $28,000.  In addition, we were
```

Press CTRL-F9 and choose Add.

(Regardless of the operation you are going to perform, you must *always* choose Add for your first number to place it in the total.) Your number will be highlighted and the item count and total will be displayed on the prompt line (your number appears in the total in the active math format):

```
Item Count = 2

Total = 293,800.00
```

Now move the cursor under the next number in the operation—the one you want to add to or subtract from the first number, or the one you want to multiply or divide by. Your first number will remain highlighted.

```
《▌.,2.,,,,_,,,3.,,,,_,,4.,,,,Δ,,,,5.,,,,_,,,,6.,,,,_,,,,7.,,,,》,,,,8,,,,▪,,,,9,,,,

Dear Mr. Jorkins:

     As I will indicate at our annual meeting next week, we
had a very successful first quarter.  Our store took in over
$▓▓▓,▓▓▓  Our expenses for rent during this period came to
$6,200 and labor costs to $28,000.  In addition, we were
```

Press CTRL-F9.

Now select Add, Subtract, Multiply, or Divide, depending on what you want to do. You will see your second number highlighted, and the new item count and total will be displayed on the status lines. For example, if you subtracted the second number from the first, you would see

```
Item Count = 1

Total = 300,000.00
```

Repeat this procedure for each number in your file that you want included in the operation. As you perform operations on the numbers, the item count and total on the status lines will change to reflect the operations.

Inserting a Total into Your File

You can insert the total displayed on the second status line into your file at any location. It does not matter whether the total was arrived at by Block Add or by one of the four math operations.

To insert a total into your file, move the cursor to where you want the total to appear:

```
Our profit for the quarter was _
```

Press CTRL-F9 and choose Insert Total.

Your total will appear in the designated location and also remain on the second status line.

Finding an Average

After you have added a group of numbers with Add or Block Add, you can use DisplayWrite 4 to find the average of your numbers. Say you have used Block Add to add up all your food costs for the first six months of the year and have discovered that the total is $2,467.00:

```
Item Count = 6

Total = 2,467.00
```

Now you want to find the average amount you spend on food each month. Do *not* clear the total or exit the Math feature. Instead,

press CTRL-F9 and choose Options for Math.

You will see the Math Options menu shown in Figure 20-2. From the Math Options menu, choose Active Math Format/View Average. Your average will be displayed:

`Average = 411.17`

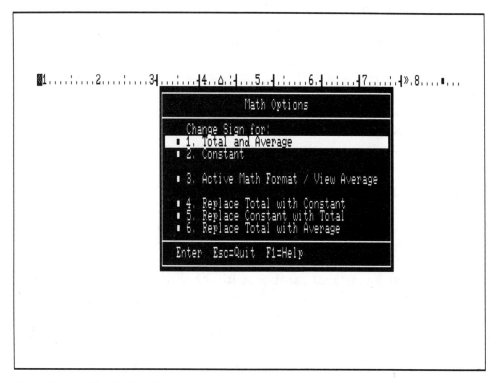

Figure 20-2. The Math Options menu

Press ESC to return to the typing area.

Making the Average Your New Total

For certain calculations, you may want the figure for the average to replace the figure for the total on the second status line. To replace the existing total with the average,

press CTRL-F9 and choose Options for Math.

Then, from the Math Options menu,

choose Replace Total with Average.

You are returned to the typing area. Your average appears on the second status line as the new total and the item count is returned to zero.

You insert the average into your file the way you would insert any other total. (See the section "Inserting a Total into Your File" earlier in this chapter.)

Using a Constant

A *constant* is a numerical value that does not change (such as the number of weeks in a year — 52). You can enter a constant into the DisplayWrite 4 Math function and perform calculations using that constant with other numbers. Say you have to pay a 6% sales tax on purchases; you can enter 6% as a constant into the system and use it to calculate your tax. Or if your file includes monthly figures but you want quarterly projections, you can enter the constant 3 so that the monthly figures can be multiplied by 3 to get quarterly figures.

You can enter only one constant at a time into DisplayWrite 4. When you enter a second constant, it replaces the first. The constant does not have to appear anywhere in your file.

Entering the Constant into the System

To enter a constant into the system, you can be anywhere in the typing area of your file.

Press CTRL-F9 and choose Use a Constant.

Then, from the Use a Constant menu,

choose Enter or Change Constant.

In the Enter or Change Constant menu, type the constant you want. You may type a hyphen (-) before the number for a negative constant or a percent sign (%) after it for a percentage.

Press ENTER.

You will see a zero total and item count on the prompt line.

Note: Whenever you press ESC to exit the Math feature, the constant resets to zero (no constant).

Performing Calculations with a Constant

To use the constant, move the cursor under any part of the number on which you want to perform calculations.

Press CTRL-F9 and choose Add.

You will see your number highlighted and added to the item count and total on the status lines.

Press CTRL-F9 and select Use a Constant.

If you want to check that you have the correct constant or if you want to change the constant, choose Enter or Change Constant. Otherwise, select the operation you want to perform. If you want your number multiplied by the constant, choose Multiply Total. If you want your number divided by the total, choose Divide Total. If you want to calculate the percentage, make sure your constant is a number followed by a percent sign and choose Multiply Total. You will see your new item count and total displayed on the status line.

You may use the constant with as many numbers from your file as you want. If you want the item count and total to keep accumulating, don't clear the total. If you want to start over with a new number, press CTRL-F9 and choose Clear Total to clear the total.

Making the Constant Your New Total

For certain calculations, you may want the constant to replace your existing total and become your new total. If so,

press CTRL-F9 and choose Options for Math.

When you see the Math Options menu,

choose Replace Total with Constant.

You are returned to the typing area. If you look at the item count and total displayed on the status lines, you will see that your constant is now your new total and the item count has been returned to zero. Your constant has not changed.

Making the Total Your New Constant

For certain calculations, you may want the total to replace your existing constant and become the new constant. If so,

press CTRL-F9 and select Options for Math.

When you see the Math Options menu,

choose Replace Constant with Total.

You are returned to the typing area.

If you look at the item count and total displayed on the status lines, you will see that these items have not changed. However, the number displayed as your total is now also your new constant.

Changing the Sign of the Total and Average or of the Constant

For certain math calculations, you may want your total and average or your constant to be displayed with the opposite sign. For example, if your total appears on the second status line as a positive number, you may want to convert it to a negative number.

To change the sign of a total and average or of a constant,

press CTRL-F9 and choose Options for Math.

Then, from the Math Options menu,

either choose Total and Average or choose Constant.

You will be returned to the typing area. If you changed the sign of your total, you can look at the second status line and see that the total now appears with the opposite sign.

If you insert the total and average or the constant anywhere in your file, it will appear with the changed sign. However, any totals and averages or constants that you previously inserted into your file will not be changed.

Deciding How Your Numbers Will Look

Until now, your totals and averages have all been displayed in the same format. For example, they all show two decimal places after a decimal point *even if the numbers you were working with did not contain any decimal points*. They all use a period as the decimal point symbol and a comma as the thousands separator symbol. However, you do not have to use this format; DisplayWrite 4 gives you a choice of four preset formats and, in addition, lets you design your own in the Profiles menu (see Chapter 15).

Selecting a Different Format for Your Numbers

To select a different format for your numbers, go to the typing area.

Press CTRL-F9 and choose Options for Math.

Then, from the Math Options menu,

choose Active Math Format/View Average.

The top line of the screen shows the average displayed in the currently active format (format 1 is the default). Below that you can see how numbers will look displayed in each of the four preset formats:

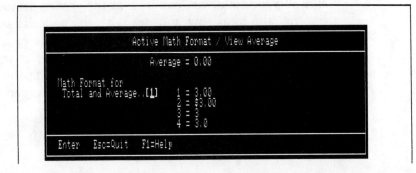

Table 20-2 shows you the differences in each format and also shows you the choices you can make in the Profiles menu if you want to create a customized number format.

To select a different format, type the number of the desired format and press ENTER. You will be returned to the typing area.

Perform your math calculations. Totals will be displayed in the format you just chose. When you press ESC to continue creating or revising your file, format 1, the default setting, becomes active again.

Designing Your Own Number Format

If none of the available formats is suitable for your work, you can customize your number format by going to the Profiles menu as described in Chapter 15.

From the Profiles menu,

choose Revise Profile.

Then type the profile name.

Press ENTER, choose Text, and then choose Math Format.

You will see the Math Format menu:

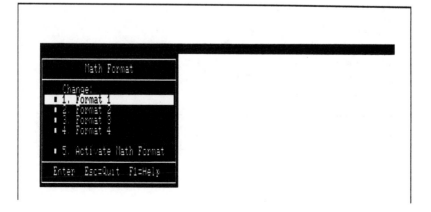

Format Item	Format 1	Format 2	Format 3	Format 4	Choices You Can Make in Profiles Menu
Decimal point symbol	period	period	period	period	period, comma, colon
Thousands separator symbol	comma	comma	comma	none	period, comma, none, space
Number of digits to the right of the decimal point	2	2	0	1	0-15
Rounding rule	1-4 down &5-9 up	1-4 down &5-9 up	1-4 down &5-9 up	1-4 down &5-9 up	1-4 down &5-9 up, 1-9 up, 1-5 down &6-9 up, 1-9 down, none
Leading characters (positive numbers)	none	$	none	none	up to eight characters
Trailing characters (positive numbers)	none	none	none	none	up to eight characters
Leading characters (negative numbers)	-	-$	-	-	up to eight characters
Trailing characters (negative numbers)	none	none	none	none	up to eight characters

Table 20-2. How Your Numbers Will Look

Customizing a Format   You can customize any of the four existing formats from the Math Format menu.

To customize a format, choose the number of the format you want to change. You will see the Change Math Format menu shown in Figure 20-3. Make the desired changes from the choices that follow.

- Decimal Point Character. You can choose a period, a comma, or a colon for your decimal point symbol.

- *Thousands Separator Character.* You can choose a comma, a period, or a space as your thousands separator, or you can choose to have no separator.

- *Number of Positions Past Decimal Point.* You can choose up to 15 digits to the right of the decimal. However, since the *total* number of digits can only be 15, digits to the right of the decimal exceeding the total will be rounded off.

- *Rounding Rule.* You can decide how numbers will be rounded off. You can also choose not to have numbers rounded off at all.

- *Leading Characters and Trailing Characters.* You can select up to eight characters to appear before and eight characters to appear after each number. In all four formats, the default leading character before negative numbers is a hyphen (a minus sign). Format 2 also has a dollar sign as a leading character before both positive and negative numbers.

When you are finished making changes in the Change Math Format menu,

press ENTER

to return to the Math Format menu.

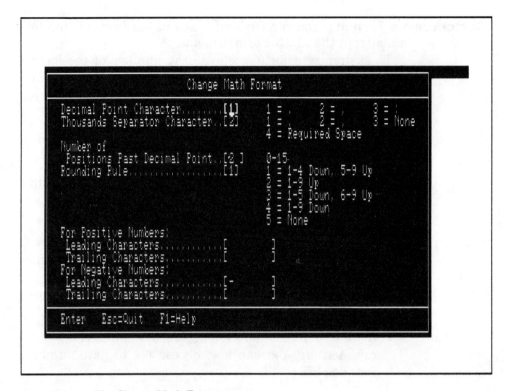

Figure 20-3.   The Change Math Format menu

Choosing a Different Default Math Format   The Math Format menu also lets you change the default math format. If you find, for example, that you almost always want to display totals with dollar signs in front of them, you would want the default format to be format 2 instead of format 1. To change the default format,

choose Active Math Format

and type the number of the format that you want as the new default setting.

Press ENTER.

When you are finished making changes in the Math Format menu,

press ESC

until you return to the End/Save menu.

Choose End and Save

to save your changes. You will be returned to the Profiles menu. When you next use Math, your number format changes will be in effect.

21

Keystroke
Programming
(Macros)

This chapter shows you how to save a series of keystrokes so you can execute a series of commands or insert a text block into your file by pressing just two keys.

What Keystroke Programming Is

On the left side of your keyboard or across the top are 10 or 12 keys called *function keys.* You have been using these keys, either alone or together with the CTRL key, as long as you have been using DisplayWrite 4. There is also another way you can use these keys.

DisplayWrite 4 lets you program these function keys: You can save a series of keystrokes, called a *keystroke program* (also called a *macro*) on disk, and then you can simply press the ALT or the SHIFT key simultaneously with one of the function keys to replay the keystroke series without doing any typing. Each keystroke program can contain up to 500 keystrokes.

There are two kinds of keystroke series that you will find useful to store in a keystroke program. One kind consists of text that you find yourself typing frequently. For example, if you had to type the text box in Figure 21-1 frequently, you would find it handy to simply press ALT or SHIFT and a function key to have the text automatically typed for you.

The second kind of useful keystroke program consists of a series of operations that you instruct DisplayWrite 4 to perform. For example, say you frequently save your file, paginate it using the default settings, and then print three copies in nondraft mode. You can save on disk the keystrokes necessary for this procedure and then recall them simply by pressing ALT or SHIFT and a function key. Table 21-1 shows the keystrokes required for this procedure with keystroke programming and without it. You can even instruct the system

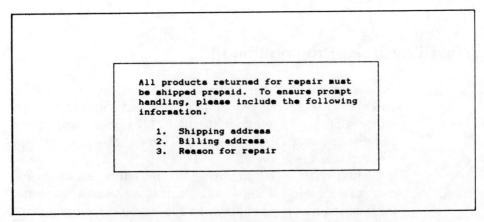

Figure 21-1. You can write a keystroke program for frequently used text

to pause at certain points during the execution of a keystroke program so you can type in information that may change each time (such as the file name).

Programming your function keys is a two-step process. First you "capture," or enter, the series of keystrokes in the computer's memory. At this stage, you can revise the program to add or eliminate keystrokes. When you have captured the keystrokes to your satisfaction, you save them on disk. To recall the series of keystrokes, you need only press the ALT or SHIFT key along with the designated function key.

With Keystroke Programming	Without Keystroke Programming
SHIFT-F1	F2 (to exit the typing area)
	TAB three times (to position cursor on Paginate, End, and Save)
	ENTER (to choose Paginate, End, and Save)
	ENTER (to paginate using defaults)
	4 (to choose Print)
	TAB (to position cursor at Options for Printer choice)
	ENTER (to select Options for Printer)
	ENTER (to select Printer 1)
	n (to select nondraft mode)
	ENTER (to return to Options for Printer # menu)
	ESC (to return to Print menu)
	ENTER (to display Print Document menu)
	TAB three times (to position cursor at Number of Copies choice)
	3 (to indicate that you want three copies)
	ENTER (to begin printing)

Table 21-1. Keystrokes Required to Save, Paginate, and Print Three Copies of a File in Nondraft Mode

The First Step: Capturing the Keystrokes in Memory

To begin capturing keystrokes, go to the DisplayWrite 4 area where capture is to begin. If you want to capture text, go to a typing area. If you want to capture a procedure (such as saving a file), go to a menu or a typing area.

For example, you can create a simple keystroke program that will insert Keep codes before and after a block of text. (Remember that Keep codes keep a block of text together on one page when you print your file.) The program will have to insert a Begin Keep code into your file, pause for you to move the cursor to the end of the block you want kept together, and then insert an End Keep code into your file.

To create such a keystroke program, type text in the typing area until you get to the point where you want to begin keeping text on one page. This is the point where you will begin capturing keystrokes. (You can have only one keystroke program in memory at any one time. When you begin typing a keystroke program, any keystroke program previously in memory is wiped out.)

Press CTRL-F1 (the Key Program key).

You will see the Keystroke Programming menu shown in Figure 21-2.

Choose Capture.

Notice that "Capt" is displayed on the top status line:

"Capt" is displayed on the top status line

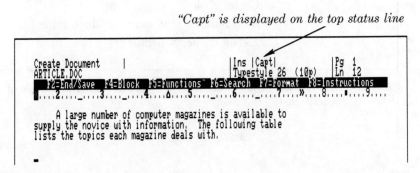

Now each keystroke that you type will be captured in the keystroke program. Since you first need to capture the keystrokes to begin the Keep feature,

press F8, choose Begin, and then choose Keep.

A Begin Keep code is inserted into your text. (Don't set Display All Codes to Yes to see it or these keystrokes will be captured too.)

The next step is to instruct the keystroke program to pause so that you can type in the text to be kept together. (Such data is called *variable information* because it may be differ-

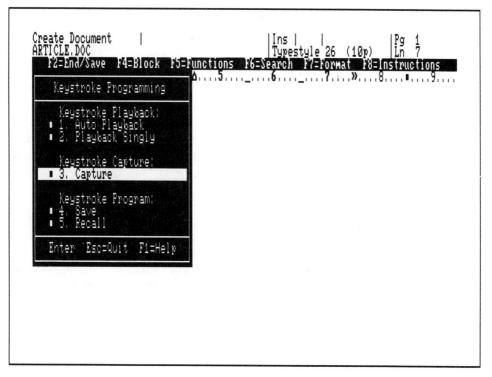

Figure 21-2. The Keystroke Programming menu

ent each time you use this keystroke program.) To insert a pause,

press CTRL-F1 and choose Pause.

"Capt" is highlighted on the status line, showing that keystroke capture is temporarily suspended. Type in the text you want kept together. When you are finished typing variable information,

press CTRL-F1 and choose Continue Capture.

(If you were done with your keystroke program, you would choose End Capture.)
Now you must capture the keystrokes necessary to insert an End Keep code into your text.

Press F8, choose End, and then choose Keep.

When you have captured all the necessary keystrokes,

press CTRL-F1 and choose End Capture.

Your Keep keystroke program is now in memory for you to use whenever you want to.
When you are creating your own keystroke programs, remember that 500 is the maximum number of keystrokes you can capture for each program.

Running a Keystroke Program in Memory

Before saving a keystroke program permanently on your disk, you should try it to see if it works. In fact, if you want to use the program only for the current work session, you do not need to save it to disk at all. To play back a keystroke program, go to the point where you want to begin using it. (If you are adding text, you should be in the typing area. If you are performing a procedure, you should be at the point in the system where the procedure is to begin.) In the case of the Keep keystroke program, you would position the cursor at the point where you wanted to begin keeping text together on a page.

Press CTRL-F1 and choose Auto Playback.

During playback, "Play" is displayed on the top status line. The system first plays back the keystrokes that put the Begin Keep code into your text. When it comes to the pause, playback ceases and you will see a message telling you that you may now type in text.

Type in the text you want between the Keep codes. Then, to resume playback and insert the End Keep code,

press CTRL-F1 and choose Auto Playback again.

Playback resumes and an End Keep code is inserted into your text.

If you want to interrupt playback before it is completed,

press CTRL-F1 and choose End Play.

Now, if you set Display All Codes to Yes, you will see the Begin Keep and End Keep codes in your file.

Note: If for any reason an error message is displayed during Auto Playback, the system will switch to Playback Singly so you can revise your program. The next section will show you how to revise a keystroke program.

Revising a Keystroke Program in Memory

Suppose your keystroke program does not work the way you want it to. You can revise a keystroke program while it is in memory, either by adding or by deleting keystrokes. This way you make all changes and corrections *before* you save the keystroke program to disk. The procedures for deleting and for adding keystrokes are presented separately here, but after you learn the procedures, you can make both additions and deletions in the same passage through a keystroke program.

Deleting Keystrokes   To delete keystrokes from a keystroke program,

press CTRL-F1 and choose Playback Singly.

You will see the first keystroke in the program highlighted on the top status line. In the case of the Keep program, you would see "Instr," since the first keystroke in the program is F8 and this key is called the Instruction, or Instr, key:

Each keystroke is displayed on the top status line

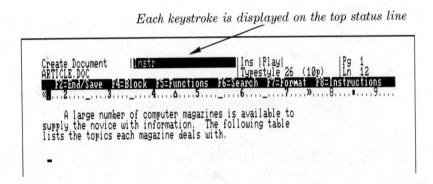

To play back the keystroke and keep it in the program,

press ENTER.

To delete the keystroke from the program,

    press DEL.

You will then see your next keystroke displayed on the status line. Repeat the process.

    When you come to a pause, you can press DEL to delete it the way you would delete any other keystroke in the program. If you don't want to delete it, continue until you see the "pause" message telling you that playback has been stopped to allow typing. Then

    press CTRL-F1 and choose Playback Singly.

Continue deleting keystrokes as necessary. When you have finished your deletions, you can remain in Playback Singly mode and continue going through your program keystroke by keystroke, or you can leave this mode. To leave it,

    press CTRL-F1.

Then either choose Automatic Playback to play back the remainder of the keystroke program quickly, or choose End Play to discontinue playback.

    If you remain in Playback Singly mode, you will see the message

`> Last keystroke was played back.`

When all keystrokes have been played, select End Play to terminate the playback.

    Note: As you play back keystrokes singly for revision, the system is actually playing back the keystrokes that you do not delete. If, for example, you play back the keystrokes in your Keep keystroke program, a Begin Keep code and End Keep code are inserted into your file at the cursor location.

Adding Keystrokes If you want to add keystrokes to a keystroke program,

press CTRL-F1 and choose Playback Singly.

The first keystroke in your program appears highlighted on the top status line.

Press ENTER

until you get to the point where you want to add new keystrokes. The status line should show the first keystroke that will *follow* your additions, as shown here:

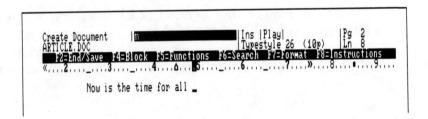

```
Create Document        |m              |Ins |Play|        |Pg  2
ARTICLE.DOC                            |Typestyle 26  (10p) |Ln  8
     F2=End/Save  F4=Block  F5=Functions  F6=Search  F7=Format  F8=Instructions
«....2...._...3...._....4....Δ....5...._....6....._...7....»....8....■....9....

          Now is the time for all _
```

Press CTRL-F1. Then choose Capture.

Type all the keystrokes that you want to add to your keystroke program. When you are finished adding keystrokes,

press CTRL-F1 and choose End Capture.

You will see the Keystroke Programming menu with four choices.

- Choose Auto Playback if you are finished adding keystrokes and want to play back the remaining keystrokes quickly.

- Choose Playback Singly if you want to continue playback stroke by stroke. You can then add or delete keystrokes later in the program.

- Choose End Play to terminate the keystroke program.

- Choose Capture if you decide to add still more keystrokes.

Adding a Pause   When revising a keystroke program, you may also add
pauses to capture variable information. During Playback
Singly, when you come to the place where you want to insert
a pause,

> press CTRL-F1 and choose Capture; then press CTRL-F1 and
> choose Pause.

A pause is inserted into your keystroke program. Then

> press CTRL-F1 again.

Choose Continue Capture if you want to add more keystrokes
to your program. Choose End Capture if you are finished
capturing keystrokes.

Some Pointers for Successful
Keystroke Programming

The following information will help you avoid errors when
you create and use a keystroke program.

- On a floppy-disk system, do not create a keystroke program for a procedure that requires disk changes.

- Keystroke programming will stop if you invoke the Help
  function. When you are done using Help, keystroke programming will resume. The keys used in Help cannot be
  captured as part of the keystroke program.

- Capture and playback are suspended if you choose DOS
  Commands from the DisplayWrite 4 menu and resume
  when you return to DisplayWrite 4.

The Second Step: Saving the Keystroke Program on Disk

If all DisplayWrite 4 could do was create a keystroke program and keep it in memory, it would hardly be worth your time to create one. First, you can keep only one program in memory at a time, and second, as soon as you shut off your computer, your carefully constructed keystroke program would be gone forever. This section will show you how to save your keystroke program and how to play it back by pressing a programmable function key (SHIFT or ALT plus one of your regular function keys F1 through F12).

To save a keystroke program on disk, first capture the keystrokes as described in the previous section. Make any necessary revisions. Then

press CTRL-F1 and choose Save.

You will be prompted for the keystroke program name.

For the keystroke program name, press either the ALT or the SHIFT key simultaneously with one of the function keys F1 through F12. For example,

press SHIFT-F1.

Your keystroke program will be saved and you will see a message like

> Saved keystrokes are stored in "C:\DW4\SF01.KEY."

This means that your keystroke program is saved on your hard disk in the \dw4 directory in a file called SF01.KEY. On a floppy-disk system, your keystroke program is saved in the default drive where your data files are.

Table 21-2 lists the names your files will be saved under. Notice that the third column of the table is blank so you can jot down a description of your own keystroke programs. The combination of SHIFT or ALT with the 12 function keys lets you define 24 programmable function keys. (If you only have 10 function keys, you can define only 20 programmable function keys.)

If you don't want to save your keystroke program under a function key name, you can respond to the Keystroke Program Name prompt by typing in any file name you want to. Pick a name that reminds you of what is in the keystroke

Key	Name of File Containing Keystrokes	Description of Keystroke Program
SHIFT-F1	SF01.KEY	
SHIFT-F2	SF02.KEY	
SHIFT-F3	SF03.KEY	
SHIFT-F4	SF04.KEY	
SHIFT-F5	SF05.KEY	
SHIFT-F6	SF06.KEY	
SHIFT-F7	SF07.KEY	
SHIFT-F8	SF08.KEY	
SHIFT-F9	SF09.KEY	
SHIFT-F10	SF10.KEY	
SHIFT-F11	SF11.KEY	
SHIFT-F12	SF12.KEY	
ALT-F1	AF01.KEY	
ALT-F2	AF02.KEY	
ALT-F3	AF03.KEY	
ALT-F4	AF04.KEY	
ALT-F5	AF05.KEY	
ALT-F6	AF06.KEY	
ALT-F7	AF07.KEY	
ALT-F8	AF08.KEY	
ALT-F9	AF09.KEY	
ALT-F10	AF10.KEY	
ALT-F11	AF11.KEY	
ALT-F12	AF12.KEY	

Table 21-2.   How Your Keystroke Programs Are Saved on Disk

program. However, if you name your keystroke program with a file name, you will not be able to recall the keystrokes simply by pressing a programmable function key. (See the next section for a description of how to recall keystrokes stored this way.) DisplayWrite 4 will provide the default extension .KEY if you don't specify any other.

If you do save your keystroke program with a file name (as opposed to a function key), you can also add a Keystroke Program Comment of up to 44 characters to help remind you of what is in the program. You will see the comment when you press F3 to list your files and choose Comments with Directory. After you have typed in the name and the optional comment,

press ENTER to save the program

Keystroke programs are saved in the directory specified in the Profiles menu. For hard-disk users, the default is the \dw4 directory. For floppy-disk users, it is the default drive. If you want the program saved elsewhere, you can specify the drive and path as part of the name. For example, if you have a floppy-disk system and want the keystroke program saved on your program disk in drive A rather than on your data disk in drive B, type **a:** before the name. (Make sure you have room on your program disk before doing this.)

Using the Saved Keystroke Program

Using your saved keystroke program is the reward for all your previous labor.

Playing Back a Keystroke Program Saved Under a Function Key Name

To use a keystroke program saved under a function key name, you simply press the appropriate programmed function key (SHIFT-F1 through -F12 or ALT-F1 through -F12), and all your keystrokes are played back.

If you inserted a pause, the system will pause for you to type in variable information. After you type the information,

press CTRL-F1 and choose Auto Playback.

The remaining keystrokes will be played back.

Playing Back a Keystroke Program
Saved Under a File Name

If you saved your keystroke program under a file name, the playback process involves a few more steps. To play back a keystroke program saved under a file name,

press CTRL-F1 and choose Recall.

Then type the name of the keystroke program and

press ENTER.

You will see the message

> Saved keystrokes recalled from "C:\DW4\FILE.KEY.

Press CTRL-F1 and choose Auto Playback.

Revising a Saved Keystroke Program

To revise a saved keystroke program, you must first load it into the computer's memory.

Press CTRL-F1 and choose Recall.

Then, in response to the prompt, press the appropriate programmed function key (SHIFT-F1 through -F12 or ALT-F1 through -F12), or type the file name of the program and press ENTER.

After you see the message

```
> Saved keystrokes recalled from "C:\DW4\FILE.KEY.
```

press CTRL-F1 and choose Playback Singly.

Revise your keystroke program, adding or deleting keystrokes as necessary. When revisions are complete,

press CTRL-F1 and choose End Play.

Then, to replace the original program with the revised program,

press CTRL-F1 and choose Save.

When prompted for the file name, press SHIFT or ALT together with the appropriate function key, or type the file name and press ENTER. For example, if your program was previously saved under SHIFT-F1, press SHIFT-F1.

You will be told that the file already exists. At this point, press ENTER to replace the old keystroke program with the revised program, or press ESC to abandon the revisions.

Deleting a Keystroke Program

You can delete the keystroke program the way you would delete any other file. You can also delete the program by replacing it with another keystroke program as just described.

Changing the Default Directory
for Saving and Recalling Keystrokes

DisplayWrite 4 lets you choose the directory your keystroke programs will be stored in. To make the selection, choose Profiles from the DisplayWrite 4 menu (see Chapter 15 for complete information on profile tasks). Choose Revise Profile and enter the name of the profile you want to revise. Then

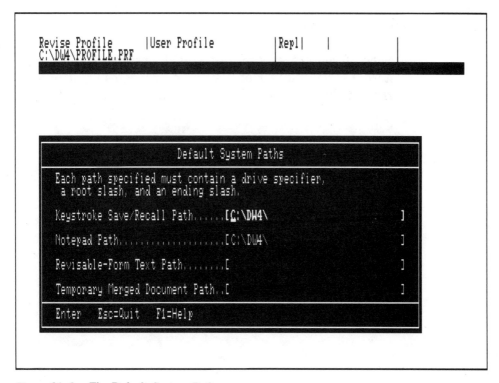

Figure 21-3. The Default System Paths menu

choose System Paths. You will see the Default System Paths menu shown in Figure 21-3.

Type the drive and path identifying the directory you wish to use for storing your keystroke programs. (Paths are also explained in Appendix C.) If you leave this item blank (by pressing ALT-8), keystroke programs will be stored in the current directory.

Press ESC and choose End and Save

from the End Save menu. You will be returned to the Profiles menu, and your keystroke programs will have been saved in the directory you specified.

Note: If you are using a floppy-disk system, do not try to store a large number of keystroke programs on your program disks; there simply isn't room.

22

Keyboard
Changes

This chapter shows how you can invoke special keyboard extensions to use symbols and characters that are not engraved on your keyboard. It also shows you how to design your own keyboard extensions so that nonengraved characters that you use frequently are readily accessible.

What Keyboard Extensions Are

DisplayWrite 4 lets you see on your screen and print on your printer many more characters than are engraved on your physical keyboard. There are characters and symbols for scientific and technical work, for writing in foreign languages, and for special business purposes.

DisplayWrite 4 provides four *keyboard extensions* that contain these characters and symbols. You can use characters and symbols from *any* of these extensions in the typing area at any time. In addition, you can revise these keyboard extensions to include different characters and symbols, if the ones currently included are not satisfactory for your work.

Figure 22-1 shows the four keyboard extensions. You do not have to purchase anything extra to use these keyboard extensions (unless you need a different print element for your printer). They are all part of your DisplayWrite 4 program.

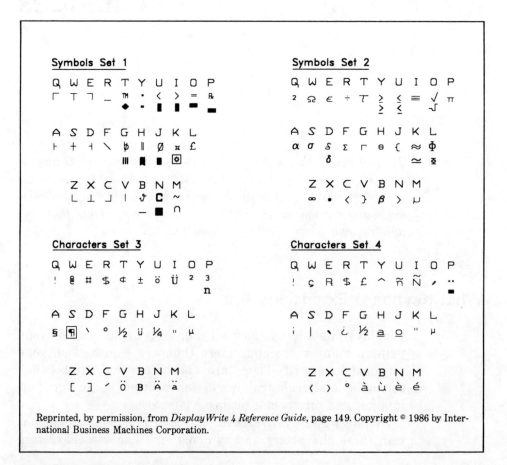

Reprinted, by permission, from *DisplayWrite 4 Reference Guide*, page 149. Copyright © 1986 by International Business Machines Corporation.

Figure 22-1.   The four keyboard extensions

In the figure, the first line of characters in each set shows the characters on your keyboard; the second line shows the EBCDIC characters; the third line shows the ASCII characters *if they are different from the EBCDIC characters*. Any symbol enclosed in a box will print as an underscore on an IBM Proprinter.

Printing Keyboard Extension Characters

If you have a dot matrix printer, you simply print your file in the usual way, and the keyboard extension characters will be printed out. The following is an example of dot matrix output that contains keyboard extension characters.

100+2 ≥ π√8

However, if your printer uses a print element such as a daisy wheel, thimble, or cartridge, the print element obviously must have the characters you want. Some printers will prompt you to change the print element when necessary.

The sections that follow show you how to select the characters that you will print.

EBCDIC or ASCII?

In Chapter 12 you learned that DisplayWrite 4 stores information in a form called EBCDIC. Information is displayed on your PC screen in a form called ASCII if you are in Character mode and in EBCDIC if you are in APA mode. Sometimes the EBCDIC version of a keyboard extension character is different from the ASCII version.

What will you get when you print? That depends on your printer. The 5152-2 Graphics and the 3852 Model 2 Color Jetprinter will print the ASCII version. The 5216 Wheelprinter (with appropriate wheel), 5223 Wheelprinter E (with appropriate wheel), 5219 FFTDCA, and 5140 PC Convertible

System printer print the EBCDIC version. The 4201 Pro-printer XL can print in both ASCII and EBCDIC. The 3812 Pageprinter can also print either EBCDIC or ASCII, depending on how you program it, and the Quietwriters can also print either, depending on the cartridge installed.

Using a Character from the Active Keyboard Extension

A keyboard extension must be *active* before you can use it. The default active keyboard extension is Symbols Set 1. To use a character from Symbols Set 1, in the typing area, place the cursor where you want the character to appear. Then you simply hold down the ALT key and type the characters you want. (Use Figure 22-1 for reference.)

For example, let's say you have an EBCDIC printer and want to use the trademark symbol in your file. You type text in the usual way until you come to the point where you want to insert the symbol. You can see from Figure 22-1 that the trademark symbol is on the T key. Therefore, you simply press ALT and type T simultaneously and you will see the trademark symbol on your screen. (ASCII displays will show a diamond.)

The top status line will read "Keyboard Change" because the cursor is under a Keyboard Change code. If you set Display All Codes to Yes, you will see that Keyboard Change codes have been inserted before and after the trademark symbol.

Using Another Keyboard Extension

If you want to use another of the three extensions, you must first make it the active extension.

To do this, in the typing area,

press CTRL-F5.

Then, in the Edit Options menu, set the keyboard extension to the extension you want as the active extension.

Press ENTER.

The keyboard extension you chose is now the active extension. It will remain active until you exit from DisplayWrite 4, *even if you save the file you are working on and edit a different file.*

For example, let's say you want to use a character from Symbols Set 2. You press CTRL-F5 to display the Edit Options menu, tab to Keyboard Extension, type 2 (to choose Symbols Set 2), and press ENTER. Now you can proceed exactly as you did previously, except that you will be using characters from Symbols Set 2 instead of from Symbols Set 1: In the typing area, position the cursor where you want to use the symbol.

```
《....2....._....3....._....4.....∆....▯.....6....._....7.....》....8....■....9....
         The area of a circle is _
```

Then press ALT and type the character or characters. You will see the extension character from Symbols Set 2.

```
《....2....._....3....._....4.....∆....▯.....6....._....7.....》....8....■....9....
         The area of a circle is π▪
```

Note: If you find you most often use characters from a keyboard extension other than Symbols Set 1, you can make one of the other extensions your default active keyboard extension. You do this through the Profiles menu. (When you revise the profile, choose Work Station and then choose Keyboard/Mouse Options.)

Designing Your Own Keyboard Extension

If the four keyboard extensions do not contain the characters or symbols you need, you can revise them. When you revise a keyboard extension, you replace a character or symbol that you don't use with a character that you do. You can use any of the symbols in Table 22-1 or any of the characters in Table 22-2. Remember that your printer must be able to print the character or symbol you choose. You revise keyboard extensions through the Profiles menu.

To revise a keyboard extension, choose Revise Profile from the Profiles menu and enter the name of the profile you want to revise. Choose Work Station and then choose Revise Keyboard Extensions. You will see the Revise Keyboard Extensions menu.

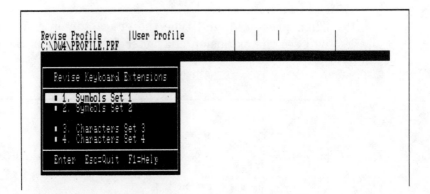

Symbols Set Chart

Keyboard Extension Choices	EBCDIC Graphic Character Names	EBCDIC		ASCII	
		Char	Hex	Char	Hex
1	Space		40		20
2	Required Space		41		20
3	Equal Sign Superscript	=	42	—	5F
4	Minus Sign Superscript	–	43	—	5F
5	Plus Sign Superscript	+	44	—	5F
6	Infinity Symbol Superscript	∞	45	—	5F
7	Pi Superscript	π	46	—	5F
8	Delta Superscript	Δ	47	—	5F
9	Right Arrow Superscript	→	48	—	5F
10	Slash Superscript	/	49	—	5F
11	Left Bracket	[	4A	[	5B
12	Dagger	†	4B	—	5F
13	Less Than Sign	<	4C	<	3C
14	Left Parenthesis	(	4D	(	28
15	Copyright Symbol	©	4E	⌐	A9
16	Radical	√	4F	√	FB
17	Less Than or Equal Sign	≤	50	≤	F3
18	Macron Accent	–	51	—	5F
19	Left Angle Bracket Superscript	‹	52	▮	DE
20	Right Angle Bracket Superscript	›	53	▮	DD
21	Prescription Symbol	℞	54	▬	DC
22	"Is Not an Element of" Symbol	∉	55	—	5F
23	"Therefore" Symbol	∴	56	—	5F
24	Increase	↗	57	—	5F
25	Decrease	↘	58	—	5F
26	Double Dagger	‡	59	—	5F
27	Right Bracket	]	5A	]	5D
28	Middle Dot, Product Dot	•	5B	•	F9
29	Not Equal Sign	≠	5C	¬	AA
30	Right Parenthesis	)	5D	)	29

Reprinted, by permission, from *DisplayWrite 4 Technical Reference*, pages 26-32. Copyright © 1986 by International Business Machines Corporation.

Table 22-1. The Symbols Set Chart

Symbols Set Chart

Keyboard Extension Choices	EBCDIC Graphic Character Names	EBCDIC Char	EBCDIC Hex	ASCII Char	ASCII Hex
31	Diaresis Accent	¨	5E	■	FE
32	Circumflex Accent	^	5F	^	5E
33	Minus Sign, Hyphen	-	60	-	2D
34	Greater Than or Equal Sign	≥	61	≥	F2
35	Or Symbol	∨	62	—	5F
36	And Symbol	∧	63	—	5F
37	Parallel Symbol	‖	64	▒	B1
38	Angle Symbol	∠	65	—	5F
39	Left Angle Bracket	〈	66	—	5F
40	Right Angle Bracket	〉	67	—	5F
41	Minus or Plus Sign	∓	68	—	5F
42	Lozenge	¤	69	—	5F
43	Minute Symbol	′	6A	'	27
44	Female Symbol	♀	6B	♀	0C
45	Male Symbol	♂	6C	♂	0B
46	Underscore	_	6D	—	5F
47	Greater Than Sign	>	6E	>	3E
48	Integral Symbol	∫	6F	—	5F
49	Intersection, Logical Product	∩	70	∩	EF
50	Union, Logical Sum	∪	71	—	5F
51	"Is Included In" Symbol	⊂	72	—	5F
52	"Includes" Symbol	⊃	73	—	5F
53	Circle Plus, Closed Sum	⊕	74	—	5F
54	Right Angle Symbol	∟	75	∟	1C
55	(Unassignable)		76		5F
56	Circle x, Closed Product	⊗	77	—	5F
57	Breve Accent	˘	78	—	5F
58	Grave Accent	`	79	`	60
59	Divide Sign	÷	7A	÷	F6
60	Plus or Minus Sign	±	7B	±	F1

Table 22-1. The Symbols Set Chart (*continued*)

Symbols Set Chart

Keyboard Extension Choices	EBCDIC Graphic Character Names	EBCDIC		ASCII	
		Char	Hex	Char	Hex
61	Degree Symbol	o	7C	o	F8
62	Acute Accent	´	7D	ˏ	27
63	Seconds Symbol	″	7E	''	22
64	Registered Trademark Symbol	®	7F	•	FA
65	Double Overline	=	80	▪	DF
66	Alpha Small	α	81	α	E0
67	Beta Small	β	82	β	E1
68	Psi Small	ψ	83	—	5F
69	Phi Small	ø	84	ø	ED
70	Epsilon Small	ε	85	ε	EE
71	Pi Small	π	86	π	E3
72	Lambda Small	λ	87	—	5F
73	Eta Small	η	88	—	5F
74	Iota Small	ι	89	—	5F
75	Upper Left Box Corner	⌐	8A	⌐	DA
76	Left Middle Box Side	⊢	8B	⊢	C3
77	Lower Left Box Corner	L	8C	L	C0
78	Center Box Bar Vertical			8D			B3
79	Upper Left Parenthesis Section	⌠	8E	—	5F
80	Lower Left Parenthesis Section	⌡	8F	—	5F
81	Permille Symbol	‰	90	—	5F
82	Theta Small (Open Form)	ϑ	91	—	5F
83	Kappa Small	κ	92	—	5F
84	Omega Small	ω	93	—	5F
85	Mu Small	μ	94	μ	E6
86	Nu Small	ν	95	—	5F
87	Omicron Small	o	96	—	5F
88	Rho Small	ρ	97	—	5F
89	Gamma Small	γ	98	—	5F
90	Theta Small	θ	99	—	5F

Table 22-1. The Symbols Set Chart (*continued*)

Symbols Set Chart

Keyboard Extension Choices	EBCDIC Graphic Character Names	EBCDIC Char	EBCDIC Hex	ASCII Char	ASCII Hex
91	Middle Box Top	⊤	9A	⊤	C2
92	Box Cross, Box Corner	+	9B	+	C5
93	Middle Box Bottom	⊥	9C	⊥	C1
94	Trademark Symbol	™	9D	◆	04
95	Upper Right Parenthesis Section	⎞	9E	—	5F
96	Lower Right Parenthesis Section	⎠	9F	—	5F
97	"Congruent To" Symbol	≅	A0	≈	F7
98	Tilde Accent	~	A1	~	7E
99	Sigma Small	σ	A2	σ	E5
100	Tau Small	τ	A3	τ	E7
101	Xi Small	ξ	A4	—	5F
102	Multiply Sign	×	A5	—	5F
103	Delta Small	δ	A6	δ	EB
104	Chi Small	χ	A7	—	5F
105	Upsilon Small	υ	A8	—	5F
106	Zeta Small	ζ	A9	—	5F
107	Upper Right Box Corner	⎤	AA	⎤	BF
108	Right Middle Box Side	⊣	AB	⊣	B4
109	Lower Right Box Corner	⎦	AC	⎦	D9
110	Center Box Bar Horizontal	—	AD	—	C4
111	Lower Right/Upper Left Brace Section	⌠	AE	—	5F
112	Upper Right/Lower Left Brace Section	⌡	AF	—	5F
113	Zero Subscript	₀	B0	—	5F
114	One Subscript	₁	B1	—	5F
115	Two Subscript	₂	B2	—	5F
116	Three Subscript	₃	B3	—	5F
117	Four Subscript	₄	B4	—	5F
118	Five Subscript	₅	B5	—	5F
119	Six Subscript	₆	B6	—	5F
120	Seven Subscript	₇	B7	—	5F

Reprinted, by permission, from *DisplayWrite 4 Technical Reference*, pages 26-32. Copyright © 1986 by International Business Machines Corporation.

Table 22-1. The Symbols Set Chart (*continued*)

Symbols Set Chart

Keyboard Extension Choices	EBCDIC Graphic Character Names	EBCDIC		ASCII	
		Char	Hex	Char	Hex
121	Eight Subscript	₈	B8	—	5F
122	Nine Subscript	₉	B9	—	5F
123	Perpendicular Symbol	⊥	BA	—	5F
124	Total Symbol	◊	BB	—	5F
125	Large Bullet, Closed Circle	●	BC	●	FA
126	Pound Sign	£	BD	£	9C
127	International Currency Symbol	¤	BE	¤	0F
128	Yen Sign	¥	BF	¥	9D
129	Left Brace	{	C0	{	7B
130	Del, Delt, Nabla	∇	C1	—	5F
131	Infinity Symbol	∞	C2	∞	EC
132	Psi Capital	Ψ	C3	—	5F
133	Phi Capital	Φ	C4	Φ	E8
134	Left Arrow	←	C5	←	1B
135	Pi Capital	Π	C6	—	5F
136	Lambda Capital	Λ	C7	—	5F
137	Paragraph Symbol (USA)	¶	C8	¶	14
138	Up Arrow	↑	C9	↑	18
139	Syllable Hyphen	–	CA	–	2D
140	Solid Diamond	♦	CB	♦	04
141	Caron Accent	ˇ	CC	—	5F
142	Bottle Symbol	♦	CD	—	5F
143	Vertical Line Unbroken	|	CE	|	B3
144	Substitute Blank	♭	CF	‖‖	B0
145	Right Brace	}	D0	}	7D
146	Double Underscore	=	D1	—	5F
147	Section Symbol (USA)	§	D2	§	15
148	Omega Capital	Ω	D3	Ω	EA
149	Partial Differential Symbol	∂	D4	—	5F
150	Sine Symbol	∿	D5	∿	7E

Reprinted, by permission, from *DisplayWrite 4 Technical Reference*, pages 26-32. Copyright © 1986 by International Business Machines Corporation.

Table 22-1. The Symbols Set Chart (*continued*)

Symbols Set Chart

Keyboard Extension Choices	EBCDIC Graphic Character Names	EBCDIC		ASCII	
		Char	Hex	Char	Hex
151	Down Arrow	↓	D6	↓	19
152	Liter Symbol	λ	D7		5F
153	Gamma Capital	Γ	D8	Γ	E2
154	Theta Capital	Θ	D9	Θ	E9
155	Open Square	□	DA	■	DB
156	Solid Square, Histogram	■	DB	■	FE
157	Slash Square (Cancelled) Square	Ø	DC	/	2F
158	Overline	—	DD	—	5F
159	Upper Summation Section	Γ	DE	—	5F
160	Lower Summation Section	L	DF	—	5F
161	Backslash	\	E0	\	5C
162	Numeric Space		E1		20
163	Sigma Capital	Σ	E2	Σ	E4
164	Right Arrow	→	E3	→	1A
165	Xi Capital	Ξ	E4	—	5F
166	"Proportional To" Symbol	α	E5	—	5F
167	Delta Capital	Δ	E6	Δ	7F
168	Identity Symbol	≡	E7	≡	F0
169	Upsilon Capital	Υ	E8	—	5F
170	"Approximately Equal To" Symbol	≅	E9	≈	F7
171	"Equivalent To" Symbol, Cycle Symbol	~	EA	∩	EF
172	Logical Not	¬	EB	¬	AA
173	Arrow Indicator	►	EC	—	5F
174	Solid Triangle	▲	ED	—	5F
175	Upper Integral Section	⌠	EE	⌠	F4
176	Lower Integral Section	⌡	EF	⌡	F5
177	Zero Superscript	^{0}	F0	—	5F
178	One Superscript	^{1}	F1	—	5F
179	Two Superscript	^{2}	F2	^{2}	FD
180	Three Superscript	^{3}	F3	^{n}	FC

Reprinted, by permission, from *DisplayWrite 4 Technical Reference*, pages 26-32. Copyright © 1986 by International Business Machines Corporation.

Table 22-1.   The Symbols Set Chart (*continued*)

Symbols Set Chart

Keyboard Extension Choices	EBCDIC Graphic Character Names	EBCDIC		ASCII	
		Char	Hex	Char	Hex
181	Four Superscript	4	F4	—	5F
182	Five Superscript	5	F5	—	5F
183	Six Superscript	6	F6	—	5F
184	Seven Superscript	7	F7	—	5F
185	Eight Superscript	8	F8	—	5F
186	Nine Superscript	9	F9	—	5F
187	Zero Slash	Ø	FA	▓	B2
188	One Eighth	1/8	FB	—	5F
189	Three Eighths	3/8	FC	—	5F
190	Five Eighths	5/8	FD	—	5F
191	Seven Eighths	7/8	FE	—	5F

Table 22-1.   The Symbols Set Chart (*continued*)

Characters Set Chart

Keyboard Extension Choices	EBCDIC Graphic Character Names	EBCDIC Char	EBCDIC Hex	ASCII Char	ASCII Hex
1	Space		40		20
2	Required Space	–	41	–	20
3	a Circumflex Small	â	42	â	83
4	a Diaeresis Small	ä	43	ä	84
5	a Grave Small	à	44	à	85
6	a Acute Small	á	45	á	AO
7	a Tilde Small	ã	46	–	5F
8	a Overcircle Small	å	47	å	86
9	c Cedilla Small	ç	48	ç	87
10	n Tilde Small	ñ	49	ñ	A4
11	Left Bracket	[	4A	[	5B
12	Period	.	4B	.	2E
13	Less Than Sign	<	4C	<	3C
14	Left Parenthesis	(	4D	(	28
15	Plus Sign	+	4E	+	2B
16	Exclamation Point	!	4F	!	21
17	Ampersand	&	50	&	26
18	e Acute Small	é	51	é	82
19	e Circumflex Small	ê	52	ê	88
20	e Diaeresis Small	ë	53	ë	89
21	e Grave Small	è	54	è	8A
22	i Acute Small	í	55	í	A1
23	i Circumflex Small	î	56	î	8C
24	i Diaeresis Small	ï	57	ï	8B
25	i Grave Small	ì	58	ì	8D
26	Sharp s Small	β	59	β	E1
27	Right Bracket	]	5A	]	5D
28	Dollar Sign	$	5B	$	24
29	Asterisk	*	5C	*	2A
30	Right Parenthesis	)	5D	)	29

Table 22-2.   The Characters Set Chart

Characters Set Chart

Keyboard Extension Choices	EBCDIC Graphic Character Names	EBCDIC		ASCII	
		Char	Hex	Char	Hex
31	Semicolon	;	5E	;	3B
32	Circumflex Accent	^	5F	^	5E
33	Minus Sign, Hyphen	–	60	–	2D
34	Slash	/	61	/	2F
35	A Circumflex Capital	Â	62	–	5F
36	A Diaeresis Capital	Ä	63	Ä	8E
37	A Grave Capital	À	64	–	5F
38	A Acute Capital	Á	65	–	5F
39	A Tilde Capital	Ã	66	–	5F
40	A Overcircle Capital	Å	67	Å	8F
41	C Cedilla Capital	Ç	68	Ç	80
42	N Tilde Capital	Ñ	69	Ñ	A5
43	Vertical Line Broken	¦	6A	¦	7C
44	Comma	,	6B	,	2C
45	Percent Sign	%	6C	%	25
46	Underline, Continuous Underscore	–	6D	–	5F
47	Greater Than Sign	>	6E	>	3E
48	Question Mark	?	6F	?	3F
49	o Slash Small	ø	70	o	6F
50	E Acute Capital	É	71	É	90
51	E Circumflex Capital	Ê	72	–	5F
52	E Diaeresis Capital	Ë	73	–	5F
53	E Grave Capital	È	74	–	5F
54	I Acute Capital	Í	75	–	5F
55	I Circumflex Capital	Î	76	–	5F
56	I Diaeresis Capital	Ï	77	–	5F
57	I Grave Capital	Ì	78	–	5F
58	Grave Accent	`	79	`	60
59	Colon	:	7A	:	3A
60	Number Sign	#	7B	#	23

Reprinted, by permission, from *DisplayWrite 4 Technical Reference*, pages 19-25. Copyright © 1986 by International Business Machines Corporation.

Table 22-2. The Characters Set Chart (*continued*)

Characters Set Chart

Keyboard Extension Choices	EBCDIC Graphic Character Names	EBCDIC		ASCII	
		Char	Hex	Char	Hex
61	At Sign	@	7C	@	40
62	Apostrophe	'	7D	'	27
63	Equal Sign	=	7E	=	3D
64	Quotation Marks	''	7F	''	22
65	O Slash Capital	Ø	80	Ó	4F
66	a Small	a	81	a	61
67	b Small	b	82	b	62
68	c Small	c	83	c	63
69	d Small	d	84	d	64
70	e Small	e	85	e	65
71	f Small	f	86	f	66
72	g Small	g	87	g	67
73	h Small	h	88	h	68
74	i Small	i	89	i	69
75	Left Angle Quotes	«	8A	«	AE
76	Right Angle Quotes	»	8B	»	AF
77	eth Icelandic Small	ð	8C	—	5F
78	y Acute Small	ý	8D	—	5F
79	Thorn Icelandic Small	þ	8E	—	5F
80	Plus or Minus Sign	±	8F	±	F1
81	Degree Symbol	°	90	°	F8
82	j Small	j	91	j	6A
83	k Small	k	92	k	6B
84	l Small	l	93	l	6C
85	m Small	m	94	m	6D
86	n Small	n	95	n	6E
87	o Small	o	96	o	6F
88	p Small	p	97	p	70
89	q Small	q	98	q	71
90	r Small	r	99	r	72

Table 22-2.   The Characters Set Chart (*continued*)

Characters Set Chart

Keyboard Extension Choices	EBCDIC Graphic Character Names	EBCDIC		ASCII	
		Char	Hex	Char	Hex
91	a Underline Small (Ordinal Indicator, Female)	a	9A	a	A6
92	o Underline Small (Ordinal Indicator, Male)	o	9B	o	A7
93	ae Diphthong Small	æ	9C	æ	91
94	Cedilla Accent	˛	9D	▪	FE
95	AE Diphthong Capital	Æ	9E	Æ	92
96	International Currency Symbol	¤	9F	¤	0F
97	Micro Symbol, Mu	μ	A0	μ	E6
98	Tilde Accent	~	A1	~	7E
99	s Small	s	A2	s	73
100	t Small	t	A3	t	74
101	u Small	u	A4	u	75
102	v Small	v	A5	v	76
103	w Small	w	A6	w	77
104	x Small	x	A7	x	78
105	y Small	y	A8	y	79
106	z Small	z	A9	z	7A
107	Exclamation Point Inverted	¡	AA	¡	AD
108	Question Mark Inverted	¿	AB	¿	A8
109	Eth Icelandic Capital	Ð	AC	–	5F
110	Y Acute Capital	Ý	AD	–	5F
111	Thorn Icelandic Capital	Þ	AE	–	5F
112	Registered Trademark	®	AF	•	FA
113	Cent Sign	¢	B0	¢	9B
114	Pound Sign	£	B1	£	9C
115	Yen Sign	¥	B2	¥	9D
116	Peseta Sign	Pt	B3	Pt	9E
117	Florin Sign	f	B4	f	9F
118	Section Symbol (USA)	§	B5	§	15
119	Paragraph Symbol (USA)	¶	B6	¶	14
120	One Quarter	¼	B7	¼	AC

Table 22-2. The Characters Set Chart (*continued*)

Characters Set Chart

Keyboard Extension Choices	EBCDIC Graphic Character Names	EBCDIC		ASCII	
		Char	Hex	Char	Hex
121	One Half	½	B8	½	AB
122	Three Quarters	¾	B9	■	FE
123	Logical Not, "End of Line" Symbol	¬	BA	¬	AA
124	Logical Or, Vertical Line Unbroken	|	BB	|	B3
125	Macron Accent, Overline	–	BC	–	5F
126	Diaeresis Accent	..	BD	■	FE
127	Acute Accent	´	BE	´	27
128	Double Underscore	=	BF	–	5F
129	Left Brace	{	C0	{	7B
130	A Capital	A	C1	A	41
131	B Capital	B	C2	B	42
132	C Capital	C	C3	C	43
133	D Capital	D	C4	D	44
134	E Capital	E	C5	E	45
135	F Capital	F	C6	F	46
136	G Capital	G	C7	G	47
137	H Capital	H	C8	H	48
138	I Capital	I	C9	I	49
139	Syllable Hyphen	–̂	CA	–̂	2D
140	o Circumflex Small	ô	CB	ô	93
141	o Diaeresis Small	ö	CC	ö	94
142	o Grave Small	ò	CD	ò	95
143	o Acute Small	ó	CE	ó	A2
144	o Tilde Small	õ	CF	–	5F
145	Right Brace	}	D0	}	7D
146	J Capital	J	D1	J	4A
147	K Capital	K	D2	K	4B
148	L Capital	L	D3	L	4C
149	M Capital	M	D4	M	4D
150	N Capital	N	D5	N	4E

Table 22-2. The Characters Set Chart (*continued*)

Characters Set Chart

Keyboard Extension Choices	EBCDIC Graphic Character Names	EBCDIC Char	EBCDIC Hex	ASCII Char	ASCII Hex
151	O Capital	O	D6	O	4F
152	P Capital	P	D7	P	50
153	Q Capital	Q	D8	Q	51
154	R Capital	R	D9	R	52
155	i Dotless Small	ı	DA	—	5F
156	u Circumflex Small	û	DB	û	96
157	u Diaeresis Small	ü	DC	ü	81
158	u Grave Small	ù	DD	ù	97
159	u Acute Small	ú	DE	ú	A3
160	y Diaeresis Small	ÿ	DF	ÿ	98
161	Reverse Slash	\	E0	\	5C
162	Numeric Space		E1		20
163	S Capital	S	E2	S	53
164	T Capital	T	E3	T	54
165	U Capital	U	E4	U	55
166	V Capital	V	E5	V	56
167	W Capital	W	E6	W	57
168	X Capital	X	E7	X	58
169	Y Capital	Y	E8	Y	59
170	Z Capital	Z	E9	Z	5A
171	Two Superscript	²	EA	²	FD
172	O Circumflex Capital	Ô	EB	¨	5F
173	O Diaeresis Capital	Ö	EC	Ö	99
174	O Grave Capital	Ò	ED	—	5F
175	O Acute Capital	Ó	EE	—	5F
176	O Tilde Capital	Õ	EF	—	5F
177	Zero	0	F0	Ō	30
178	One	1	F1	1	31
179	Two	2	F2	2	32
180	Three	3	F3	3	33

Reprinted, by permission, from *DisplayWrite 4 Technical Reference*, pages 19-25. Copyright © 1986 by International Business Machines Corporation.

Table 22-2. The Characters Set Chart (*continued*)

Characters Set Chart

Keyboard Extension Choices	EBCDIC Graphic Character Names	EBCDIC		ASCII	
		Char	Hex	Char	Hex
181	Four	4	F4	4	34
182	Five	5	F5	5	35
183	Six	6	F6	6	36
184	Seven	7	F7	7	37
185	Eight	8	F8	8	38
186	Nine	9	F9	9	39
187	Three Superscript	³	FA	ⁿ	FC
188	U Circumflex Capital	Û	FB		5F
189	U Diaeresis Capital	Ü	FC	Ü	9A
190	U Grave Capital	Ù	FD	—	5F
191	U Acute Capital	Ú	FE	—	5F

Table 22-2.   The Characters Set Chart (*continued*)

Select the extension you want to revise. Now you are ready to make revisions.

Let's say that you want to replace the Left Middle Box Side symbol (ALT-A) of Symbols Set 1 with the Two Superscript symbol. Choose Symbols Set 1 from the Revise Keyboard Extensions menu. You will see the first page of the Revise Symbols screen in Figure 22-2 (the second page gives you the rest of the alphabet). Then look through Table 22-1, the Symbols Set Chart, until you find the Two Superscript symbol. You see from the chart that the Keyboard Extension Choice for the Two Superscript symbol is 179.

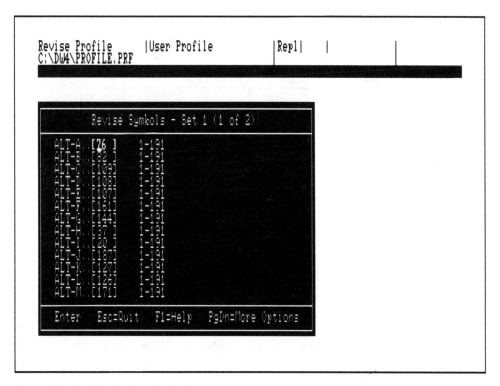

Figure 22-2. The Revise Symbols screen

Now, on the Revise Symbols menu,

Type **179** for ALT-A.

This will replace the current Keyboard Extension Choice for ALT-A. Do this for every symbol in Symbols Set 1 that you want to change. Use Figure 22-3 to keep a record of your choices.

When you are finished,

press ENTER

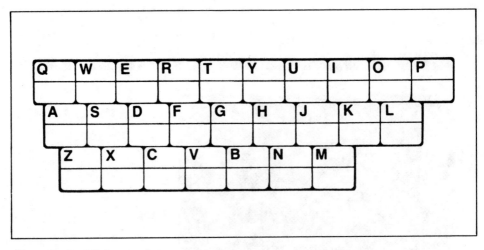

Figure 22-3. Mark your choices on this figure

to return to the Revise Keyboard Extensions menu. Then press ESC until you see the End/Save menu.

Choose End and Save

to save your revisions. You will be returned to the Profiles menu.

Typing a Character with an Accent Over It

Look at Characters Set 4 in Figure 22-1. Notice that some of the characters, such as ALT-U and ALT-I, have symbols over them. To display and print such a character, you just type the keyboard extension character in the usual way.

However, there is also a character, ALT-D, that is simply an accent mark. For this accent mark to be useful, you must be able to type two characters in the same cursor location—the accent mark and the character itself.

Note: You can also overstrike with an ordinary apostrophe to create an accent.

To type the accent mark over a character, first make Characters Set 3 the active extension. Next,

press ALT-D. Then press CTRL-BACKSPACE (the Required Backspace key).

Then type the character. You cannot see both the accent mark and the character in the same cursor location on your screen. However, if you set Display All Codes to Yes, you will see the accent to the left of the Required Backspace code and the character to the right of the code. When you print your file, the accent will print above the character.

Table 22-3 shows the keys used for keyboard changes.

Key	Function
ALT	When pressed simultaneously with a keyboard character (A-Z), lets you use a character from the active keyboard extension
CTRL-BACKSPACE	Puts a Required Backspace code into your file. Used when you want a character to print with an accent mark over it
CTRL-F5	The Keyboard Change item lets you change the active keyboard extension

Table 22-3.   Keys Used in Keyboard Extensions

PRODUCING REPETITIVE DOCUMENTS

23

Using Get
and Merge for
Form Letters

*This chapter describes repetitive documents and the methods
of producing them in DisplayWrite 4. It will teach you how to
use the Get function with Stop codes to produce a few copies
and the Merge function to produce many copies.*

What Repetitive Documents Are

A repetitive document is a document such as a form letter, in
which most of the text does not change from one copy to
another, but some of the text—like names and addresses—is
different in each copy.

DisplayWrite 4 provides you with many methods of producing repetitive documents, all of which spare you the
tedium of retyping each document from scratch. The method
you choose depends on how many copies of a given document
you need and how complex the document is.

The simplest method is to type the form letter once and then use the DisplayWrite 4 Copy utility or the DOS COPY command to copy the file. You then simply type the new name and address over the old and change any other information that needs to be changed. This method is perfectly suitable if you have to produce only two or three copies of your document.

The Shell Document and Variable Information

If you need to produce more than two or three copies of your document, DisplayWrite 4 has more powerful methods. These other methods involve producing a file containing all the text that does not change. This file is called the *shell document*. In the shell document, you reserve places for the *variable information*. This is the information that changes from document to document. Figure 23-1 shows you two copies of the same shell document, each containing different variable information.

How DisplayWrite 4 Produces
Repetitive Documents

If you have only a small number of copies to produce, you can store the shell document on disk, reserving places for the variable information with Stop codes. You then use the Get function to retrieve the shell for each repetitive document. After retrieving the shell, you type in the variable information.

Another method, suitable for producing larger quantities of documents, is to store the shell document in one file and all the variable information in another file, called a *variables document* or *fill-in*. Then you use the DisplayWrite 4 Merge with Named Variables feature to combine the information in the shell with the information in the fill-in. These two methods are discussed in this chapter.

October 25, 1985

Dear (Bob and Sue),

Thank you for coming to our wedding and sharing
this special day with us. We love the (vase) you gave
us. It goes perfectly (on our end table).

We are looking forward to seeing you (in July).

Yours,

Paul and Sara

October 25, 1985

Dear (Marcie),

Thank you for coming to our wedding and sharing
this special day with us. We love the (throw rug) you
gave us. It goes perfectly (in our hallway).

We are looking forward to seeing you (in two weeks).

Yours,

Paul and Sara

Figure 23-1. One shell with two sets of variable information

Chapter 24 will teach you how to create a "paragraph library"—a collection of paragraphs from which you make choices to produce a variety of form letters. For example, if you are running a collection agency, you might want one opening paragraph for those who have paid their bills and another for those who have not. You can insert variable information into paragraphs from a paragraph library by using either Stop codes or the DisplayWrite 4 Merge with Named Variables feature.

Chapter 25 teaches you how to produce repetitive documents using the DisplayWrite 4 Merge with File feature. This feature lets you merge a DisplayWrite 4 shell file with variable information stored in a data file generated by another program, such as a spreadsheet or database management program. Using Merge with File, you can produce a great many copies of repetitive documents quickly.

As you gain experience in producing repetitive documents, you will be able to gauge which method is best for you.

Using Get with Stop Codes

The first step in using Get to produce repetitive documents is to store a shell document on disk.

Choose Create Document

from the DisplayWrite 4 menu and name your shell file. Pick a name that will remind you of the file's contents.

Selecting a Format

The format of the shell should be the same as the format you want for the final repetitive document. Ordinarily, you would design a format for a file by going to the typing area, pressing CTRL-F7, and choosing Document Format. When you later created a file for your final repetitive document, you could design the same format for that file.

There are two disadvantages to this method: first, you have to create the same format twice; second, you have to remember all the format settings of your shell file. Fortunately, there is a more convenient method.

When you are in the typing area, position your cursor at the beginning of the file. Then, instead of pressing CTRL-F7,

press F7.

You will see the Format menu. Make all the format changes you want (as described in Chapter 10). When you are finished,

press ESC

to return to the typing area. The cursor will be under a Format Change code:

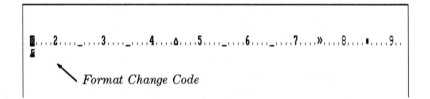

Format Change Code

The advantage of this method is that you do not have to enter the format again for your repetitive document. When you later use Get to put a copy of the shell into your repetitive document, the Format Change code (containing your format specifications) will be transferred along with the rest of the file.

Entering the Stop Codes

Type text in the usual way until you come to the first place where you want to insert variable information. (This can be at the very beginning of the file.) Type any spaces or punctuation that you want to precede the variable information. Then set Display All Codes to Yes.

Press CTRL-6 (the Stop key).

This inserts a Stop code in your text.

Stop Code

Then type any punctuation or spaces that you want after the Stop code. Do *not* press ENTER to reserve blank lines for variable information that is several lines long. You will enter the appropriate carriage returns when you type the variable information itself.

Continue typing your shell document, inserting a Stop code each time you come to a place where you need variable information. Remember to include all necessary spaces and punctuation both before and after the Stop code. Your completed shell might look like Figure 23-2.

Press F2 and choose End and Save

to save the file.

```
«,,,,2,,,,,_,,,3,,,,,_,,,,4,Δ,,,,_,,,5,,,,,_,,,,6,,█,,,,,,,»,,,,,_,,,,8,,,,,█,,,,9,,,,
ℙ→   →    →    →    →    →    →    October 25, 1985◄
◄
Dear ■,◄
◄
  →    Thank you for coming to our wedding and sharing ◢
this special day with us.  We love the ■ you gave us.  ◢
It goes perfectly ■,◄
◄
  →    We are looking forward to seeing you ■,◄
◄
  →    →    →    →    →    →    →    Yours,◄
◄
◄
  →    →    →    →    →    →    →    Paul and Sara_
```

Figure 23-2. A shell file with Stop codes

Producing the Repetitive Document

To create the repetitive document, choose Create Document from the DisplayWrite 4 menu. Name your file and go to the typing area.

Press CTRL-F6 (the Get key).

You will see the Get File menu shown in Figure 23-3. For File Name, type the name of the shell file. Then

press ENTER.

You will be returned to the typing area with your shell

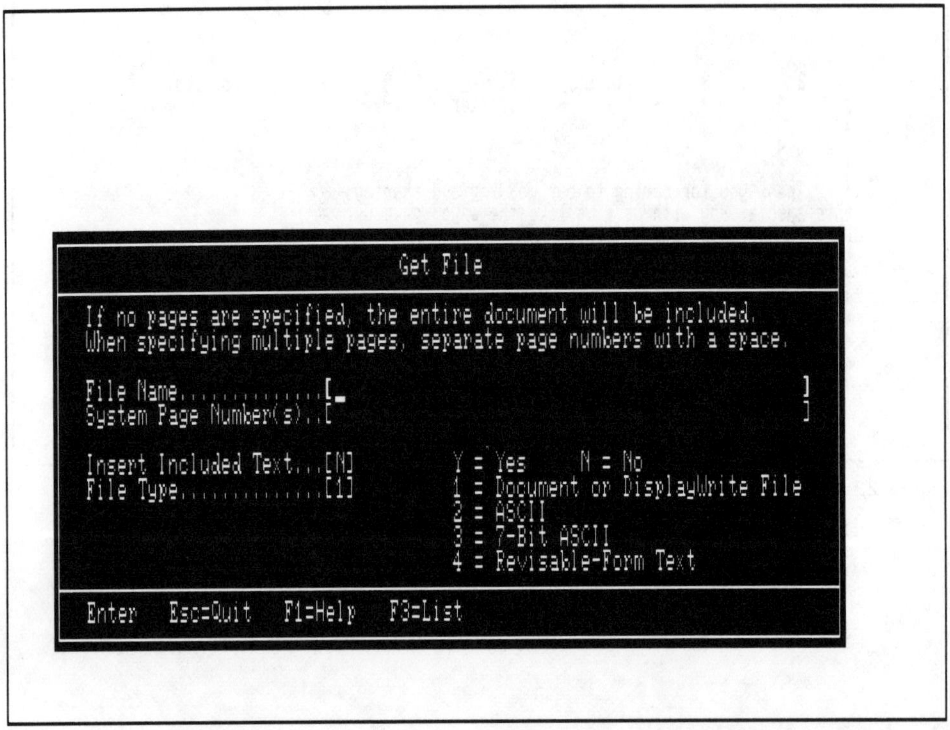

Figure 23-3. The Get File menu

document on the screen. Now set Display All Codes to Yes.

Press CTRL-N (the Next key)

to take you to the first Stop code. Type the first piece of variable information. If you are entering short lines (perhaps for a three-line address), press ENTER to end each line just as you would usually do.

When you have completed typing the first piece of variable information,

press CTRL-N.

The cursor will jump to the next Stop code. (Notice that as the cursor moves, the line lengths are readjusted if necessary.) Repeat this procedure until you have typed in all your variable information. If you need to readjust the line containing the last Stop code, just move the cursor to any other line. Your completed document might look like Figure 23-4.

To produce the next copy of the repetitive document, position the cursor at the end of your file. Then

press CTRL-R

to insert a Required Page End code into your file. This step is important because it ensures that each copy of the repetitive document begins on a new page, even after pagination.

Now use Get to retrieve the shell document again, and fill in the variable information just as you did before. Insert a Required Page End code into your file when you are finished.

Continue in this way until you have completed all of your repetitive document copies. However, do not put a Required

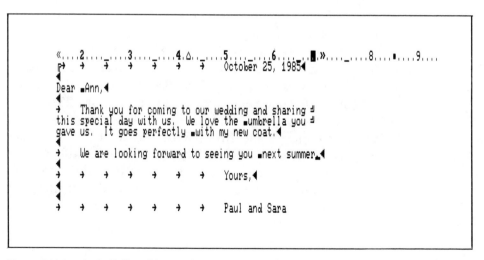

Figure 23-4. A shell file with variable information filled in

Page End code after your final copy. Instead,

press F2 and choose Paginate, End, and Save.

You are now ready to print your file.

Note: If your shells are several pages long and you plan to use page numbering, use the Copy utility to make a separate file for each document rather than using Required Page End codes; otherwise your numbering will be incorrect.

Using Merge with Named Variables

The DisplayWrite 4 Merge Documents function takes a little longer to set up than does the use of Get with Stop codes. However, you will more than make up the time if you are producing a sizable number of documents.

Using the Merge with Named Variables feature, you give each piece of variable information a unique name. When you produce the shell, you reserve places for the variable information by name, as shown in Figure 23-5.

Then you create another file, called a variables document or fill-in, that is composed of a number of pages. Each page of the fill-in gives variable information—identified by variable names—for one repetitive document. Figure 23-6 is an example of one page of a fill-in file.

When you merge the fill-in with the shell, the variable names in the fill-in will be matched with the variable names in the shell to produce copies of the repetitive document. A completed copy of a repetitive document produced this way will look like Figure 23-7.

```
█....¦...2,....¦...3,....¦...4,.Δ..¦...5,....¦...6,...¦...7,..».,..8,...■...9
→                                    October 1, 1985◄
◄
!address!◄
◄
Dear !name!:◄
◄
→    Thank you for sending in your application for our "!subject!" class.◄
◄
→    The enrollment fee is $!cost! and is due in full at the first ◿
class session on !date!.  The group will meet from !time! each !day! through ◿
November.◄
◄
→    We are looking forward to seeing you there.◄
◄
→    →    →    →    →    →    →    →    →    Sincerely,◄
◄
→    →    →    →    →    →    →    →    →    Joan Crupp◄
↨    →    →    →    →    →    →    →    →    Registrar
```

Figure 23-5.   A shell with variable names

```
«....2..█....3,....¦....4,...Δ....5,....¦....6,....¦....7,..»,...8,...■....9,...
!address!Ms. Angela Mills◄
2642 Arch Lane◄
Logan, CA 94001◄
!name!Ms. Mills◄
!subject!Computers and Conscience◄
!cost!125◄
!date!October 15◄
!time!7:00 p.m. to 9:00 p.m.◄
!day!Tuesday_
```

Figure 23-6.   A page of a fill-in file

```
                                        October 1, 1985


     Ms. Angela Mills
     2462 Arch Lane
     Logan, CA 94001

     Dear Ms. Mills:

          Thank you for sending in your application form for our
     "Computers and Conscience" class.

          The enrollment fee is $125 and is due in full at the
     first class session on October 15.  The group will meet from
     7:00 p.m. to 9:00 p.m. each Tuesday through November.

          We are looking forward to seeing you there.

                                        Sincerely,



                                        Joan Crupp
                                        Registrar
```

Figure 23-7.   A completed copy of a repetitive document created by using Merge with Named Variables

Creating the Shell

To create the shell,

choose Create Document

from the DisplayWrite 4 menu and name your shell file. Pick a name that will remind you of the file's contents. Then, in the typing area,

press CTRL-F7

and set the format that you want for your finished repetitive document.

Type your file in the usual way until you get to the place where you want to insert the first piece of variable information. (Again, this can be at the beginning of the file.) Include any spaces, punctuation, and blank lines that you want to precede the variable information. Set Display All Codes to Yes.

Press F8 and choose Merge Instructions.

Then

choose Variable.

In the Variable menu, type the name you want for the first piece of variable information and

press ENTER.

Figure 23-8 lists the rules for naming variables. Select a name that describes the variable information. For example, if the variable information is an address, "address" is a suitable variable name.

You will see the variable name on the screen, enclosed by Variable codes (Display All Codes must be set to Yes):

```
«▮...¦_..¦2_...¦_...¦3_...¦_...¦4_¦Δ¦_...¦5_...¦_...¦6_...¦_...¦7_...¦»...¦8....▮....¦9
◀
→    →   →   →   →   →   →   →   →    October 1, 1985◀
◀
!address!_
```

1. Each type of variable information must have a unique name.
2. Variable names can contain letters, numbers, and spaces (spaces are changed into underscores) but must *always* begin with a letter.
3. Punctuation characters cannot be used.
4. A variable name can contain a maximum of 16 characters, including spaces.
5. Variable names are case-sensitive. (A variable name containing uppercase letters is considered to be a different variable name from the same name containing lowercase letters.)

Figure 23-8. Naming variables

Do *not* press ENTER to reserve blank lines for variable information that is several lines long. You will enter the appropriate carriage returns when you type the variable information. Type any punctuation or spaces that you want to follow the variable name.

Continue typing text until you get to the next place where you need variable information; press F8 again and repeat the procedure. Make sure you give a new name to each new type of variable information. (However, if you want to use the same variable information more than once in the document — for example, to place an address at both the top and the bottom of a letter — use the same variable name each time.)

If your shell is several pages long and you want to end a page at a particular place,

press CTRL-R

to put a Required Page End code into your file. Otherwise, page endings will be adjusted during the merge process. Make sure you allow space for variable information when you plan your page breaks.

Revising Variable Names

If you want to change a variable name, place the cursor under the Variable code for that variable name.

Press CTRL-F8.

You will see the Variable menu. For Variable Name, type in the revised variable name. (Remember, you can press ALT-8 to erase the old variable name.)

Press ENTER.

You will be returned to the typing area and will see your revised variable name on the screen.

When you are finished typing your shell with variable names,

press F2 and choose End and Save

to save the file.

Printing a Reference Copy

You will find it handy to print a reference copy of the shell as a record of the variable names you have selected. Do not be concerned about uneven margins in your printed shell document. The lines will be properly adjusted in the final, merged printout.

Creating the Fill-In

In the fill-in document, you will enter the variable information for each copy of the repetitive document on a separate system page.

To create the fill-in file,

choose Create Document

from the DisplayWrite 4 menu, and name your file.

In the typing area,

press CTRL-F7 and choose Document Comment.

Then, in the Document Comment menu, set Preserve Page Numbers to Yes. You must do this to prevent pagination, so that the set of variable information for each copy of the repetitive document remains on its own page. (You do not need to make any other format selections for your fill-in file; the default settings are fine.) Next,

press CTRL-F5.

When you see the Edit Options menu, you need to make two changes:

1. Set Display All Codes to Yes.

2. Set Auto Page End to No.

Next,

press ENTER

to return to the typing area. You are now ready to begin typing your fill-in.

Press F8 and choose Merge Instructions.

Then

select Variable.

In the Variable menu, type the first variable name *exactly as you did in the shell document.* Use your printed reference copy to remind you of the names you used. Then, without typing a space, type the variable information that goes with that variable name *for one copy of the repetitive document only.* (For example, if your variable name is "address," type one person's address.) Include all carriage returns that are part of the variable information. Your document will look like this:

```
«....2...._...,.....4....∆....5...._...,..6...._.....7....»,...8....▪....9...
!address!Ms. Angela Mills◀
2642 Arch Lane◀
Logan, CA 94001_
```

Press ENTER.

Type the next variable name and the next piece of variable information for that copy of the repetitive document. Each variable name must begin on a new line. Use each variable name *only once* in the fill-in even if you used it more than once in the shell.

Continue until you have typed all the variable names and variable information for one copy of the repetitive document.

Press CTRL-E

to take you to the next system page. There you can enter variable names and variable information for the next copy of the repetitive document. Repeat this procedure for each copy. However, do not press CTRL-E after the last page of the fill-in. When you are finished,

Press F2 and choose End and Save

to save the fill-in file.

Note: To avoid having to type the variable names for each page of the fill-in, you can store the variable names (one to a line) in the Notepad. Then, for each page of the fill-in, you Recall from Notepad the list of names. When you have typed the fill-in information for one variable name, you can use CTRL-N (the Next key) to move the cursor to the end of the next variable name.

Using One Fill-In with Several Different Shells

Perhaps you have a number of different form letters, all containing some identical variable information. For example, you may use the same set of addresses on a number of different form letters. However, each form letter also has certain items that are different. For example, one form letter may require customers' phone numbers, while another may not.

You can create one fill-in file that includes all the variable names and variable information that you need for *all* these form letters. During the merge process, variable names in your fill-in that are not found in the shell are ignored.

Producing the Merged Documents

Merged documents are not printed from the Print menu as other files are; nor do you use pagination on merged documents—even those containing footnotes. Pagination, footnote resolution, and printing are all performed as part of the Merge with Named Variables task.

When you produce your final merged documents, you have three choices:

- You can simply print the final documents.

- You can print the documents *and* save them to disk.

- You can save them to disk for printing at a later time.

However, if you have a floppy-disk system, beware of saving large numbers of repetitive documents on your disk because your disk will fill up very quickly.

To print the final merged documents, from the Display-Write 4 menu,

choose Merge and then choose Named Variables.

You will see the two-page Merge with Named Variables menu shown in Figures 23-9*a* and 23-9*b*.

Type in the name of the shell file and the name of the variables document (the fill-in file).

If you want to merge only some pages of the fill-in (if, for example, you have a letter you want sent to just some of your customers), tab to System Page Numbers and type the system page numbers you want merged, separating each from the next with a space. You may select up to ten separate pages. Your entry might look like this:

1 3 4 5 8 10

The next two choices, Merged Document Name and Print Merged Document, let you determine whether your repetitive document will be printed, stored, or both.

- If you want your final documents printed but not stored, make no changes in these items.

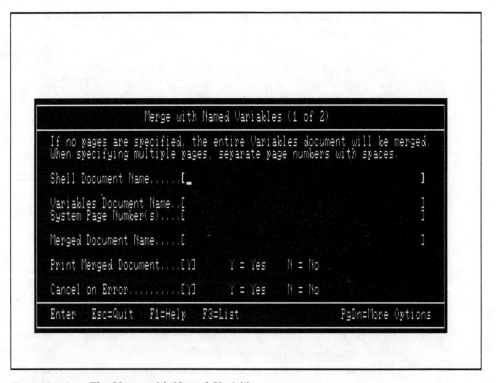

Figure 23-9a. The Merge with Named Variables menu, page 1

- If you want your final documents printed *and* stored, tab to Merged Document Name and type a name for the merged document.

- If you want your final documents stored but not printed, tab to Merged Document Name and type a name for the merged document. Then tab to Print Merged Document and set it to No.

Notice that the default setting of the next menu item, Cancel on Error, is Yes. If you want merging to continue regard-

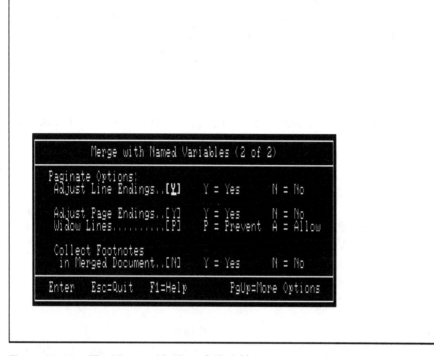

Figure 23-9*b*.   The Merge with Named Variables menu, page 2

less of whether you have errors, change the setting to No. With a No setting, the merge will proceed but the merged document will display a list of errors.

The Adjust Line Endings and Adjust Page Endings items are similiar to choices you encounter during pagination. The final choice, Collect Footnotes in Merged Document, lets you collect all of your footnotes at the end of the merged document, rather than having each footnote at the bottom of the appropriate page. This choice is useful if you are planning to revise a batch of footnotes at one time. (Make sure you select a Merged Document Name if you plan to revise footnotes; otherwise, they will be printed but not stored.)

When you have made all desired menu changes, make sure that your printer is on (unless you are saving the merge but not printing it). Then

press ENTER

to begin merging. Your final documents will be printed or stored on disk according to your instructions.

If you want to cancel the merge operation,

press CTRL-BREAK.

Table 23-1 lists the keys used for Get and for Merge with Named Variables.

Key	Function
CTRL-F5	The Display All Codes choice lets you see your Stop codes or variable names
CTRL-6	Puts a Stop code into your shell
CTRL-F6	Lets you insert the shell document into the repetitive document you are working on
F7	Lets you establish a format for your shell that you can transfer with Get to your repetitive document
F8	The Merge Instructions choice followed by the Variable choice inserts a Variable code at the beginning and end of your variable name
CTRL-F8	When positioned under a Variable code, lets you revise a variable name
CTRL-N	Locates the next Stop code or named variable
CTRL-R	Inserts a Required Page End code into your text, separating copies of a repetitive document produced by Get, so that each will print on a separate physical page

Table 23-1. Keys Used for Get and for Merge with Named Variables

24

Creating
a Paragraph
Selection
Document

This chapter shows you how to create a library of frequently used paragraphs that you can choose from and insert into your file as needed.

What a Paragraph Selection Document Is

In your work you may find yourself inserting certain set paragraphs of text into your files over and over again. Such a set text block is often called *boilerplate*. DisplayWrite 4 lets you create a *paragraph selection document* (also called a *paragraph library*) to store these paragraphs so you can call them into your files as needed. This spares you the tedium of retyping the paragraphs each time.

Using the techniques you learned in Chapter 23, you can personalize the paragraphs from the library with variable information—the information that changes from document to document. The combination of these two approaches—selecting paragraphs from a paragraph library and then individualizing them with variable information—lets you produce highly personalized form letters with a minimum of typing. Figure 24-1a shows a selection of paragraphs from a paragraph library. Figure 24-1b shows the same paragraphs with the addition of some variable information. The variable information is circled.

As you produce your own form letters, you will discover that DisplayWrite 4 often offers you several ways of accomplishing a single task. With practice, you will be able to tell which method is best for you. If the paragraphs you are producing contain any variable information, or if you are using Include instructions in your file (see the section "Using Merge to Assemble the Form Letter"), be sure to read Chapter 23 before you read further in this chapter.

```
We are pleased to inform you that your grant request has
been approved by our selection committee.

We are sorry to inform you that your grant request has not
been approved by our selection committee.  The members felt
that other projects better suited the needs of the community
at this time.

Although your project was not chosen for funding, it was one
that attracted our special attention, and we want to invite
you to resubmit your proposal next year.

As you know, our Foundation receives many more grant re-
quests than it can accommodate.  Therefore, our refusal in
no way reflects on the value of your proposed project.  We
wish you every success securing funds elsewhere.

We would like you to set up an appointment with our project
coordinator, Ms. Whimple, as soon as possible, so we can get
the paper work started.  Please call 555-6789.

We are looking forward to hearing from you.
```

Figure 24-1a. Paragraphs from a paragraph library

Figure 24-1b. Paragraphs from a paragraph library that contain variable information

Making the Library

In the paragraph library, each paragraph will be stored on a separate system page. If you want to include variable information, you must insert a variable name in the paragraph text when you type it.

To create your paragraph library, choose Create Document from the DisplayWrite 4 menu and name your paragraph library file. In the typing area,

press CTRL-F7 and select Document Comment.

Set Preserve Page Numbers to Yes. Then

press ENTER

to return to the typing area. This procedure prevents pagination and ensures that each paragraph remains on a separate page.

Then, if your paragraphs are longer than one page,

press CTRL-F5 and set Auto Page End to No.

This keeps pages from ending in incorrect places after the paragraphs from the library have been inserted into your file.

If you are planning to insert variable names into your paragraph library, set Display All Codes to Yes.

Now type the first paragraph.

```
«....2...._...3.....,....4....∆....5...._▉...6.....,...._7....»,...8....■....9..
We are pleased to inform you that your grant request has
been approved by our selection committee.▲
```

If you are inserting variable names, position the cursor where you want the first piece of variable information to appear.

Press F8, choose Merge Instructions, and then choose Variable.

Next, type the variable name and

press ENTER.

The variable name will be embedded in your text. Repeat the procedure at each location where you want variable information.

```
«....2...._....3...._....4....∆....5....▮..6...._....7....»....8....▪....9...
We are pleased to inform you that your grant request !amount! has ⏎
been approved by our selection committee.▲
                                                            ↑
                                                    Variable Name
```

After you are finished typing the first paragraph,

   press ENTER

to insert a required carriage return for each blank line you want in the final document after the paragraph. Then, to begin a new system page for the next paragraph,

   press CTRL-E.

Repeat the process for each paragraph in the library. However, after you type the last paragraph, do not press CTRL-E. Instead,

   press F2 and choose End and Save.

Printing a Reference Copy of the Library

You will want to print a reference copy of your paragraph library to refer to when you are deciding which paragraphs to include in a final document. If you want the reference copy to have page numbers, you can create a header or footer that includes system page numbers (see Chapter 11). Each paragraph will print on a separate page, numbered with the system page number. The system page numbers of your paragraph library will *not* appear when you later retrieve paragraphs from it to insert in other files.

If you want a more compact reference copy, use the DOS COPY command or the DisplayWrite 4 Copy utility to make a copy of the paragraph library. On the copy, set Preserve Page Numbers to No. Paginate and print the reference copy. By hand, write in the system page number next to each paragraph.

If you use variable names, your margins may appear misaligned in the reference copy. They will be properly adjusted in the merged document.

Assembling a Form Letter Without Variables

If your final form letter does not contain variable names, DisplayWrite 4 provides a number of ways that you can assemble the final document. If you have variable names in your paragraph library, or if you are using them anywhere else in your letters, go to the section "Assembling a Form Letter with Variables" later in this chapter.

Using Get to Assemble Form Letters

If your final letter does not contain variable names, then Get is the easiest method of assembling the final document. Choose Create Document from the DisplayWrite 4 menu to create the shell file (the file that contains information that does not change from letter to letter). Name the file, go to the typing area, and design the format you want for your completed documents. Type any text that you want to precede the paragraphs from the paragraph library. Next, position the cursor where you want your first paragraph to appear:

```
█....2.....__....3....._....4....Δ....5......__....6.....__...7....»....8....■....9..
                              November 15, 1985
Mr. Joseph Fielding
92 Arrow Lane
Lawrence, IL 60018

Dear Mr. Fielding:

■
```

Then

    Press CTRL-F6.

You will see the Get File menu.

    For File Name, type the name of the paragraph library. Then, for System Page Numbers, type the numbers of the system pages where your paragraphs are stored. (Type them in the order you want them to appear in the final letter.) Separate each number from the next with a space (use your reference copy to refresh your memory). For example, if you want to include paragraphs 2, 3, and 6,

    type **2 3 6**; then press ENTER.

    You will see the selected paragraphs inserted into your file at the cursor location. Then type any text that follows the text from the paragraph library and call in more paragraphs from the paragraph library if necessary. It is best if the paragraphs in the paragraph library have the same format as your form letter. If this is not possible (for example, when you use your paragraph library with form letters in several different formats), the paragraphs retrieved through Get will take on the format of your form letter during pagination (unless they contain F7 Format codes). Your completed form letter will resemble Figure 24-2.

If you want to produce another version of the repetitive document using paragraphs from the paragraph library,

press CTRL-R.

This inserts a Required Page End code into your file.

Now you can begin the next letter (use the Block Copy feature to copy the constant text). For each letter you can incorporate a different selection of paragraphs from the library.

```
                                    November 15, 1985

Mr. Joseph Fielding
92 Arrow Lane
Lawrence, IL 60018

Dear Mr. Lawrence:

We are sorry to inform you that your grant request has not
been approved by our selection committee.  The members felt
that other projects better suited the needs of the community
at this time.

Although your project was not chosen for funding, it was one
that attracted our special attention, and we want to invite
you to resubmit your proposal next year.

We are looking forward to hearing from you.

                         Sincerely,


                         Peter Green
                         President
                         ACME Arts Foundation
```

Figure 24-2.   A form letter assembled with Get

When you have assembled all your letters,

press F2 and choose Paginate, End, and Save.

You are now ready to print the letters.

Using Merge to Assemble Form Letters

You can also assemble your form letter through the Merge menu by using an *include instruction* in your shell file. The include instruction tells DisplayWrite 4 what paragraphs from the library to include in the completed form letter. The advantage of this method is that you can assemble, paginate, and print all in one operation. The disadvantage is that you can produce only one letter at a time.

To use Merge to assemble a form letter that does not contain variable information,

choose Create Document

from the DisplayWrite 4 menu and name your shell file. Pick a name that will remind you of the file's contents. Then go to the typing area and set the format that you want for your final assembled documents. Set Display All Codes to Yes.

Begin typing the shell. When you get to the location where you want paragraphs from the paragraph library included,

press F8 and choose Merge Instructions.

Then, from the Merge Instructions menu,

choose Include.

You will see the Include menu. (Notice that it looks a lot like an abbreviated Get File menu, and in fact, it works essentially the same way.) For Document Name, type in the name of the paragraph library:

paralib.doc

Then tab to System Page Number and type the system page numbers of the paragraphs you want to include (in the order you want them included), with a space separating each number from the next:

2 3 6

You can choose up to ten paragraphs. (If you want to select more than ten paragraphs, or if you are choosing paragraphs from more than one library, you will have to enter additional Include instructions.)

Press ENTER

to return to the typing area.

You will see the Include code embedded in your text *even with Display All Codes set to No.* With Display All Codes set to Yes, you will see the entire Include instruction:

```
«....2.....█....3...._....4.....∆....5...._....6....._....7.....»....8.....▮....9....
◄
→   →   →   →   →   →   →   →   →   June 6, 1987◄
◄
Dear Mr. Jones:◄
◄
→    Here are the instructions for processing your claim:◄
◄
→   →   /Include,CLAIM.DOC,1,3,5/◄
▲
```

Type any text that comes after the Include instruction.

If you have paragraphs stored in several different paragraph libraries, you can insert paragraphs from them into the same file. Just enter different Include instructions and specify the different library names. Then

press F2 and choose End and Save.

To assemble and print the form letter, from the Display-Write 4 menu,

choose Merge. Then choose Includes Only.

Complete the Merge with Includes Only menu the same way you completed the Merge with Named Variables menu (see Chapter 23). Fill in the Shell Document Name, and, if you want the letter saved on disk, the Merged Document Name. Then make any other changes in the menu that you need to. Turn your printer on.

Press ENTER

to begin the Merge. Your file will be printed with the designated text inserted into it.

Note: Do not put a Required Page End code at the end of your file to produce a second version of the document because Required Page End codes do not work properly with Merge.

Using Get to Include Text

There is one other way to activate an Include instruction. This method inserts the included text while you are in the typing area and lets you print your file in the usual way. You can use Get to insert the file that contains the Include instruction into another file that you are currently working on.
First,

press CTRL-F6

to display the Get File menu. Then, for File Name, type the name of the file containing the Include instruction. Tab to Insert Included Text and set it to Yes.

Press ENTER.

This begins a "nesting" process.
The Include instruction "gets" the specified paragraphs and inserts them into the file specified in the Get File menu.

The system then "gets" the file you specified (with the paragraphs included) and inserts that into the current file. In the typing area, you see the assembled file.

Revising an Include Instruction

You revise Include instructions the same way you revise variable names. In the typing area, set Display All Codes to Yes. Position the cursor under the Include instruction. Then

press CTRL-F8.

You will see the Include menu. Revise the Include instructions as necessary. When you have completed your revision,

press ENTER

to return to the typing area.

Assembling a Form Letter with Variables

If you have used variable names in your paragraph library, or if you are using them anywhere in your form letter, you must use the Merge feature to create the letters. You will make a shell document and a fill-in as you learned to do in Chapter 23, with the following difference: you must include additional instructions to retrieve the selected paragraphs from the library and to replace any variable names in these paragraphs with the correct variable information.

Creating the Shell

Choose Create Document from the DisplayWrite 4 menu and name your shell file. Pick a name that will remind you of the file's contents. Then, in the typing area, set the format that you want for your final assembled documents. Set Display All Codes to Yes.

Begin typing the shell. When you get to a place where you want variable information, insert a variable name as you learned to do in Chapter 23. (Press F8, choose Merge Instructions, and then choose Variable. Type the variable name and press ENTER.) Continue in this way until the cursor is at the location where you want to place your paragraphs from the library.

```
▓....2...._...3...._...4....Δ....5...._...6...._....7....»....8.....■....9.
  →    →    →    →    →    →    →     November 15, 1985◄
◄
!address!◄
◄
Dear !name!:◄
◄
▬
```

Now you must enter a special variable name that will later instruct DisplayWrite 4 to insert the specified paragraphs from your paragraph library into your shell. You may pick any name you want *as long as you have not used it in the shell already.* Insert this variable name the same way you insert any other. In the following screen display, the variable name is "library".

```
«▓....2...._...3...._...4....Δ....5...._...6...._....7....»....8.....■....9..
  →    →    →    →    →    →    →     November 15, 1985◄
◄
!address!◄
◄
Dear !name!:◄
◄
!library!_
```

Position the cursor where you want to type any text that follows the paragraphs from the library. (If you inserted blank lines after your paragraphs in the library, don't insert the same blank lines again in your shell, or you will have twice as many blank lines as you want.) Type in the text, including any variable names. When you are finished,

press F2 and choose End and Save.

Print a reference copy. The reference copy will look like Figure 24-3. It will show the variable names in the shell but not the variable names in the library paragraphs.

Creating the Fill-In

Now you must create a fill-in file.

Choose Create Document

from the DisplayWrite 4 menu and name your file. In the typing area,

press CTRL-F7 and choose Document Comment.

Then set Preserve Page Numbers to Yes.

Press ENTER

to return to the typing area. In the Edit Options menu, set Auto Page End to No and set Display All Codes to Yes. You are now ready to begin typing the fill-in file.

To enter all your variable names and variable information, you will need to consult both of your reference copies — the one showing the variable names in your shell, and the other showing the variable names in your paragraph library.

Enter the first variable name that appears in your shell. (Press F8, choose Merge Instructions, and then choose Vari-

```
                                            November 15, 1985
        !address!

        Dear !name!:

        !library!
                                            Sincerely,


                                            !signature!
                                            !title!
                                            Acme Arts Foundation
```

Figure 24-3. A shell for form letters to be assembled with Merge with Named Variables

able. Type the variable name and press ENTER.) Then, without typing a space, type the associated variable information for one copy of the document and press ENTER. For example, if your first variable name is "address", type one person's address. Remember that each variable name begins on a separate line. Continue typing variable names and associated variable information until you come to the variable name that is to instruct DisplayWrite 4 to insert specified paragraphs from the library.

Insert the special variable name exactly as you inserted all other variable names. Now, on the same line, you are going to insert a special Include instruction into your file that will tell DisplayWrite 4 what paragraphs to insert during the merge process.

To specify the paragraphs,

press F8 and choose Merge Instructions.

Then, from the Merge Instructions menu,

choose Include.

You will see the Include Instruction menu.

For Document Name, type the name of the paragraph library. For System Page Number, type the system page numbers of the paragraphs you want to include, with a space separating each number from the next.

You can choose up to ten paragraphs. (If you want to select more than ten paragraphs, or if you are choosing paragraphs from more than one library, you will have to enter additional Include instructions.)

Press ENTER

to return to the typing area. You will see your Include instruction next to the variable name.

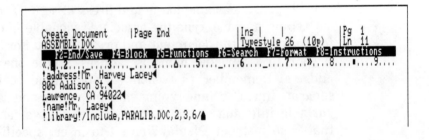

Note: If you are going to use the same paragraphs from the paragraph library for all copies of the repetitive document in a merge, you can enter the Include instruction in the shell instead of entering a special variable name. However, if the paragraphs themselves include variables, you will have to enter the variable information for them in the fill-in.

Press ENTER

to move to the next line.

Now enter the first variable name appearing in your selected paragraphs and, next to it, type the associated variable information. Continue typing variable names and information until you have used each of the variable names appearing in your selected paragraphs.

Now enter any variable names and associated variable information that appear in your shell *after* the paragraphs from the library. A completed page of your fill-in might look like the screen that follows:

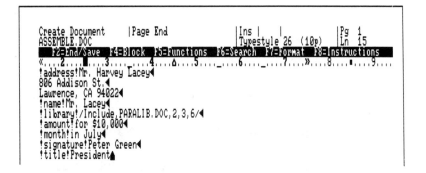

This takes you to the next system page, so you can enter variable names and variable information for the next copy. You can choose a different selection of paragraphs with the Include instruction if you wish to. When you are finished entering names and variable information for all your copies, do not press CTRL-E. Instead,

press F2 and choose End and Save.

Printing the Letters

To produce the final form letters—collecting the selected paragraphs from the paragraph library and merging the variable information from the fill-in into the shell—you use the Merge feature exactly as you do for any other documents containing variable names. From the DisplayWrite menu,

Key	Function
CTRL-F6	Displays the Get File menu, which lets you insert the selected paragraphs into your file
F8	The Merge Instructions choice followed by the Variable choice lets you insert a Variable name into your file
	The Merge Instructions choice followed by the Include choice lets you designate paragraphs to be inserted into your text during the merge process
CTRL-F8	When the cursor is positioned under an Include instruction, it lets you revise the instruction; under a variable name, it lets you revise the variable name

Table 24-1. Keys Used with Paragraph Libraries

choose Merge. Then choose Named Variables.

From the Merge with Named Variables menu, enter the names of your shell file and your variables document (your fill-in file). Then, to begin the merge,

press ENTER.

Each completed form letter will contain the particular selection of paragraphs you specified, and the letters will be further personalized with variable information.

Table 24-1 lists the keys you use when working with paragraph libraries.

25

Merging with
Data Files

*This chapter shows you how to merge a shell produced by Dis-
playWrite 4 with information from a data file produced by
another program.*

The DisplayWrite 4 Merge
with Data File Feature

In Chapter 23 you learned how to produce repetitive documents by saving text that does not change in a DisplayWrite
4 shell and merging it with a fill-in containing variable
information (information that changes from document to
document). DisplayWrite 4 has another feature, Merge with
Data File, that lets you merge your DisplayWrite 4 shell with
variable information extracted from a data file created by
another program.

There are a number of reasons that you might want to merge with information in a data base rather than in a fill-in file. Data bases can store huge amounts of information. Also, you can sort the information and select subsets for processing. With Merge with Data File, you can produce tremendous numbers of repetitive documents with minimal typing.

What a Data File Is

A *data file* is simply a collection of data ordered in a certain way. For a business, a data file might include a list of customers' names, addresses, and phone numbers and the dates of recent purchases. Within the data file, information is stored by *records*, each record containing the information about, say, one customer. Each item in a record is called a *field*, and each different category in a record is identified by a field name. DisplayWrite 4 recognizes two types of fields: *character* and *numeric*. A numeric field may contain *only* numbers, plus an optional decimal point and an optional plus or minus sign. Fields containing *any* other characters are designated as character fields. Figure 25-1 shows part of a data file with a record, field, and field name identified.

Merge with Data File can be used only if the field names in the data file *are identical* to the variable names in your DisplayWrite 4 shell, as shown in Figures 25-2a and 25-2b. Then, during Merge with File, the names are matched and variable information is extracted from the data file to produce copies of the repetitive document. Each record produces one copy of the repetitive document.

What Types of Data Files Work

Merge with Data File works with BASIC and program files like PDS, WKS, WRK, DIF, SYLK, dBASEII and with DOS ASCII files. However, the files must be designed according to certain rules. Since each field name must be identical to its

```
              Field Name
                 /
                /
   TITLE  FNAME       LNAME        STREET            CITY       ST   ZIP

   Mr.    Fred        Barnes       1268 A. St.       Dale       CA   94002
   Mrs.   Angel       Barnes       1268 A. St.       Dale       CA   94002
   Ms.    Lauren      Hemsley      34 Far View Dr.   Oaks       CA   93002
   Ms.    Amy         Stark        827 Sunset Lane   Ridge      CA   93742
   Mr.    Louis       Harvey       45 King St.       Hamilton   CA   94704
   Mr.    Ronald      Clark        872 Alta Vista    Hamilton   CA   94704
```

Record   *A Field Within*
                                a Record

Figure 25-1. Part of a data file

corresponding variable name, the rules for naming variables listed in Figure 23-8 also apply to naming fields. In addition, to work with Merge with Data File, data files must contain

- A maximum of 65,000 records

- A maximum of 100 fields and 2000 characters per record

- A maximum of 500 characters per character field

- A maximum of 15 numbers per numeric field plus an optional decimal point and an optional leading plus or minus sign for a total field length of 17

Eight data file formats work with Merge with Data File; examples of programs that use these formats are shown in

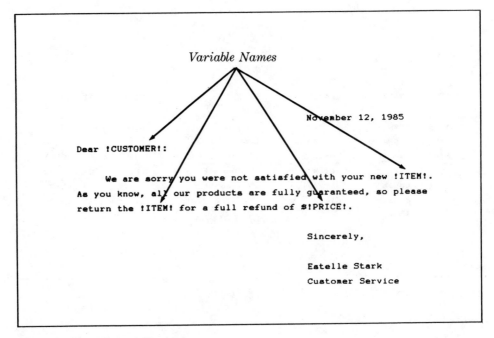

Figure 25-2a. The variable names

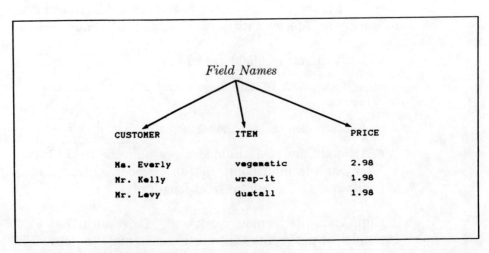

Figure 25-2b. The field names

Table 25-1. In addition, Merge with Data File can work with *user-supplied* programs as long as these programs are created in accordance with specified work file formats.

The *DisplayWrite 4 Technical Reference* manual that comes with your DisplayWrite 4 program gives specific rules for creating data files with the eight supported formats and with user-supplied programs so that they can work successfully with DisplayWrite 4.

File Descriptions If you are using a BASIC sequential or fixed-length data file format, you will need to create a *file description* before you can use Merge with Data File. The file description is created with DisplayWrite 4 and contains a description of every field in your data file. With a user-supplied program, you need to create a file description only if one is not automatically generated by the program itself.

Data File Format	Example of User Program
BASIC Sequential	BASIC Sequential, release 2.1
dBASE II	dBASE II, version 2.4
DIF	Lotus 1-2-3, release 1A
	VisiCalc, version 1.1
Fixed-length	BASIC random (character-type data only), release 2.1
PDS	IBM Personal Decision Series Data Edition, version 1.0
SYLK	Multiplan, version 1.1
WKS	Lotus 1-2-3, release 1A
WRK	Symphony, release 1.0

Table 25-1. Data File Formats That Work with Merge with File

See the section "Creating a File Description" later in this chapter to learn how to create file descriptions.

Creating a Shell

You can create a shell for Merge with Data File using the procedures that you learned in Chapter 23. This shell works as explained in that chapter except that instead of merging with data from a fill-in file, the shell merges with variable information extracted from a data file.

Whenever you come to a place where you want variable information to go, you *must* select, for the variable name, the corresponding field name in the data file. Insert the variable name in the usual way (press F8, choose Merge Instructions, choose Variable, type the name, and press ENTER). After you complete your shell, save it and print a reference copy.

There is also, however, another type of shell that you can create for Merge with Data Files. This shell has much more flexibility than the regular shell because it includes *special instructions*. These instructions can tell the system to print text on a specific line (handy for printing forms); to perform certain math calculations and insert the results into final documents; and to print certain text depending on whether or not a certain field in a record is empty.

The next three sections will show you how to include special instructions in your shell. Make sure to set Display All Codes to Yes when you are including special instructions. Otherwise, you will not be able to see the instructions on your screen.

Using Skip to Line Instructions

For certain repetitive documents, such as forms, you may want some text to be printed on a specific line. With an ordinary file, you simply look at the status line to see what line you are on. With repetitive documents, though, because a short variable name in the shell may be replaced by variable information that is several lines long in the final document, it is more difficult to determine where text will be placed.

To solve this problem, DisplayWrite 4 lets you put Skip to Line instructions in the shell that tell the system to begin printing text on a specific line. To use Skip to Line, type the shell until you get to the point where you want text to be printed on a specific line. Then

press F8 and choose Merge Instructions.

From the Merge Instructions menu,

choose Skip to Line Number.

Then type the number of the next line that you want to print on. (Make sure the number you designate is greater than the number of the line you are currently on.) You may even designate a half line. For example,

type **50.5** and press ENTER.

If Display All Codes is set to Yes (which it should be), you will be able to see the Skip to Line instruction inserted into your text:

```
▌....2...._...3...._...4....∆....5...._...6..._...7....».....8.....■....9.
Permission is granted for the use of the material as ◄
stipulated above.◄
/Skip to Line,50.5/◄
▪
```

The little arrow after the Skip to Line instruction is a *Zero Index Carrier Return code (ZICR)*. A ZICR returns you to the left margin without moving you down a line in your file, thereby letting you display the instruction on your screen without using up an actual line in your file. (You can insert a ZICR into your file at any time by pressing CTRL-Z.)

Now type the text or variable names for text that you want printed on the specified line. The status line will not show the designated line number because the "skipping" is not done until the actual merge. Continue typing text if necessary. You may use Skip to Line instructions in a file as often as you like. Just be careful to keep within the bounds of the last typing line selected in your format. When you merge your file, text will be printed on the designated lines.

Note: You must make sure that the paper in your printer is positioned to correspond with your DisplayWrite 4 instructions. Your Skip to Line instructions cannot be executed properly if the paper in your printer is scrolled up or down so that, say, line 50 is actually printed on line 40 or line 60 of your paper.

Using Math Instructions

The Math instruction allows DisplayWrite 4 to perform calculations during the Merge with Data File process and to print the results of the calculations at designated locations in your repetitive documents.

The Math instruction will add, subtract, multiply, or divide numbers from designated numeric fields in your data file. You can also perform calculations by using a constant typed directly into the Math instruction itself or by using the results of a previous calculation.

Although the Math instruction works with only two numbers at a time, you can produce calculations involving more than two numbers by using a series of Math instructions in your shell. For example, let's say you offer a special discount of 10% to preferred customers. You could type one Math instruction to calculate the discount:

DISCOUNT = PRICE × .10

You could then type a second instruction to calculate the final price:

FINAL—PRICE = PRICE − DISCOUNT

In these Math instructions, PRICE is a field name from your data file, .10 is a constant, and DISCOUNT and FINAL— PRICE are calculation results called *math answers*.

Type each Math instruction on a separate line in the shell document. If you have several such instructions, make sure they are in the correct order—the Math instruction to be executed first must come before the Math instruction to be executed second. Also, make sure that the Math instruction comes *before* the place in the file where the answer is to be inserted. To avoid problems, it is a good idea to put all math instructions at the beginning of the shell.

To put the first of these two Math instructions in the shell,

press F8 and choose Merge Instructions.

Then, when you see the Merge Instructions menu,

choose Math.

You will see the Math menu shown in Figure 25-3*a*.

The first thing you must do is to select a variable name for your first math answer. Tab to Math Answer Variable Name.

Type **DISCOUNT**.

Then tab to First Number. Type the field name of a numeric field from your data file, or a constant, or a math answer

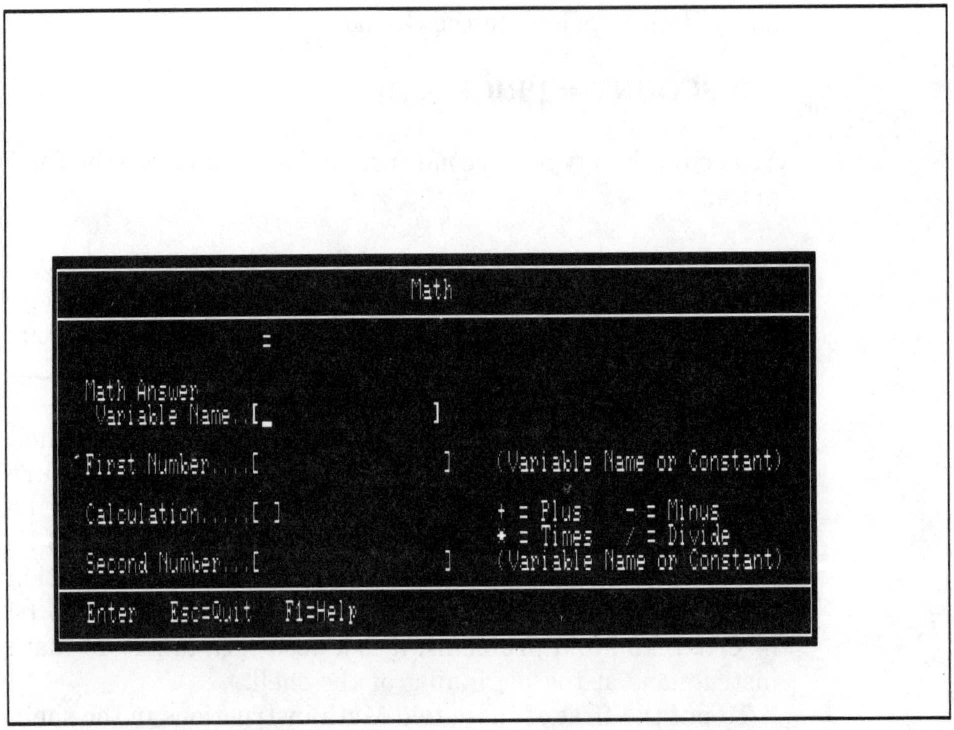

Figure 25-3a. The Math menu

from a previous calculation. In this case, you want the field name PRICE.

Type **PRICE**.

Then tab to Calculation and select the desired operation. In this case,

type * (for Times).

Now tab to Second Number. Here again you can type a field name, or a constant, or a math answer from a previous

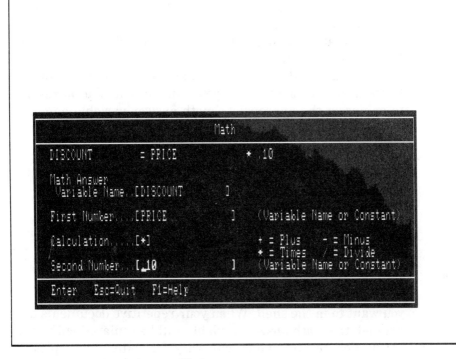

Figure 25-3b. The Math menu filled out

calculation. Here you want a constant.

Type **.10** and press ENTER.

Your completed menu will look like Figure 25-3b. Notice that as you type each item, it is included in an equation at the top of the menu. To return to the shell,

press ENTER.

You will see the Math instruction in your file with a Zero Index Carrier Return after it.

Now you can repeat the process to produce the second Math instruction. Use FINAL—PRICE as the Math Answer Variable Name, PRICE as the First Number, −(Minus) as the Calculation, and DISCOUNT as the Second Number. Return to the shell.

Type your shell in the usual way. When you come to the location in your shell where you want the calculation results to go, insert the appropriate math answer variable name:

```
«....2....._....3.....,....4.....Δ....5...._....6...._....∎....»....8....∎....9....
/DISCOUNT = PRICE * .10/←
/FINAL_PRICE = PRICE - DISCOUNT/←
◄
→    Since you are one of our preferred customers, we are ⌐
happy to offer you our new !product! at the special price of !FINAL_PRICE!.▲
                                                             ↑
                                                      Math Answer
```

You can insert the math answer variable name as often as you want to in the shell. When your repetitive documents are printed, the math answer variable will be replaced with your calculation results, which can vary for individual copies of the final document.

Revising a Math Instruction   To revise a Math instruction, move the cursor under the instruction. Then

press CTRL-F8.

You will see the Math menu. Make the desired changes. To return to the typing area,

press ENTER.

Using If Statements (Conditional Text Instructions)

Sometimes a field in a particular record of a data file is empty, but the same field in another record is not. A common example is a field containing customers' middle initials. Some customers use middle initials; others don't. Another example is a field showing customers' payments. This field would contain data if a customer had paid but would be empty if the customer hadn't paid. DisplayWrite 4 lets you put If Statements into your shell to tell it what to do with fields that contain entries for some records but not for others. Your If Statement goes in the shell instead of the ordinary variable name. There are three possibilities:

1. If the field is not empty, you want the field contents or some other text to be printed.

2. If the field is empty, you want to ignore it.

3. If the field is empty, you want certain text to be printed.

Ordinarily, you insert necessary spaces in the shell after a variable name to separate the variable information from whatever constant text or other comes next. Otherwise, your printed documents would read

Mr.BillC.Taylor

instead of

Mr. Bill C. Taylor.

However, if a field is empty for some records, you don't always want to insert a space; if it turns out that nothing is printed in that location, you would end up with unnecessary spaces. DisplayWrite 4 lets you decide when to include spaces as part of the If Statement, as you will see.

Let's look at two situations that encompass the three possibilities. In the first situation, you want the field contents to be printed if they exist. However, if the field is empty, you want it ignored. In the second situation, you want the field contents to be printed if they exist and other text to be printed if the field is empty.

Situation 1   We will use the "middle initial" example here. Let's say you want customers' middle initials to be printed if that information is in the field but you want the field ignored if it is empty.

To create the If Statement, type the shell until you get to the location where you would ordinarily insert the variable name for the middle initial field. (Let's say this name is MI.) However, instead of inserting the variable name, you are going to insert the If Statement.

Press F8 and choose Merge Instructions.

Then, from the Merge Instructions menu,

choose If Variable Not Empty.

From the Test Variable menu, type the name of the field to be searched:

Type **MI**; then press ENTER.

You will be returned to the typing area and see the first part of your If Statement on the screen:

`/If Not Empty, MI/_`

Now you must tell DisplayWrite 4 what to print if the field is not empty. In this case you want the contents of the field MI plus a space. (You can actually choose the contents of any field or any text.) To include the contents of the field MI,

press F8 and choose Merge Instructions.

Then, in the Merge Instructions menu,

select Variable.

Type the variable name (the field name). In this case,

type **MI**; then press ENTER.

Then type a space to separate the middle initial from text that comes after it.
To end the If Statement,

press F8 and choose Merge Instructions.

Then, from the Merge Instructions menu,

select End "If" Test.

You will be returned to the typing area. Your complete If Statement will look like this:

```
/If Not Empty, MI/!MI! /End If/_
```

When copies of the repetitive documents are printed, the middle initial will be printed if the field is not empty. If the field *is* empty, the entire conditional statement will automatically be ignored and the field will be passed over.

Situation 2 Now let's look at a situation in which a dentist is sending appointment reminder notices to patients. The appointments are recorded in a field called APPT—DATE. However, some patients have not called for appointments, so their APPT—DATE field is empty. When sending notices to these patients, the dentist wants the message "Please call for appointment." in the APPT—DATE location.

For this situation, you need two If Statements. The first one is exactly like Situation 1. (You tell the system to print the contents of a field plus a space if the field is not empty.) The second If Statement tells the system to print "Please call for appointment." if the field is empty.

To create these instructions, move the cursor to the location in the shell where the variable name APPT—DATE would ordinarily go. Produce the first If Statement exactly as described in Situation 1, but use the variable name APPT—DATE instead of MI. Your instruction should look like this:

```
/If Not Empty, APPT_DATE/!APPT_DATE! /End If/_
```

Now you are going to insert the second instruction directly following the first.

Press F8 and choose Merge Instructions.

Then, from the Merge Instructions menu,

choose IF Variable Empty and then type the variable name
APPT—DATE

in the Test Variable menu. Then

press ENTER.

This returns you to the typing area. You can see the If Empty instruction inserted into your file.

Now type the text that you want to appear if the field is empty. (You can specify the contents of any field in the data file, or any text.) Remember to type a space (or spaces) after the text. In this case,

type **Please call for appointment.**

Next,

press F8, and choose Merge Instructions, and choose End "If" Test.

You will be returned to the typing area and can see your second If Statement on the screen:

```
/If Empty, APPT_DATE/Please call for appointment.  /End If/_
```

When your copies of the repetitive documents are printed, the appointment date will be printed if the patient has made an appointment. Otherwise, the "Please call for appointment." message will be printed.

Selecting a Math Format for a Numeric Variable

When you type a variable name in the Variable menu for use with Merge with Data File, you can also select a number format for that numeric variable. You can do this with any numeric variable in your shell, including a math answer. If you leave this item blank, numeric variables will be printed in the default format (as specified in the Profiles menu).

You select the number format for a variable at the time you insert the variable name into your shell. However, after you type the variable name in the Variable menu, instead of pressing ENTER, tab to Output Format and type the number (from 1 through 4) that represents the format you want. Then press ENTER to return to the typing area.

Creating a File Description

Before you can use the DisplayWrite 4 Merge with Data File feature with a fixed-length or BASIC sequential data file, you must create a file description for it. The file description contains a description of each field in the file, listing the field's name, type, and length. If you are merging with a user-supplied program data file, you may also need to create a file description if the program does not generate its own.

If you are using a data file with a PDS, WKS, WRK, DIF, SYLK, or dBASE II file format, you do not need to create a file description. In this case, go on to the section "Producing the Final Documents."

To create a field description for a file,

choose Merge from the DisplayWrite 4 menu.

Then, from the Merge menu,

choose Data File Description: Create.

Type the name you want for your file description. The system will append the extension .DES if you don't supply any other.

Press ENTER.

You will see the Create/Revise Data File Description menu:

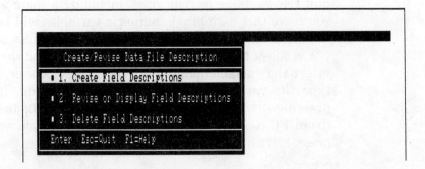

```
   Create/Revise Data File Description
▪ 1. Create Field Descriptions
▪ 2. Revise or Display Field Descriptions
▪ 3. Delete Field Descriptions
Enter  Esc=Quit  F1=Help
```

Creating a Field Description

From the Create/Revise Data File Description menu,

choose Create Field Description.

You will see the Field Description menu.

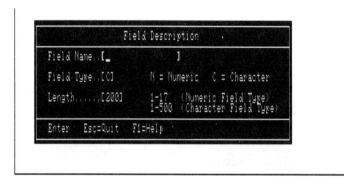

Begin with the first field in your data file and fill out the menu. In Figure 25-1, this would be the TITLE field. (The order in which you enter the field descriptions *must* match the order of the fields in your data file.)

- *Field Name.* The field name must be the same as the variable name in the shell.

- *Field Type.* Numeric fields can contain *only* numbers, an optional decimal point, and an optional plus or minus sign. All other fields are character fields. Thus a field containing the entry *07-416* would be a character field because it contains a dash.

- *Length.* For fixed-length files, the field length you specify must be identical to the field length in the data file. For BASIC sequential files, the field length you specify must be equal to or longer than the longest entry in that field.

When you have completed the menu,

press ENTER.

You will see the message

> Field is added to File Description.

Now repeat the process for each field in your data file. When you have created a field description for every field in your file,

press ESC three times

to return to the DisplayWrite 4 menu.

Revising a File Description

You can revise a file description by adding, deleting, and changing field descriptions. You can also display existing field descriptions without revising them. To revise or display a file description, from the DisplayWrite 4 menu,

choose Merge; then choose Data File Description: Revise.

Type the name of the file description you want to revise. Then

press ENTER.

You will see the Create/Revise Data File Description menu. There are three choices on this menu.

Create Field Descriptions   Select this option if you have added more fields to your data file and need to create additional field descriptions. You do this exactly the same way that you originally created field descriptions. The new field descriptions are added to the end of the current list of field descriptions.

Revise or Display Field Descriptions   When you select this option, the screen displays a list of all your field names in the order of their field descriptions. Choose the field whose description you want to revise.

The field description for that field will be displayed with your current settings. Make the desired changes and press ENTER to return to the Revise Field Description menu. You will see the message

> Field Description is changed.

If necessary, revise any other field descriptions. Then

press ENTER

to return to the Create/Revise Data File Description menu.

Delete Field Descriptions   When you select this option, you will see a list of your field descriptions with Keep and Delete choices:

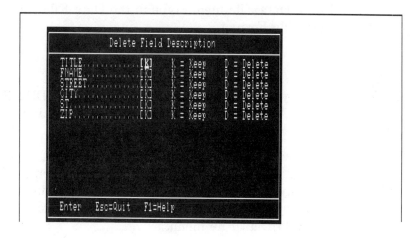

Type **d** (for Delete) next to each field description that you want to delete. Then

press ENTER.

You will see

```
> Field Descriptions deleted = #.
```

Press ESC twice

to return to the DisplayWrite 4 menu.

Producing the Final Documents

To produce final copies of your repetitive documents,

choose Merge

from the DisplayWrite 4 menu. Then, from the Merge menu,

choose Merge with Data File.

In the Data File menu, type in the Data File Name and the Data File Format.

Press ENTER.

- If you specified PDS, WKS or WRK, DIF, SYLK, or dBASE II as the file format, the Merge with Data File menu will be displayed.

- If you specified Fixed Length or BASIC Sequential as the file format, the File Description menu will be displayed. Type the file description name in the File Description menu. Then press ENTER to go to the Merge with Data File menu.

- If you specified User-Supplied, the File Description menu will be displayed. If your user-supplied program produces its own file description, *do not type anything in this menu.* Simply press ENTER. If you created a file description for your user-supplied program, type the file description name in the File Description menu. Then press ENTER to go to the Merge with Data File menu.

You will see the two-page Merge with Data File menu. Type in the Shell Document Name.

The next two choices—Merged Document Name and Print Merged Document—let you determine whether your repetitive documents will be printed, or stored, or both. (If you decide to store them, they will all be saved in one large file, not in a separate file for each document.)

- If you want your final documents printed but not stored, make no menu changes in these items.

- If you want your final documents printed *and* stored, type a name for the merged document.

- If you want your final documents stored but not printed, type a name for the merged document. Then set Print Merged Document to No.

Make any other changes you want.
To begin the merge process,

press ENTER.

During merging, the Merge with Data File Status screen is displayed. Your final documents will be printed or stored on disk according to your specifications.

Stopping and Restarting Merge with Data File

If you want to stop merging,

press CTRL-BREAK.

If you are planning to restart the process later, look at the

Key	Function
F8	The Merge Instructions choice followed by the Variable choice inserts a Variable code into your shell around the variable name
	The Merge Instructions choice followed by any of the last three menu items puts If Statements into your shell
	The Merge Instructions choice followed by the Skip to Line Number choice lets you put a Skip to Line instruction into your shell
	The Merge Instructions choice followed by the Math choice lets you insert Math instructions into your shell
CTRL-F8	If pressed when the cursor is under a Math instruction, it lets you revise the instruction
CTRL-BREAK	Stops Merge with Data File

Table 25-2.   Keys Used for Merge with Data File

Merge with Data File Status screen and jot down the restart number.

To resume merging, return to the Merge with Data File menu. Fill out the menu items as you did before, but this time also

choose Restart Number

and enter the number that was displayed on the Status screen when you previously canceled. To restart the merge,

press ENTER.

Table 25-2 lists the keys used for Merge with Data File.

APPENDIXES

Making Your Own Printer Table

DisplayWrite 4 provides a printer function table DEFAULT.PFT for use with nonsupported printers. This table lets you perform simple printing tasks, but you will not be able to use any of your printer's advanced features with DEFAULT.PFT.

DisplayWrite 4 also lets you create your own printer function table or revise an existing table (one that has been provided for a supported printer). You create and revise printer description tables through the Profiles menu. Creating or revising a printer description table enables you to use your printer's advanced features even if your printer is not supported.

To create or revise a printer description table, you must have a list of the control codes used by your printer. These codes are usually provided in your printer manual.

Who Should Create the Table

The *DisplayWrite 4 Technical Reference* manual that comes with DisplayWrite 4 warns that "The Printer Function Table tasks are intended for use by programmers, technicians, or experts on printer functions." There are several reasons why it is difficult for a computer novice to create or revise a printer table.

One reason is that when you create or revise a printer function table, control sequences must be entered in hexadecimal form, but your printer manual may give the values in ASCII or decimal form. An ASCII Reference Table at the end of the "Printer Function Table Tasks" document that you will print out shows conversion among the three forms, but it still takes some know-how.

The second reason is that it often takes a *sequence* of controls to perform a desired action. For example, to set a certain pitch, you must make sure that a previously used pitch is turned off. Figuring out the sequences required by your printer takes familiarity with printer functions.

Despite these warnings, you can do no damage by attempting to create a printer function table even if you aren't very experienced. If your table doesn't work properly, just don't use it.

Creating a Printer Function Table

Before you begin creating your own printer function table, you must make certain preparations.

Revising the Active Profile

Revise the active profile so that DEFAULT.PFT is the printer function table being used by your printer.

Printing the Files

Print the file PFTNOTES.PRN (found on your *original* Volume 1 disk) with the DisplayWrite 4 Print feature or with the DOS Print function. This file is a 16-part document called "Printer Function Table Tasks" that guides you through the creation of your own table. On-screen help is also available with the F1 key.

Print the file PFTTEST.DOC (found on your *original* Volume 3 disk) with the DisplayWrite 4 Print feature. This test document shows you which printer functions you need to change when you create your table. One line, for example, reads "This is bold text." If the line, in fact, illustrates bold-face, you do not need to change that function; if the line doesn't, you do. The test document includes examples of vertical line spacing, horizontal character spacing, advanced printing functions, paper position, and typestyles.

Note: If you are using a page printer, set Paper Handling to Manual feed before you print out PFTTEST.DOC.

Print the file PFTWS.PRN (found on your *original* Volume 3 disk) with the DisplayWrite 4 Print feature or DOS Print. Use this worksheet to define and write down the control sequences required by your printer.

Filling Out the Worksheet PFTWS.PRN

Before you fill out the worksheet, read sections 1 through 5 of "Printer Function Table Tasks." These sections explain how the printer function table tasks work and in what form values must be entered in your printer function table. You should also familiarize yourself with section 16, which lists the ASCII characters with both their decimal and hexadecimal values.

Next, referring to the test document PFTTEST.DOC to see

which printer functions need changing, fill in the worksheet with the values supplied by your printer's manual for each function.

Creating the Table

To create the printer function table, follow these steps:

1. Choose Create Table from the Profiles menu. You will see a screenful of information about printer function table tasks.

2. Press ENTER to display the Create Printer Function Table Selection menu. Type in the name you want for your new table, the printer you are defining it for, and the paper handling choice. Press ENTER.

3. You will see the Create Printer Function Table menu. Using PFTTEST.DOC as a reference, select the menu items representing areas in which you need to make changes. Enter the control sequences as indicated on your worksheet. *Make sure you enter all sequences in hexadecimal form.*

4. When you are finished, select Function Selection Tests from the menu to verify the print functions you defined in your table. These tests will let you make final choices about text appearance and let you coordinate your choices with the DisplayWrite 4 Print function.

5. Save the printer function table you just created.

6. Revise the active profile so that the new table is the printer function table being used by your printer.

7. Print the PFTTEST.DOC with the DisplayWrite 4 Print feature to check that your new table is working properly. If it is not, revise it.

Revising a Printer Function Table

Your own nonsupported printer may be quite similar to one of the printers supported by DisplayWrite 4. In this case, you may be able to use an existing printer function table with only minor revisions.

The first step is to copy the printer function table for the supported printer, giving the copy the name you want for your own printer function table (use the extension .PFT). For example, you could copy IBM5152.PFT and call the copy CUSTOM.PFT. You will make all revisions on the copy.

Now proceed exactly as described in the previous section "Creating a Printer Function Table," with the following differences:

1. Revise the active profile so it contains the name of the printer function table you are about to revise—in this case, CUSTOM.PFT.

2. Select Revise Table instead of Create Table from the Profiles menu, and type in the name of the table.

3. If you need to revise a control sequence in a menu, delete the existing sequence with ALT-8 and type in the sequence you want. If the control sequence contains a variable "n", delete the sequence with ALT-8 and then press ENTER to reset the menu to its default values.

B

Using DisplayWrite 4 with Emulation Programs

You can use DisplayWrite 4 with certain *emulation* programs. These programs include the following:

- IBM PC Support/36 Organizer
- IBM PC 3270 Emulation
- IBM TopView Program

Switching to and from the Emulation Program

To use DisplayWrite 4 with an emulation program:

1. Load the emulation program.
2. Load DisplayWrite 4.

3. From the DisplayWrite 4 menu or the Create Document or Revise Document typing area, press the "hot key" to switch to the other application. If you are in Character mode, you must use the hot key provided by the other program. If you are in APA mode, use ALT-7 (the Application Change key).

4. Perform whatever tasks you wish to with the other program. When you are finished, exit from the program by the usual method.

5. Press ESC to return to DisplayWrite 4.

Note: If your computer is connected to an IBM System/36, you may be able to return to DisplayWrite 4 from the IBM PC Support/36 Organizer by selecting DisplayWrite 4 from a menu.

Using DisplayWrite 4 with TopView

The original DisplayWrite 4 Volume 1 disk contains two files, DW4.PIF and DW4.TBL, that enable DisplayWrite 4 and TopView to work together.

When you use TopView with DisplayWrite 4, be aware of the following limitations:

- You cannot use a mouse in DisplayWrite 4 when you are running under TopView.

- If you want to issue DOS commands, use the TopView DOS Service function as you will not be able to use DisplayWrite 4's DOS Commands feature.

- You cannot use the TopView Quit function while you are in DisplayWrite 4. You must exit from DisplayWrite 4 to return to DOS.

Using TopView's Window Function

In order to use the TopView Window function with Display-Write 4, you must remove the last character from the end of the Program Parameters in TopView's Change Program Information menu. Then replace the last character as follows:

- Replace the last character with a "t" if your display uses BW80/MONO Character mode. This is for color displays that can display only in two colors or for monochrome displays.

- Replace the last character with a "w" if your display uses C080/MONO Character mode. This is for displays that can use all 16 colors or for monochrome displays.

In TopView's Change Program Information menu, set "Writes directly to the screen" to No.

Using TopView's Scissors Function

To use TopView's scissors function to copy column text into a DisplayWrite file, follow these steps:

1. Put DisplayWrite 4 into Insert mode.

2. Position the cursor; then select Scissors.

3. Block the area that includes the columns to the left and right of the column you want to move, as well as the column itself.

4. Use the Paste feature to insert the columns into your DisplayWrite 4 file.

5. Delete the unnecessary columns.

6. Delete any unnecessary Carrier Return codes. (DisplayWrite 4 inserts a Carrier Return code at the end of each text line inserted with the Scissors function.)

Note: See the *DisplayWrite 4 Technical Reference* manual for complete instructions on using DisplayWrite 4 with emulation programs and also for instructions on using DisplayWrite 4 with the IBM PC Local Area Network Program.

C

Working with
Subdirectories

The directory that is created on a disk when you format it is called the *root* directory. The root directory on a double-sided floppy disk can hold up to 112 files; the root directory on a hard disk can contain 512. DOS and DisplayWrite 4 have a special feature that lets you use *subdirectories* so you can subdivide large numbers of files into useful groups. Because of the limited storage capacity of floppy-disk systems, subdirectories are generally used only with hard-disk systems.

What Subdirectories Are

The subdirectory feature lets you group your files into categories. You can have one category for letters, one for reports, one for bills, one for payments, and so on. Each category is a subdirectory. Each subdirectory can contain files or other subdirectories or a combination of both. Like the root directory, each subdirectory on a hard disk can contain up to 512 entries. Figure C-1 shows a simple subdirectory structure on a disk. Here the root directory contains two subdirectories, minutes and reports. The minutes subdirectory contains two files; the reports subdirectory also contains two files but it also contains another subdirectory, products, which contains three files.

Subdirectories are often simply called *directories*. The directory that you see when you start DOS and issue the DIR command is called the *current* directory. However, you can make a different directory the current directory with the DOS CHDIR command or by loading a program or batch file that changes the current directory. In DisplayWrite 4, you can change both the current directory and the default drive with F3 (the List key).

Note: The terms *subdirectory* and *directory* are used interchangeably in the rest of this appendix.

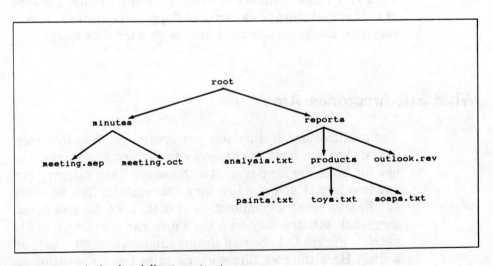

Figure C-1. A simple subdirectory structure

What a File Specification Is

If the file you want to work with is not in the current directory, you must locate it by typing more than the file name. You must type a *file specification* that consists of three parts:

- The drive specifier, consisting of the drive letter plus a colon. (If the file you want is on the default drive, you don't need a drive specifier.)

- The path, composed of a series of directory names separated by backslashes (\ ) leading to the directory containing the file. (If the file you want is in the current directory, you don't need a path.)

- The file name, which must be separated from the last directory name with a backslash.

A complete document specification might look like this:

C: \dw4 \data \sales \august.doc

This document specification would tell DOS or DisplayWrite 4 to look in the root directory of drive C for a subdirectory called dw4, then to look in that subdirectory for another subdirectory called data, then to look in that subdirectory for another subdirectory called sales, and finally to look in that subdirectory for august.doc.

The first backslash in the path tells DOS or DisplayWrite 4 to begin at the root directory. If you leave out the first backslash, the search will begin at the current directory. (If the root directory is the current directory, you can leave out the first backslash.)

For a fuller discussion of the subdirectory concept, read your DOS manual.

Note: In DOS you can use only a backslash (\ ) to separate directories, but in DisplayWrite 4 you can use either a backslash (\ ) or a slash (/).

DOS Commands Used for Directories

DOS has commands for making a directory, for changing to a different directory, and for deleting a directory.

Making a Directory in DOS

Directories can be made only in DOS, not in DisplayWrite 4, and the rules for naming them are the same as the rules for naming files. You must make a higher-level subdirectory before you can make any lower-level subdirectories contained in it. For example, in Figure C-1 you would make the subdirectory reports before you would make the subdirectory products.

You make a directory with the MKDIR or MD command. For example, to make the subdirectory reports, turn on your computer and monitor. When you see the DOS prompt (usually C> on a hard-disk system),

type **mkdir reports** and press ENTER.

(In this case, you don't need a drive specifier because you want the directory on your default drive, and you don't need a backslash because you are already at your root directory.) You will be prompted for your next command, signifying that the directory has been created.

To create a directory named products in the reports directory,

type **mkdir reports \products** and press ENTER.

Note: You can leave DisplayWrite 4 temporarily with the DOS Commands choice on the DisplayWrite 4 menu, make a directory, and resume DisplayWrite 4. This process is described in the section "Creating a Directory in Display-Write 4."

Changing the Current Directory in DOS

You change to a new current directory with the CHDIR or CD command. To make the products subdirectory your current directory, boot your system. When you see the C> prompt,

type **chdir reports \products** and press ENTER.

The products subdirectory is now the current directory.

Removing a Directory in DOS

You remove a directory with the RMDIR or RD command. To remove a directory, you must first delete all the files in the directory, and you must always delete a lower-level subdirectory before you delete the higher-level one containing it. Subdirectories can be removed only in DOS.

To remove a subdirectory, boot your system. When you see the DOS prompt, type the RMDIR command followed by a space, the drive specifier, and the path of the subdirectory you want to delete. For example, if you want to delete the products subdirectory,

type **rmdir reports \products**

(Here again, you don't need a drive specifier or a backslash because you are already on the default drive and in the root directory.) The product subdirectory is erased.

Note: If you have been using the slash when working with subdirectories in DisplayWrite 4, remember that you must return to the backslash in DOS. This is particularly important when you are using DOS to delete individual files in a subdirectory. If you use the slash instead of the backslash, DOS may delete all the files from the highest-level directory in the path. If you see the message "Are you sure?" after you try to delete a file, DOS is warning you that it is planning to delete more than one file.

Working with Directories in DisplayWrite 4

DisplayWrite 4 has several features that make it easy to create, use, and display directories.

Creating a Directory in DisplayWrite 4

To create a directory while you are in DisplayWrite 4, choose DOS Commands from the DisplayWrite 4 menu. When you enter DOS from DisplayWrite 4, the directory that you were in while working with DisplayWrite 4 is still the current directory. For example, if you load and save documents from a subdirectory of your dw4 directory called data, then data will still be the current directory when you choose DOS Commands. When you are prompted to type a command, create your directory with the MKDIR command. For example,

type **mkdir sales**

This is all you need to do to create a directory sales that is a subdirectory of your data directory.

Type **exit** and press ENTER

to return to DisplayWrite 4.

Changing the Current Directory in DisplayWrite 4

You can make your new directory the current directory directly from DisplayWrite 4. You do not have to do this in DOS. To makes sales the current directory, press F3 and choose Current Directory.

You will see the Change Current Directory menu filled in with your default drive and current directory. Tab to Current Directory.

Type **sales** and press ENTER.

Your current directory is now sales. Any files that you save will be saved automatically in your sales subdirectory. If you display the Change Current Directory menu again, the screen will indicate **c:\dw4\data\sales** for Current Directory.

Displaying a Directory in DisplayWrite 4

To display a directory in DisplayWrite 4,

press F3 and choose Directory.

The Directory menu is displayed. If you simply press ENTER without specifying a directory, you will see a list of files in your current directory. If you want to see a list of files in any other directory, you must type in the directory name with a drive and a path. For example, to see a list of files in your dw4 directory,

type **C:\dw4** and press ENTER.

In this example, you will see a listing of your program files.

Note: When you display a subdirectory, you will see two special entries. The first, a period (.), tells DOS that a subdirectory is being displayed. The second, two periods (..), tells DOS what the next-higher-level directory is.

Modifying
the Batch File

When you type the command *dw4* to load DisplayWrite 4 into your computer, you are actually executing a series of commands that are stored in a special file called a *batch file*. On a hard-disk system, the batch file is stored in the root directory of the hard disk; on a floppy-disk system, the batch file is stored on your working disks.

The batch-file commands instruct the program to run in a certain way. For example, they tell the system where to find the program files and where to store the text files. They also tell the system whether you are in Character or APA mode and what printers to use. The batch file also returns you to the root directory of your hard disk or to drive A of your floppy-disk system when you leave DisplayWrite 4.

You can view the commands in your batch file easily with the DOS TYPE command. To view the commands, load DOS. If you have a floppy-disk system, insert your Volume 0 floppy disk in drive A,

type **type dw4.bat**, and press ENTER.

You will see a list of the commands on your screen.

The original batch file is created for your system during the installation process. However, you can redesign the original batch file or create additional batch files in order to use a different configuration.

You do this through the Create Batch File choice on the Profiles menu. You can specify the following options:

- *Drive and directory for storing data files.* You can specify a drive, path, and directory on a hard-disk system or a drive for a floppy-disk system.

- *Primary program path or drive.* On a hard-disk system, the primary program path specifies the path from which DisplayWrite 4 loads program files. The system first looks for the programs in the temporary program path (if it exists). If they are not found, it then looks for them in the primary program path and finally in the secondary program path. On a floppy-disk system, the primary program drive specifies the drive from which the system loads the DisplayWrite 4 program files.

- *User profile path and name.* This option tells Display-Write 4 what profile to activate when you load the program.

- *Display mode.* This option selects the display mode. The choices are APA mode, Character mode for color displays that can use only two colors, and Character mode for displays that use 16 colors or that use monochrome displays.

- *Printer attached to LPT#?* This option lets you specify whether a printer is attached to each of the three LPT ports. A Yes choice means that a printer is attached to the port; a No choice means either that no printer is attached or that printer output is redirected to a COM port.

- *Temporary program path.* This specifies where Display-Write 4 stores and retrieves programs and temporary program data. You can specify a hard disk or a virtual drive in extended memory. A floppy-disk system cannot use a temporary program path. When loading programs, DisplayWrite 4 first looks for them in the temporary program path, then in the primary program path, and finally in the secondary program path. The system saves temporary program data in a special file in the temporary program path called DW4A0100.$$P. This file occupies up to 52K of space on your disk. However, using a temporary program path reduces the amount of memory required to run DisplayWrite 4 by about 31K.

- *Secondary program path.* This option specifies a directory or drive from which DisplayWrite 4 will load programs if they are not found in the temporary program path (if it exists) or in the primary program path. The system will issue an error message if the program is still not found.

Creating the New Batch File

To create a new batch file,

choose Profiles

from the DisplayWrite 4 menu. When you see the Profiles menu,

choose Create Batch File.

You will see a screenful of information explaining where your batch file will be stored. Read the screen. Then

press ENTER

to display the two-page Batch File Options menu.

Make configuration changes as desired. For example, if you want your display to be in APA mode instead of in the default Character mode, tab to Display Mode and type an "a" to select APA mode. When you have completed all changes,

press ENTER.

You will be prompted for the name of your new batch file. Type in the name (without the .BAT). You *cannot* use the name of an existing batch file.

Press ENTER.

You will be returned to the Profiles menu.

Using the New Batch File

If you have a floppy-disk system, copy the new batch file to each of your working disks.

To load DisplayWrite 4 with the new batch file, at the DOS prompt, type the name of the new batch file (without the .BAT) and press ENTER. Then proceed exactly the same way you usually do. You can also use the original batch file whenever you want to by typing **dw4** at the DOS prompt.

If you want the new batch file to replace the old so that in effect you are *revising* the original batch file instead of creating an additional one, erase the original batch file from all of your working disks. Then rename the new batch file dw4.bat and copy it to all of your working disks. Now, at the DOS prompt, you can type **dw4** just as you usually do, and your revised batch file will load.

Trademarks

FONTastic®	Koch Software Industries
IBM®	International Business Machines Corporation
Quietwriter®	International Business Machines Corporation
Wheelprinter™	International Business Machines Corporation
Wheelprinter E™	International Business Machines Corporation
IBM Personal Computer AT®	International Business Machines Corporation
IBM Personal Computer XT™	International Business Machines Corporation
PC Em-U-Print™	Koch Software Industries
Proprinter™	International Business Machines Corporation

Index

CURSOR MOVEMENT KEYS

Key	Action
↑ (up arrow)	Moves cursor up one line
↓ (down arrow)	Moves cursor down one line
← (left arrow)	Moves cursor left one space
→ (right arrow)	Moves cursor right one space
CTRL-← (CTRL-left arrow)	Moves cursor to first character of current or previous word
CTRL-→ (CTRL-right arrow)	Moves cursor to first character of next word
HOME	Moves cursor to beginning of line
END	Moves cursor to end of line
CTRL-HOME	Moves cursor to beginning of page
CTRL-END	Moves cursor to end of page
PGUP	Moves screen window up
PGDN	Moves screen window down
CTRL-PGUP	Moves screen window left
CTRL-PGDN	Moves screen window right

© 1987 Osborne McGraw-Hill

FUNCTION KEYS (F1-F12)

Key	Action
F1 (the Help key)	Provides on-screen help
CTRL-F1 (the Key Program key)	Displays the Keystroke Programming menu
F2	Displays the End/Save menu
CTRL-F2 (the Menu Restore key)	Restores menu choices to their default values
F3 (the List key)	Displays the List Services menu
F4 (the Block key)	Displays the Block menu
CTRL-F4 (the Notepad key)	Displays the Notepad menu
F5 (the Functions key)	Lists the keys used to perform various functions
CTRL-F5 (the Edit Options key)	Displays the Edit Options menu
F6 (the Search key)	Displays the Search menu
CTRL-F6 (the Get key)	Displays the Get File menu
F7 (the Format key)	Displays the Format menu
CTRL-F7 (the Document Options key)	Displays the Document Options menu
F8 (the Instructions key)	Displays the Instructions menu
CTRL-F8 (the View/Revise key)	When the cursor is under the appropriate code, this key lets you revise footnotes, formats, math instructions, outlines, typestyles, variables, and voice notes
F9 (the Table key)	Displays the Table menu
CTRL-F9 (the Math key)	Displays the Math menu
F10 (the Spell key)	Displays the Spell menu
F11 or ALT-1 (the Cursor Draw key)	Displays the Cursor Draw menu
F12 or ALT-2 (the Line Adjust key)	Adjusts line endings

DisplayWrite 4 Made Easy

OTHER KEYS

Key	Description	Key	Description
CTRL-6 (the Stop key)	Inserts a Stop code	INS	Toggles between Insert mode and Replace mode
ALT-7 (the Application Change key)	In APA mode, lets you switch to an emulation program	CTRL-T (the Indent key)	Inserts an Indent code and sets up a temporary left margin
ALT-8 (the Erase End of Line key)	In menus, erases from the cursor to the end of the line	CTRL-H (the 1/2-Down key)	Inserts a Half Index Down code to start a subscript or end a superscript
CTRL-B (the Bold key)	Inserts Bold codes into your text that cause text to print in boldface	|→ (the TAB key)	Inserts a Tab code and moves the cursor to the next tab position
→ (the Backspace key)	Deletes characters as it backspaces	CTRL-U (the Underline key)	Inserts Underline codes into your text that cause text to print underlined
CTRL-← (the Reqd Backspace key)	Inserts a Required Backspace code	CTRL-M (the Mark key)	Inserts both Bold and Underline codes into your file. Used for marking revisions
CTRL-C (the Center key)	Inserts a Center code to center text	CTRL-N (the Next key)	Locates the next Stop code or variable name
DEL	Deletes the character the cursor is under	CTRL-V (the Reqd Space key)	Inserts a Required Space code into your file
CTRL-E (the Page End key)	Inserts a Page End code and begins a new page	CTRL-O (the Outline key)	Inserts correct symbols and indentation for each outline level
ESC	Cancels menus and choices	CTRL-R (the Reqd Page End key)	Inserts a Required Page End code into your file. During pagination, the system will begin a new page when it encounters this code
CTRL-F (the Typeface key)	Displays the Change Typeface menu so you can change to a different typeface	CTRL-W (the Word Underline key)	Inserts a Word Underline code to underline a single word
		CTRL-Y (the 1/2-UP key)	Inserts a Half Index Up code to start a superscript or end a subscript
		CTRL-S (the Overstrike key)	Inserts Overstrike codes into your file, causing printed text to be overstricken with the designated character
		CTRL-Z (the ZICR key)	Inserts a Zero Index Carrier Return code

IF YOU ENJOYED THIS BOOK . . .

help us stay in touch with your needs and interests by filling out and returning the survey card below. Your opinions are important, and will help us to continue to publish the kinds of books you need, when you need them.

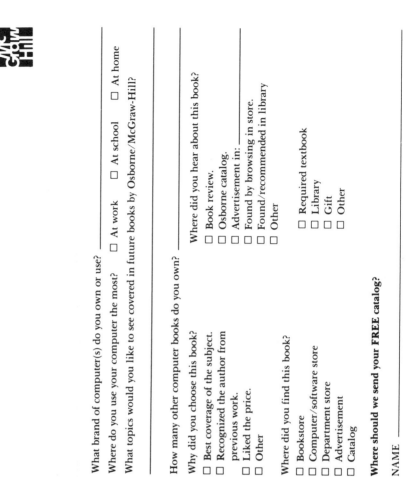

What brand of computer(s) do you own or use? _____

Where do you use your computer the most?   ☐ At work   ☐ At school   ☐ At home

What topics would you like to see covered in future books by Osborne/McGraw-Hill?

_____

How many other computer books do you own? _____

Why did you choose this book?
☐ Best coverage of the subject.
☐ Recognized the author from previous work.
☐ Liked the price.
☐ Other

Where did you find this book?
☐ Bookstore
☐ Computer/software store
☐ Department store
☐ Advertisement
☐ Catalog

Where did you hear about this book?
☐ Book review.
☐ Osborne catalog.
☐ Advertisement in:
☐ Found by browsing in store.
☐ Found/recommended in library
☐ Other

☐ Required textbook
☐ Library
☐ Gift
☐ Other

Where should we send your FREE catalog?

NAME _____

ADDRESS _____

270-4   CITY _____ STATE _____ ZIP _____

BUSINESS REPLY MAIL

FIRST CLASS   PERMIT NO. 3111   Berkeley, CA

Postage will be paid by addressee

Osborne **McGraw-Hill**

2600 Tenth Street
Berkeley, California 94710

No Postage
Necessary
If Mailed
in the
United States